"经贸汉语口语" 系列教材

第4版
The Fourth Edition

BUSINESS
CHINESE
CONVERSATION
(Elementary)

经贸初级
汉语口语

下 II

主　编：黄为之
参加编写人员：杨廷治　陈　辉　黄锡之
　　　　　　　杨天舒　成伟武

北京语言大学出版社
BEIJING LANGUAGE AND CULTURE
UNIVERSITY PRESS

© 2018 北京语言大学出版社，社图号 17352

图书在版编目（CIP）数据

经贸初级汉语口语. 下 / 黄为之主编；杨廷治等编
. — 4 版. — 北京：北京语言大学出版社，2018.9（2019.10 重印）
ISBN 978-7-5619-5157-6

Ⅰ.①经… Ⅱ.①黄… ②杨… Ⅲ.①贸易－汉语－
口语－对外汉语教学－教材 Ⅳ.① H195.4

中国版本图书馆 CIP 数据核字 (2018) 第 081685 号

经贸初级汉语口语（第 4 版）·下
JINGMAO CHUJI HANYU KOUYU (DI 4 BAN)·XIA

排版制作：	北京创艺涵文化发展有限公司
责任印制：	周 燚

出版发行：	北京语言大学出版社	
社　　址：	北京市海淀区学院路 15 号，100083	
网　　址：	www.blcup.com	
电子信箱：	service@blcup.com	
电　　话：	编辑部	8610-82303647/3592/3724
	国内发行	8610-82303650/3591/3648
	海外发行	8610-82303365/3080/3668
	北语书店	8610-82303653
	网购咨询	8610-82303908
印　　刷：	北京建宏印刷有限公司	
版　　次：	2018 年 9 月第 4 版　　印　次：2019 年 10 月第 2 次印刷	
开　　本：	787 毫米 × 1092 毫米　1/16　　印　张：18.75	
字　　数：	385 千字	
定　　价：	65.00 元	

PRINTED IN CHINA

第四版前言

当前,中国经济已经高度融合于世界经济体系,中国倡导的合作共赢、打造全球命运共同体的理念,越来越具有世界影响,中国经济在更高层次上的新一轮改革开放格局,已经形成。"一带一路"的建设对亚欧非乃至全世界经济产生重大影响;"亚投行"作为开放包容、互联互通的成果,助力于亚洲经济圈发展;"中国制造"涌现出众多高端名牌产品,引起了全世界的关注和争购;中国企业走向世界,成为全球资本市场最活跃的投资生力军;"互联网+"的万众创新,日益改变着社会经济形态和生活方式。所有这一切,正在深刻改变世界经济和国际贸易格局。我们的经贸汉语教材,应该对这种新常态、新趋势、新情况,做出及时反映和解读,这对外国留学生了解中国的现实情况,会有很大帮助。

本次修订版保留了原书的体例和基本内容,增加了四篇新课文,修改了部分课文,增加了一些练习。

黄为之

2017 年 6 月

Preface to the Fourth Edition

At present, China's economy has been highly integrated in the world economic system and embraces a new round of reform and opening up at a higher level, with its concept of win-win cooperation and global community of common destiny enjoying greater influence around the world. The Belt and Road initiative exerts deep influence on Asia, Europe, Africa and even the whole world. The Asian Infrastructure Investment Bank, as a result of openness, inclusiveness, and interconnection, promotes the development of the economic circle of Asia; with the emergence of many high-end brand-name products, "Made in China" attracts so much attention that people rush to buy them; Chinese enterprises reach out to the world and become the most active investment force in global capital market; the innovative "Internet +" changes social and economic patterns and lifestyles day by day. As a result, the world economy and international trade pattern undergo profound changes. Our business Chinese textbooks should reflect and interpret the new normal, new trend and new situation in a timely manner so as to help foreign students in understanding China's reality.

The revised edition, on the basis of the original style and basic content, modifies some texts and adds four new ones and some exercises.

Huang Weizhi
June, 2017

第三版前言

这次"经贸汉语口语"系列教材再版,主要作了四方面的修改:

一、《经贸初级汉语口语》上册,原来只有1～10课的课文配有拼音课文,现在根据外国留学生的要求,为了初学者学习口语的方便,增补了后16课的拼音课文;下册每课练习最后一题的小故事,对初学者也有一定的难度,这次修改也一并删去了。

二、世界发展很快,为能与时俱进,修改一些陈旧了的信息是必要的,如改"对外经济贸易合作部"为"商务部",改"欧洲共同体"为"欧洲联盟",改"关贸总协定"为"世贸组织";欧元流通以后,法国法郎、德国马克等已不再流通,也作了相应修改;书中引用的各种数据,有许多变化,凡是能查到的,都修改征引了最新资料,等等。

三、修改了部分课文、注释和练习,以反映社会生活和经济生活的巨大变化。

四、修订了一些打字排版的错误和书写不规范之处。

这次修订一定还有不尽如人意的地方,欢迎专家、同行、外国朋友和留学生指正。

对外经济贸易大学
黄为之
2006年5月

Preface to the Third Edition

The major changes of this edition of *Business Chinese Conversation* include the following four parts:

Firstly, unlike the previous editions of *Elementary: Volume 1* where only texts of the first 10 lessons were supplied with *pinyin*, this edition provides *pinyin* texts for the other 16 lessons for the convenience of foreigners beginning to learn spoken Chinese. Short stories in the last exercise of each lesson in *Volume 2* have been deleted to reduce the difficulty for beginners.

Secondly, changing old terms is necessary along with the development of the world. For example, "Ministry of Foreign Trade and Economic Cooperation" has been changed into "Ministry of Commerce", "European Communities" into "European Union", and "General Agreement on Tariffs and Trade" into "World Trade Organization". As francs and marks have been taken out of circulation, they are replaced by euros. Other data cited in the book have also been updated.

Thirdly, some of the texts, notes and exercises have been revised so as to mirror the great changes in social and economic lives.

Fourthly, some typos and nonstandard writings have been corrected.

We realize that this edition is not free of errors and shortcomings, and suggestions from experts, fellow teachers, foreign friends and students are welcome.

Huang Weizhi
University of International
Business and Economics,
May, 2006

再版前言

《经贸初级汉语口语》自1993年出版后，受到社会各界的热烈欢迎，被各院校和自学者广泛采用。出版的这些年来，中国的国际贸易形势发生了很大变化，有许多新的内容、新的语言需要学习；在教学实践中，我们也积累了经验，听取了各方面的意见，觉得对这本口语教材，现在进行修订、再版，是适时的。

1999年新版《经贸初级汉语口语》，在保持初版体例和优点的基础上，做了较大的修改。全书从原来的36课增加到50课，由一册分为上、下册，原有的内容作了调整，增加了经贸领域出现的新话题、新词语；减缓了学习进程的坡度，由浅入深、循序渐进的教学原则，得到了更充分的体现。我们相信，这个新版本，会在更高的水准上满足教师和学习者的需要。

1999年新版《经贸初级汉语口语》的英语翻译是黄震华教授。

对外经济贸易大学
黄为之
1999年2月

Preface to the Second Edition

Since its publication in 1993, *Business Chinese Conversation (Elementary)* has been well-received by various circles of the society, and adopted as a textbook by many universities and colleges and self-taught learners. The situation of China's international trade has witnessed great changes during the past years, which means that there are lots of new things to learn. In our teaching practice, we have also accumulated first-hand experiences and listened to suggestions from all sources. We feel that it is the right time now to revise and republish this book.

The 1999 edition of *Business Chinese Conversation (Elementary)*, while keeping the format and merits of the first edition, has undergone major and comprehensive revision. The number of lessons has been increased from 36 to 50, and the new edition consists of two volumes. The contents have also been adjusted, with new topics and new expressions in the arena of trade and economy added, and the difficulty lowered so that progressive instruction is exemplified. We believe that the new edition will better meet the needs of teachers and learners.

The English translator of the 1999 edition of *Business Chinese Conversation (Elementary)* is Professor Huang Zhenhua.

Huang Weizhi
University of International
Business and Economics,
February, 1999

原版前言

初级教材的适用对象是从零开始的初学者。

留学生学习汉语有他们自身的特殊性。一方面，他们对汉语一无所知，没有听说汉语的能力；另一方面，他们又大多是成年人，有充分发达的智能、丰富的社会阅历和科学知识；他们没有孩子那样强的语言模仿力，而同时又具有孩子不可比拟的理解力和接受力。留学生的这个特殊性，在汉语学习过程中，形成一对突出的矛盾。它一方面要求教师注意学生的零起点特点，必须像教孩子学话一样，从一字一词教起，学生也必须从一字一词学起，学习必然存在着一个日积月累、循序渐进的过程；另一方面，它又要求教师充分注意到学生的成人特点，在教学过程中，不要把学生简单地当学话的孩子对待，而应该运用各种手段调动学生的主观能动性，发挥他们的智能、阅历和知识优势，使他们既学得扎实，又学得快捷。如何认识留学生学习汉语的这种特殊性，并把这种认识运用在教材编写和教学过程中，过去往往被人们忽略。教学内容和教学进度的超前或滞后，是常有的现象。我们在编写这本初级口语时，考虑到上述情况，试图解决好留学生在学习汉语中存在的这种矛盾性，使教与学都取得最理想的效果。

初级教材具有下面一些特点：

一至四课集中学习汉语拼音，这是为零起点的初学者编写的。来自东方国家的留学生，声母和韵母的发音难点较多；而来自西方国家的留学生，声调语调的问题则较突出。这四课中，有针对性地编入了大量练习。五至十课，还有拼音练习，以巩固前四课的学习成果。通过严格的教学实践，学生就可以比较好地解决这些语音问题，为学好标准的普通话打下坚实基础。

初级教材是经贸专业汉语教材。教材内容与常见的普通汉语教材内容有极大不同。普通汉语教材中，日常衣食住行和校园生活内容，占有相当大比重，本教材则把其中的有用部分与日常经济生活巧妙地结合了起来，而以经济生活为主要内容。日常经济生活，包括买卖东西、讨价还价、货物挑选、商业服务、销售广告、经营特色、公关工作、推销技巧等，内容丰富，涉及面广，切近生活，实际有用，而教材的词汇、句型及难易程度，又都与初学者的实际水平相当。

初级教材根据语言有交际情景与交际功能属性的原理，采用了课内与课外相结合的教学体系。从第五课开始，每两课一个专题。换句话说，我们把日常经济生活分为若干个层面，每一个层面，都用两篇课文来认识它、表述它。课文"在课内"，是在教师指导下的学习。这是闭门操练，务求根基扎实。课文"在课外"，是学生走出课堂，参与社会实践。这是亲自下海，在游泳中学游泳，意在复习和运用课堂学到的语言知识。两篇课文，内容紧密相关而天地各不相同。学生学完并掌握了这两篇课文，也就学到了经济生活中一个层面的日常用语。这种教学体系，冲出了封闭式的课堂。教师在组织每一个专题课时，都可以要求学生在课前或课后，去参加相应的社会实践，为这一个专题的教学做课前准备或课后复习。本教材在进入教学过程后，必将以它生动活泼的教学形式，引起学生的极大兴趣，充分调动起学习积极性，发挥出成年人的学习优势，取得预期的效果。

初级教材在教学安排上，采用了低起点、大容量、高密度、分阶段而又大步推进的强化训练教学法。每一篇课文，生词量和篇幅长度，都超出了常见的同级普通汉语课本；整个教学过程，都以学生为主，课内课外的一切活动，都要求学生主动积极地去完成，教师只是参与、启发、引导，而决不做教授式的讲演。教学活动的单调、缓慢，学生学习的被动、疲沓，都是影响教学质量的不利因素。本教材提供了强化训练的丰富素材和各种手段，教师可以充分利用这些素材和手段，激发学生的强烈学习欲望和潜在能力，使学生进入学习的兴奋状态和紧张状态。我们所说的"紧张状态"，绝不排斥生动活泼、趣味盎然的教学气氛。恰恰相反，这种教学气氛越浓，学生也就越兴奋、越投入，知识的学习与运用也就越能达到最佳境界，一切看似不可能一下学会的东西，就有可能在最短的时间里学到手，甚至运用得熟巧。

这本教材，从内容到形式，都走了一条新路子，肯定是不完善、不成熟的，还需要在今后的教学实践中做更深入的探索，希望能听到同行教师和留学生们的批评意见。

初级教材参加编写的人员还有杨廷治、陈辉、黄锡之、杨天舒、杨立群、苏伯华、成伟武等同志，我校副校长黄震华教授负责全书的英文注释和翻译。加拿大籍专家 David Packer 先生校阅了课文译文。我校校长孙维炎教授最后审定了全书。国家对外汉语教学领导小组办公室的领导同志，对本教材的编写与出版给予了指导和帮助。我校校领导、出版社和外事处的同志们，都给本教材的出版以大力支持。在此，我对他们表示由衷的感谢。

对外经济贸易大学
黄为之
1993 年 1 月

Preface to the First Edition

This textbook is meant for Chinese beginners.

Foreign students learning the Chinese language have their own specific characteristics. On the one hand, they know nothing about Chinese, and they do not have the listening comprehension and speaking abilities concerning this target language. On the other hand, most of them are adults with fully-developed intellects, rich social experience and scientific knowledge. They do not have a language imitation ability as strong as children do, but at the same time, they have an understanding and receptive abilities with which children cannot compare. These characteristics are, in a way, contradictory. Teachers are required to pay attention to the fact that their students are starting from scratch, and they have to begin their teaching from simple words, just like teaching children to speak. Students have to start their learning from simple words too. Learning is also a process of accumulation. Also, the characteristics of the learners require the teachers to pay attention to the fact that their students are adults, and they cannot be treated as children. The teachers have to use every means to bring the students' initiative into full play, mobilizing their advantages in intelligence, experience and knowledge, so that they can learn solid knowledge quickly. The question of how to understand the special characteristics of foreign students learning Chinese and to utilize such knowledge in the compilation of textbooks and in the teaching process has often been neglected. It is common that the content and teaching schedule are either too advanced or lagging behind. In writing this book of elementary Chinese conversation, we have taken these aspects into consideration, trying to resolve the aforementioned contradictions in the foreign students' Chinese learning process, so as to bring about the most satisfactory results in both learning and teaching.

The present textbook has the following characteristics:

Lessons 1-4 concentrate on the learning of the Chinese phonetic alphabet or *pinyin*. This is for the benefit of beginners. Students from Oriental countries have more difficulties in the pronunciation of vowels and consonants, while those from Western countries have their main problems in tones and intonation. These four lessons contain a large number of exercises aiming at such problems. Phonological exercises continue in Lessons 5-10, with a view to consolidating what was learned in the first four lessons. Through strict learning and teaching practice, students can solve these phonological problems, laying a solid foundation for mastering *Putonghua* (standard Chinese).

This textbook is a Chinese teaching material for business purposes, the content of which is very different from that of ordinary textbooks, where a large proportion is devoted to such daily matters as food, clothing, shelter, means of travel, and life on campus. The present book endeavors to combine the useful parts of the above mentioned topics with daily business routines such as buying and selling, bargaining, selection of goods, commercial services, advertising, special features of management, public relations, salesmanship, etc. Emphasis is placed on these aspects and the content is such that the students are exposed to a broad range of knowledge that is realistic and practical. The book's vocabulary, sentence structures, and difficulty are suitable for beginners.

According to the principle that language has such properties as communicative situations and communicative functions, this book has adopted a system of combining learning in class and after class. Starting from Lesson 5, there are two lessons for each topic. More specifically, daily business life is divided into several parts, each of which is presented in two lessons. The "in-class" text is for learning under the teacher's instruction. It is closed-door practice, aimed at laying a solid foundation. The "after-class" text is for students to learn when they participate in social practice. As the saying goes, this is "going into the sea and learning how to swim by swimming". Its purpose is to review and use the linguistic knowledge that has been learned in class. The contents of the two texts are closely related, but with different fields of activities. When the students have learned and mastered both texts, they have also learned the daily expressions for one aspect of "economic life". This teaching system has broken down the closed-end teaching approach. In organizing the teaching of a topic, the teacher can always ask the students to take part in the corresponding social practice either before or after class, as a preview or review of the topic. After entering into the teaching process, the content of this textbook, with its active and lively teaching style, will arouse great interest among the students, motivate them to learn, and take into account the extraordinary learning capabilities of adults, so as to achieve the expected results.

The present textbook adopts the teaching method for intensive training, characterized by low threshold, large volume of content, high density, and staged and quick progressing in teaching. The number of new words and the length of the texts have both exceeded those of ordinary Chinese textbooks. The whole teaching process is student-centered. Students are required to accomplish both the in-class and after-class activities actively on their own initiative. The teacher's role is to participate, inspire, and guide, but never lecture. The monotony and slow pace in the teaching and learning activities, and the passiveness and slackness on the part of the students are negative factors affecting the learning result. This textbook provides ample materials and means for intensified training, which can be fully utilized by the teachers to stimulate the students' strong desire and potential to learn. Students respond to a lively and interesting learning atmosphere. The better the learning atmosphere, the more excited and absorbed the students will become. Hence the optimal state will be attained for learning and use of knowledge. Things that seem impossible to learn at once will be mastered within the shortest period of time by the students.

As this textbook follows a new path in both its content and form, errors and shortcomings are inevitable. Further exploration is needed in future teaching practice. Therefore, criticisms and suggestions from fellow teachers and foreign students are highly welcome.

Those who participated in the compilation of the textbook include Yang Tingzhi, Chen Hui, Huang Xizhi, Yang Tianshu, Yang Liqun, Su Bohua, and

Cheng Weiwu. The English translation of all the texts and explanations has been done by Professor Huang Zhenhua, vice president of University of International Business and Economics (UIBE). Mr. David Packer, a Canadian expert working at UIBE, assisted with the English translation. And finally Professor Sun Weiyan, president of UIBE, examined the manuscript of the whole book. Senior members from the National Office for Teaching Chinese as a Foreign Language have provided guidance and support for the compilation and publication of the book. Leading members of UIBE, and colleagues from UIBE Press and Foreign Affairs Office have also given substantial support to this book. I hereby extend my heartfelt thanks to all of them.

Huang Weizhi
University of International
Business and Economics,
January, 1993

使用说明

对外汉语教学有许多特点。就学习者来说，他们来自不同国家、不同民族，有不同经历和不同文化背景，在学习汉语时，会明显表现出各自的特殊性和彼此的差异性；就教师来说，每一个教师，都有自己的教学个性、教学经历、教学风格和教学方法。鉴于此，不可能有一个整齐划一的教法与学法，我们这里的"使用说明"，仅仅是一个建议，供使用这套"经贸汉语口语"的教师和学习者参考。事实上，许多问题已经在这套书各册的前言中说到了，这里就不再重复，现在只做如下几点补充说明。

这套"经贸汉语口语"虽然是从零学起，但它"采用了低起点、大容量、高密度、分阶段而又大步推进的强化训练教学法"。从上面一段话，我们知道，这套书涉及的内容很广，又有相当的难度，一个学期大致要学完一册书，因此，预习和复习，就显得特别重要，尤其是预习，学生更要多花些时间，多下些功夫。像课文中的生词和语法点，书中已有简明扼要的注释，学生可以自学习得，教师只需讲解其中的难点，做些熟巧练习；每一篇课文，应要求学生在预习时，通过学习生词和参看课文的英语翻译，能比较顺畅地阅读下来并基本理解，教师可通过师生互相问答，检验学生阅读与理解的程度，讲解其中的疑难问题；课文中有关文化知识的注释及课文后的一篇短文，也要以自学为主。有些练习，也当做如是处理。不要把有限的课堂时间耗费在课文及相关材料的阅读上，要以课文和这些材料为"谈资"，开展生动活泼的谈话；"大容量"，要求许多东西在课下消化；"高密度"，则要求合理有效地利用时间，强化口语训练。总之，教师与学习者，都要有一个牢固意识，这是一部口语教材，练习口语，习得一口流利的汉语，是这套教材的终极目的。

与上述问题相关的，是在教与学的过程中，如何抓住重点。以这套书的《经贸中级汉语口语》和《经贸高级汉语口语》为例，每一课都是生词量大，内容多，篇幅也相对长，试图在一个教学单元时间里（4～6课时），把课文中出现的全部生词和全部内容都学会、都掌握，一般来说，几乎是不可能的。要善于根据课文题目的提示，找出每一课的关键词、重点句和核心内容，学会和掌握这些关键词、重点句和核心内容即可，其余的，在以后的重现中会逐渐习得和熟悉。教材在编写过程中，十分重视新知识的重现率和温故而知新的学习渐进性，老师和学习者都不需担心顾此失彼。

《经贸初级汉语口语》上、下册一共54课，每课4课时，一周6课时；《经贸中级汉语口语》上、下册一共40课，每课4～6课时，一周6课时；《经贸高级汉语口语》上、下册一共32课，每课4课时，一周4课时。如果条件允许，尽可能多安排一些课外实践活动。如《经贸初级汉语口语》，每一个话题都有"课上"和"课外"两篇课文，在学习"课外"一篇课文前，一定要学生走出去，学生在社会上会得到许多新鲜的东西，"课外"课文就变活了；学习《经贸中级汉语口语》时，可以组织去观摩正式谈判，或观看正式谈判录像，也可以到市场演练货物贸易谈判，有做生意经历的学生还可以现身说法；学习《经贸高级汉语口语》时，可围绕一个文化专题组织一些参观、访问和座谈活动。社会实践方式是多种多样的，这里只是举例而已，目的是要把死的文字材料变成活的知识，变成学生可以自由表达的口语能力。

对外经济贸易大学
黄为之
2016年5月

Users' Guide

Teaching Chinese as a foreign language has its own characteristics. The learners are from different countries of different ethnic groups with different life experiences and cultural backgrounds and display their own characteristics in learning Chinese, while the teachers too have their own teaching characteristics, experiences, styles and methods. Considering this diversity, we do not want to offer a standardized teaching and learning method to use this series of Chinese textbooks. However, we'd like to offer some suggestions for teachers and learners. Since some questions have been discussed in the Preface, we only address several additional points here.

Business Chinese Conversation adopts the teaching method for intensive training characterized by low threshold, large volume of content, high density, and staged and quick progressing in teaching. With a wide range of topics, the content of certain difficulty and the curriculum requirement to finish one volume within a term, it attaches particular importance to the preview and review. Especially for preview, students should spend more time and efforts on new words and grammar points and try to learn on their own with the aid of explanations and English translation of the texts. They should read through the texts and gain basic understanding before class. Then in class the teacher can use "questions and answers" to examine their reading comprehension, and will only need to explain the difficult points. The notes on cultural knowledge and the short essays at the end of each lesson should also be learned by students themselves. Some of the exercises should also be handled this way. Don't waste class hours on reading the texts and related materials, which should instead be the "lead" to lively dialogues among the students. "Large volume of content" indicates that lots of content has to be digested after class; "high density" requires effective use of time and intensive training in speaking. All in all, teachers and learners alike should be aware that this is a series of textbooks for practicing speaking with the ultimate goal to enable learners to speak fluent Chinese.

Closely related to what's mentioned above is the question of how to grasp the key points during teaching and learning. Take *Business Chinese Conversation (Intermediate)* and *Business Chinese Conversation (Advanced)* of this series for example. In each lesson there are a large number of new words, rich content, and long texts. The attempt to master all the new words and content within a teaching unit (4-6 class hours) is almost impossible. Therefore, students should be able to focus on the key words, important sentences and core content of each lesson according to the hint of its title. As for the rest, students will achieve the mastery of them through their later reappearances. During the compilation, we put a lot of emphasis on the reoccurring rate of new knowledge and the progressiveness of learning, so the teachers and learners can rest assured of our arrangement.

Altogether the two volumes of *Business Chinese Conversation (Elementary)* have 54 lessons, with four class hours for each lesson and six class hours each week. The two volumes of *Business Chinese Conversation (Intermediate)* have 40 lessons, with four to six class hours for each lesson and six class hours each week. And the two volumes of *Business Chinese Conversation (Advanced)* have 32 lessons, with four class hours for each lesson and four class hours each week. If conditions permit, arrange as many extracurricular activities as possible. For example, in *Business Chinese Conversation (Elementary)*, there are usually one text for "in-class learning" and one for "after-class learning" under each topic. Before learning the latter one, ask the students to go outside, and they can bring in lots of fresh stuff which will enliven the learning. While teaching *Business Chinese Conversation (Intermediate)*, the teacher can arrange students to watch a real negotiation or one on the video; students can go to practice trade negotiation themselves; and those with experience in doing business can also tell their own stories about negotiation. While teaching *Business Chinese Conversation (Advanced)*, the teacher can arrange a variety of social activities like visits and discussions. Our purpose is to turn the "dead" language materials into "live" knowledge, and further into the students' ability to express themselves freely in Chinese.

Huang Weizhi
University of International
Business and Economics,
May, 2016

Contents

第二十九课 Lesson 29	坐高铁去旅行（一） Travel by High-Speed Rail (I)	1
第三十课 Lesson 30	坐高铁去旅行（二） Travel by High-Speed Rail (II)	8
第三十一课 Lesson 31	你爱吃什么（一） What Is Your Favorite Food (I)	15
第三十二课 Lesson 32	你爱吃什么（二） What Is Your Favorite Food (II)	23
第三十三课 Lesson 33	今年流行什么（一） What Is in Vogue This Year (I)	30
第三十四课 Lesson 34	今年流行什么（二） What Is in Vogue This Year (II)	38

第三十五课 Lesson 35	互联网+（一）Internet + (I)	46
第三十六课 Lesson 36	互联网+（二）Internet + (II)	53
第三十七课 Lesson 37	节日与购物（一）Festivals and Shopping (I)	61
第三十八课 Lesson 38	节日与购物（二）Festivals and Shopping (II)	69
第三十九课 Lesson 39	麦当劳和茶馆（一）McDonald's and Teahouse (I)	76
第四十课 Lesson 40	麦当劳和茶馆（二）McDonald's and Teahouse (II)	83
第四十一课 Lesson 41	味道好极了（一）The Taste Is Great (I)	92
第四十二课 Lesson 42	味道好极了（二）The Taste Is Great (II)	100
第四十三课 Lesson 43	永远别说"不"（一）Never Say "No" (I)	109
第四十四课 Lesson 44	永远别说"不"（二）Never Say "No" (II)	118

第四十五课 Lesson 45	承诺以后（一）After Making a Promise (I)	126
第四十六课 Lesson 46	承诺以后（二）After Making a Promise (II)	134
第四十七课 Lesson 47	公关工作（一）A Career in Public Relations (I)	143
第四十八课 Lesson 48	公关工作（二）A Career in Public Relations (II)	152
第四十九课 Lesson 49	选准"上帝"（一）Choose the Right "God" (I)	162
第五十课 Lesson 50	选准"上帝"（二）Choose the Right "God" (II)	171
第五十一课 Lesson 51	巧用推销术（一）Skillful Salesmanship (I)	179
第五十二课 Lesson 52	巧用推销术（二）Skillful Salesmanship (II)	187
第五十三课 Lesson 53	快递与外卖（一）Express Delivery and Takeout (I)	195
第五十四课 Lesson 54	快递与外卖（二）Express Delivery and Takeout (II)	202

英译课文 — 209
English Translation of the Texts

生词总表 — 259
Vocabulary List

第二十九课　坐高铁去旅行（一）
Lesson 29　Travel by High-Speed Rail (I)

课文 Text

在课上

王老师：同学们，假期你们想去旅行吗？

珍　妮：想，我们都准备去旅行。

王老师：你们打算怎么旅行呢？

杰　克：骑自行车！中国是自行车王国，会有许多旅行的伙伴。

珍　妮：在中国有很多自行车运动爱好者。去比较近的地方，我也喜欢骑自行车，可以锻炼身体，但是去远的地方骑车的话就比较累了。

杰　克：那就坐飞机啊。我们在美国旅行，要么自己开车，要么就坐飞机。

珍　妮：为什么不坐火车？

杰　克：美国的铁路比较少，坐火车不太方便。

珍　妮：在欧洲旅行，人们要么开私家车，要么坐火车，很少有人坐飞机。

山　口：那是因为在欧洲，从一个国家到另一个国家很近，旅途很短，火车又四通八达，所以开车、坐火车，都很方便。这跟日本的情况差不多。

王老师：可见，各个地方的情况不一样。那么，在中国呢？

珍　妮：听中国朋友说，以前中国人常常坐火车旅行，时间很长，也比较累。

山　口：不过现在私家车在中国已经普及了，中国的高速公路越来越多，所以很多家庭都喜欢开车去旅行。

杰　克：现在还有了高铁，时速可以达到二三百公里，速度提高了，价格却很便宜，所以坐高铁旅行又方便又快捷。

王老师：你们说得很对！在中国旅行，开私家车、坐高铁、坐飞机，都是不错的选择。下课以后，你们好好儿谈谈，打算怎么在中国旅行。

生 词
New Words

1. 高铁　　　gāotiě　　　high-speed rail
2. 旅行　　　lǚxíng　　　to travel
3. 假期　　　jiàqī　　　holiday
4. 打算　　　dǎsuàn　　　to plan
5. 王国　　　wángguó　　　kingdom
6. 许多　　　xǔduō　　　many
7. 伙伴　　　huǒbàn　　　fellow, companion
8. 运动　　　yùndòng　　　sport
9. 爱好者　　àihàozhě　　fan, lover (of a particular thing)
10. 锻炼　　　duànliàn　　to exercise
11. 比较　　　bǐjiào　　　relatively
12. 累　　　　lèi　　　　tired
13. 要么　　　yàome　　　either... (or...)

29 坐高铁去旅行(一)

14. 铁路	tiělù	railway
15. 私家车	sījiāchē	private car
16. 国家	guójiā	country
17. 旅途	lǚtú	journey
18. 四通八达	sìtōng-bādá	to extend in all directions
19. 情况	qíngkuàng	situation
20. 可见	kějiàn	as you see
21. 各	gè	each
22. 高速公路	gāosù gōnglù	expressway
23. 时速	shísù	speed per hour
24. 达到	dádào	to reach
25. 速度	sùdù	speed
26. 提高	tígāo	to increase
27. 却	què	but
28. 快捷	kuàijié	fast
29. 不错	búcuò	good
30. 选择	xuǎnzé	option

专　名　Proper Noun

欧洲	Ōuzhōu	Europe

注释 Notes

1 "要么……要么……",表示选择,结果是非此即彼。例如:

"要么……要么……" indicates choice. The result is either this or that. For example:

1. 你要么今天来,要么明天来,我这两天都有空儿。
2. 要么你来,要么我去,我们今天得好好谈谈!
3. 你要么打个电话,要么发个短信,把这事告诉他。

2 "可见",连词,承接上文,表示可以做出判断或结论。例如:

可见, a conjunction, is a connecting link between the preceding and following text to show that a judgment or conclusion can be made. For example:

1. 这么简单的题都写错了,可见他没有复习。
2. 这么大的事他都没告诉你,可见他没把你当朋友。
3. 杰克家有很多藏书,可见他是一个爱读书的人。

3 汉语用相邻的两个数词连用表示概数。例如:

In Chinese, adjacent numerals can be used together to indicate an approximate number. For example:

1. 走路过去十一二分钟就能到。
2. 他大概二十三四岁的样子。
3. 从这儿到书店大概五六百米。

4 "却",副词,表示转折。例如:

却, an adverb, indicates a transition. For example:

1. 我想坐公交车,他却要骑自行车。
2. 我以为上海很冷,没想到却很暖和。
3. 我喜欢看电影,哥哥却喜欢看比赛。

补充生词
Additional New Words

1. 星巴克	Xīngbākè	Starbucks
2. 地铁	dìtiě	subway
3. 挤	jǐ	crowded
4. 大巴	dàbā	bus
5. 公共交通	gōnggòng jiāotōng	public transportation
6. 科幻	kēhuàn	science fiction

29 坐高铁去旅行(一)

练习
Exercises

一、替换练习。
Substitution drills.

A：我们都准备去旅行。
B：去哪儿?
A：去上海。
B：我也跟你们一起去。

吃午饭	学生食堂
换钱	中国银行
喝咖啡	星巴克
学习	图书馆

A：你怎么去学校?
B：走路。
A：怎么不坐公交?
B：太挤。

公司	坐地铁	打的	地铁便宜
颐和园	骑车	坐出租车	太贵
旅行	坐旅游大巴	开车	太远
上海	坐高铁	坐飞机	太贵

二、把下面的词组成句子。
Rearrange the following words into sentences.

1. 旅行 哪儿 打算 你们 去 假期
2. 伙伴 认识 我 新 很多 了
3. 国家 不同 情况 的 各个
4. 中国 私家车 普及 在 已经 了
5. 四通八达 中国 的 高速公路
6. 人 选择 去 很多 坐 旅行 高铁
7. 一个 运动 是 爱好者 他 自行车
8. 周末 旅行 我们 去 开车 准备 一家

5

三、完成下面的对话。
Complete the following dialogues.

A：我是一个自行车运动爱好者。
B：_____？
A：因为骑自行车，哪儿都能去。
B：_____。

A：你们国家的公共交通怎么样？
B：_____。
A：你们怎么去旅行？
B：_____。

A：晚上去哪儿吃饭？
B：要么_____。
A：我不想去食堂。
B：_____。

A：你想看什么电影？
B：要么_____。
A：我也喜欢科幻电影。
B：_____。

四、用"却"完成下面的句子。
Complete the following sentences with 却.

1. 我说的都是真的，_____。
2. 我请他吃饭，_____。
3. 我想吃比萨，_____。
4. 他喜欢上海，_____。
5. 我已经告诉过他，_____。

6. 天气预报说今天是晴天，_____。
7. 这件事是他做错了，_____。
8. 我送她鲜花，_____。

五、谈谈你们国家的交通情况。
Talk about the transportation in your country.

第三十课　坐高铁去旅行（二）
Lesson 30　Travel by High-Speed Rail (II)

课文 Text

在课外

杰　克：山口，你回来了？

山　口：回来了。你是什么时候回来的？

杰　克：我是昨天回来的。你到什么地方去了？玩儿得怎么样？

山　口：我去敦煌了，我喜欢中国古代的文化。敦煌石窟和壁画，已经有一千多年的历史了，实在太伟大了！

杰　克：你是怎么去的？

山　口：先坐高铁到兰州，再一路玩儿到敦煌。

珍　妮：我跟你一样，我也很喜欢中国的古代文化。

杰　克：那你去哪儿了？

珍　妮：我去江南水乡了。浙江的乌镇，江苏的周庄，都是中国古代的街道和房子。小河里，一只只乌篷船来来往往，姑娘们唱着江南小调。河岸边是一排排的木楼，小桥流水，桃红柳绿，真是美极了！

30 坐高铁去旅行（二）

山　口：有这么美吗？

珍　妮：当然了。有机会，你一定要去江南看看，"上有天堂，下有苏杭"嘛。

山　口：听你这么说，我现在就想去了。对了，你是怎么去的？

珍　妮：当然是坐高铁。中国的高铁高速、安全、平稳、舒适，真是太棒了！杰克，你呢？你去哪儿了？

杰　克：我去海南了。

山　口：你也是坐高铁去的吗？

杰　克：不是，海南太远，所以我是坐飞机去的。

山　口：坐飞机，又贵又不能看沿途的风景，我还是喜欢坐高铁。

珍　妮：我觉得飞机和高铁各有各的好处。杰克，你在海南玩儿得怎么样？

杰　克：海南特别漂亮，有大海、阳光、沙滩。在海水中游泳、冲浪，在沙滩上喝可乐、听音乐，真是一种美好的享受！

山　口：那儿的外国人多吗？

杰　克：外国人多，中国人也很多。现在交通特别方便，所以冬天有很多人去海南度假。

珍　妮：那明年冬天咱们一起去吧！

生　词 New Words

1. 古代　　gǔdài　　ancient times
2. 文化　　wénhuà　　culture
3. 石窟　　shíkū　　grotto
4. 壁画　　bìhuà　　fresco

5.	历史	lìshǐ	history
6.	实在	shízài	indeed
7.	伟大	wěidà	great
8.	江南	jiāngnán	regions south of the Yangtze River
9.	水乡	shuǐxiāng	region of rivers and lakes
10.	街道	jiēdào	street
11.	河	hé	river
12.	乌篷船	wūpéngchuán	Wupeng boat, black-awning boat
13.	来往	láiwǎng	to come and go
14.	姑娘	gūniang	girl
15.	小调	xiǎodiào	melody, tune
16.	岸	àn	(river) bank
17.	桥	qiáo	bridge
18.	流	liú	to flow
19.	桃红柳绿	táo hóng liǔ lǜ	red peach blossoms and green willows
20.	极	jí	extremely
21.	天堂	tiāntáng	heaven
22.	高速	gāosù	high speed
23.	平稳	píngwěn	smooth, steady
24.	舒适	shūshì	comfortable
25.	棒	bàng	great
26.	沿途	yántú	on the way
27.	风景	fēngjǐng	scenery
28.	好处	hǎochù	advantage
29.	海	hǎi	sea
30.	阳光	yángguāng	sunshine
31.	沙滩	shātān	beach
32.	游泳	yóuyǒng	to swim
33.	冲浪	chōnglàng	to surf
34.	音乐	yīnyuè	music

35.	美好	měihǎo	wonderful
36.	享受	xiǎngshòu	to enjoy
37.	度假	dùjià	to take a holiday

专名 Proper Nouns

1.	敦煌	Dūnhuáng	Dunhuang, a city in northwestern Gansu Province, western China
2.	兰州	Lánzhōu	Lanzhou, capital of Gansu Province
3.	浙江	Zhèjiāng	Zhejiang Province
4.	乌镇	Wū Zhèn	Wuzhen, a town in Zhejiang Province
5.	江苏	Jiāngsū	Jiangsu Province
6.	周庄	Zhōuzhuāng	Zhouzhuang, a town in Jiangsu Province
7.	苏州	Sūzhōu	Suzhou, a city in Jiangsu Province
8.	杭州	Hángzhōu	Hangzhou, capital of Zhejiang Province
9.	海南	Hǎinán	Hainan Province

注释 Notes

1 "是……的",强调已经发生或完成的动作的时间、地点、方式、目的、施事和受事等。在肯定句中,"是"可以省略。否定句中"是"不能省略。例如:

"是……的" emphasizes the time, place, manner, purpose, agent, or patient, etc. of an action that has taken place or been completed. 是 can be omitted in affirmative sentences and cannot be omitted in negative sentences. For example:

1. 他是今天早上到北京的。
2. 我昨天坐飞机来的。
3. 他不是来旅行的,是来工作的。

2 "实在",副词,的确。例如:

实在, an adverb, means "indeed". For example:

1. 他实在是太忙了,你不要去打扰他。
2. 我实在没有办法,帮不了你,你不要怪我。
3. 你说得实在太对了!

"实在",也可以是形容词,形容诚实,不虚假,可以重叠使用。例如:

实在 can also be used as an adjective meaning "honesty" and may appear in the form 实实在在. For example:

1. 杰克说话很实在,你可以相信他。
2. 大娘很实在,你到了大娘家,就不要客气!
4. 我想学一点儿实实在在的本事。

3 "上有天堂,下有苏杭",意思是苏州和杭州的自然景色优美,可与天堂相比。

"上有天堂,下有苏杭" means that Suzhou and Hangzhou have such beautiful natural sceneries that can be compared to the heaven.

练 习
Exercises

一、替换练习。
Substitution drills.

A:你是<u>什么时候</u>来的?
B:我是<u>9点来</u>的。

在哪儿买	在书店买
跟谁一起来	跟朋友一起来
怎么去海南	坐飞机去

A:<u>海南</u>怎么样?
B:实在太<u>棒</u>了。

高铁	舒适
江南	美
这本书	有意思

30 坐高铁去旅行（二）

A：<u>中午</u>去哪儿吃饭？
B：当然<u>去食堂</u>。

晚上做什么　　　去看电影
吃饺子还是吃面条　　吃饺子
喝咖啡还是喝可乐　　喝可乐

二、把下面的词组成句子。
Rearrange the following words into sentences.

1. 怎么样　你　得　玩儿　家　今天　朋友　去
2. 去　假期　旅行　了　哪儿　这个　你们
3. 古色古香　喜欢　水乡　我　的　江南
4. 姑娘　好听　小调　江南　的　唱　很
5. 冬天　地方　度假　好　海南　是　的
6. 珍妮　的　坐　杭州　去　高铁　是
7. 美好　的　是　这　享受　一种
8. 喜欢　的　风景　沿途　看　我

三、完成下面的对话。
Complete the following dialogues.

A：你什么时候去旅行？
B：_____。

A：你想去哪儿？
B：_____。

A：你去过敦煌吗？
B：_____。

A：你知道敦煌的历史吗？
B：_____。

A：你喜欢海南吗？
B：_____。
A：为什么？
B：_____。

A：你是什么时候来中国的？
B：_____。
A：你是怎么来的？
B：_____。

四、把"实在"放在下面句子中适当的地方。
Put 实在 in the proper places in the following sentences.

1. 今天的作业太多了。
2. 他这个人做事，你放心！
3. 他说得太快，我听不懂。
4. 这个人麻烦，我不想和他一起去旅行。
5. 这个餐馆的饭菜不错，我很喜欢去。
6. 他是一个很的人。
7. 杰克给了珍妮许多的帮助。

五、谈谈你的一次旅行。
Talk about one of your trips.

第三十一课　你爱吃什么（一）

Lesson 31　What Is Your Favorite Food (I)

课文 Text

在课上

王老师：同学们，你们现在习惯中国的饭菜了吗？

山　口：我很习惯。

珍　妮：我也很喜欢吃中餐。

杰　克：你昨天逛王府井，还在麦当劳买汉堡包吃呢！

珍　妮：都十二点了，我饿了嘛。

王老师：中餐好吃还是西餐好吃？

珍　妮：都很好吃。

杰　克：老师，我知道北京到处都有麦当劳、肯德基，这些店的生意都很红火。难道中国人也爱吃西餐？

王老师：是的，很多人喜欢。

杰　克：为什么？

王老师：我先问你们，在你们国家，是不是也有很多中国餐馆？

杰　克：是。一个城市少的也有几个，多的可能有几十个。

王老师：他们的生意怎么样？

珍　妮：也很红火。

王老师：好，你们回答我，西方人为什么喜欢吃中餐？

珍　妮：山口，你是东方人，比较熟悉东方人的饮食习惯，你先回答老师的问题吧。

山　口：中餐很讲究色、香、味、形。

杰　克：什么色、香、味、形？

山　口：就是菜的颜色、香气、味道和形状。

杰　克：这有什么特别吗？

山　口：这么说吧，你刚坐下，还在点菜，就会闻到一股菜香；等菜摆上桌子，瞧那颜色，你就忍不住要动筷子；咬上一口，那味道，啧啧……

珍　妮：就像雀巢咖啡的广告，"味道好极了"，是不是？

杰　克：你这么说，我恨不得这就去美餐一顿。哎，还有"形"呢？

山　口：哦！那些菜的形状简直就是一件件艺术品。

珍　妮：不过，山口说的是卖米饭、炒菜的正餐，我更爱吃北京小吃。

杰　克：北京小吃，又有什么讲究？

珍　妮：我也说不清楚，明天带你去见识见识。

杰　克：说了半天，老师的问题究竟该怎么回答呢？

山　口：我想，中国人爱吃西餐，西方人爱吃中餐，大概是一种文化交流吧！

珍　妮：是为了满足好奇心，人都有好奇心！

生词
New Words

1. 习惯　　　　xíguàn　　　　custom, habit; to be accustomed to
2. 菜　　　　　cài　　　　　　food, dish, course

31 你爱吃什么（一）

3.	中餐	zhōngcān	Chinese food
4.	汉堡包	hànbǎobāo	hamburger
5.	饿	è	hungry; to starve
6.	到处	dàochù	everywhere
7.	红火	hónghuo	booming, flourishing, prosperous
8.	难道	nándào	*used to emphasize a rhetorical question*
9.	西餐	xīcān	Western food
10.	回答	huídá	to answer, to reply, to response
11.	熟悉	shúxi	to know well, to be familiar with
12.	色	sè	color
13.	香	xiāng	sweet-smelling; fragrance
14.	味	wèi	taste, flavor
15.	形	xíng	form, shape
16.	颜色	yánsè	color
17.	味道	wèidao	taste, flavor
18.	形状	xíngzhuàng	form, shape
19.	点菜	diǎn cài	to order dishes
20.	闻	wén	to smell
21.	股	gǔ	*measure word referring to smell, gas, odor, etc.*
22.	摆	bǎi	to put, to place, to arrange
23.	桌子	zhuōzi	table
24.	瞧	qiáo	to look, to see
25.	忍	rěn	to endure, to bear
26.	动	dòng	to move, to stir
27.	筷子	kuàizi	chopsticks
28.	咬	yǎo	to bite, to snap at
29.	啧啧	zézé	(*onomatopoeia*) click of the tongue

30.	恨不得	hènbude	how one wishes one could
31.	顿	dùn	*measure word referring to meal, reprimand, etc.*
32.	简直	jiǎnzhí	simply, at all
33.	艺术品	yìshùpǐn	work of art
34.	米饭	mǐfàn	(cooked) rice
35.	炒菜	chǎocài	fried dish
36.	小吃	xiǎochī	snack, refreshments
37.	见识	jiànshi	experience, knowledge, sense
38.	究竟	jiūjìng	after all, actually, exactly
39.	大概	dàgài	probably, perhaps
40.	交流	jiāoliú	to exchange, to communicate
41.	满足	mǎnzú	to satisfy, to meet
42.	好奇心	hàoqíxīn	curiosity

专　名　Proper Nouns

1.	麦当劳	Màidāngláo	McDonald's
2.	肯德基	Kěndéjī	KFC
3.	雀巢	Quècháo	Nescafé

注释 Notes

1　"难道",副词,只能用在反问句中,加重反诘的语气。"难道"有时也说"难道说",有时还跟"不成"连用,形成"难道……不成"的句式。例如:

难道 is an adverb that can only be used in a rhetorical question to stress the tone. 难道 can sometimes take the form of 难道说, or echo with 不成, constituting the sentence pattern "难道……不成". For example:

31 你爱吃什么（一）

1. 我都饿了，难道你不饿？
2. 他就在那儿，难道你看不见？
3. 他不去了，难道说我们也不去了？
4. 你这么大的人了，应该怎么说话，难道还要我教你不成？

2 "这么说吧"，提示一种解释的方式。常用于以简捷的方式解释较复杂的问题，以形象的方式表达较抽象的事物。例如：

In 这么说吧, 这么 (this way) is a demonstrative pronoun. Here it introduces a form of explanation. It is often used when one uses a simple and direct way to explain a more complicated question, or when one uses a figurative way to express something more abstract. For example:

1. A：北京的天气怎么样？
   B：这么说吧，北京的天气跟纽约差不多一样。

2. A：中国的小吃怎么样？
   B：这么说吧，你想吃什么就有什么，还一定喜欢吃。

3 "恨不得"，表示急切盼望做成某事，多用于实际做不到的事。也说"恨不能"。后面必须跟动词或动宾词组做宾语，"恨不得"和动词宾语之间常用"马上、立刻"等副词或带"一"的量词。例如：

恨不得 expresses a strong wish to finish doing something, which is often beyond one's actual ability. Another form is 恨不能. It takes a verb or a verb-object phrase as its object. 恨不得 and the verb or verb phrase are often linked by adverbs such as 马上, 立刻 (immediately) or quantifiers with 一. For example:

1. 我恨不得马上就见到他。
2. 我恨不得立刻回家休息。
3. 珍妮恨不得一下子记住这些生词。
4. 他恨不得马上飞到北京。

练 习
Exercises

一、替换练习。
Substitution drills.

A：你习惯八点钟上课吗？
B：刚来的时候不习惯，现在习惯了。

早睡早起	
用筷子	
北京的天气	
这儿的环境	

A：你难道真的饿了？
B：真的，我恨不得马上去大吃一顿。

不去逛商店	逛商店有什么意思
不想见识见识	我没有这种好奇心
不爱喝咖啡	咖啡味道太苦
不喜欢看电影	我喜欢看比赛

A：你爱吃汉堡包吗？
B：我爱吃汉堡包，可我更爱吃北京小吃。

去	西单	前门
住	宿舍	公寓
逛	公园	商店
爱	工作	玩儿

二、把下面的词组成句子。
Rearrange the following words into sentences.

1. 最 中餐 吃 我 爱
2. 饿 又 了 怎么 你
3. 我 你 帮助 难道 能 不
4. 你 一点儿 不 早 难道 能 来 吗

5. 这 生意 红火 家 的 饭店 很
6. 先生 你 菜 点 请

三、完成下面的对话。
Complete the following dialogues.

A：_____？
B：当然，我很喜欢吃中餐。
A：为什么？
B：_____。

A：_____？
B：我还没去过，也不想去。
A：难道你不喜欢_____吗？
B：喜欢，不过，_____。

A：你每天几点起床？
B：_____。
A：这是个好习惯！
B：你呢？
A：_____。
B：这个习惯可不好。

A：_____？
B：当然去过。
A：那家餐厅怎么样？
B：_____。

四、用指定的词语完成句子。
Complete the following sentences with the given words.

1. 做买卖有许多讲究，_____。（特别）

2. 我太高兴了，_____。（忍不住）

3. 爸爸打电话来说，他明天来北京看我，_____
   ____。（恨不得）

4. 做中国菜有很多讲究，_____。（见识）

5. 我看你今天很发愁，你能说说_____？（究竟）

五、下面是在饭店里的一段对话，熟读后表演。

Familiarize yourself with the following dialogue in the restaurant, and then perform it.

山　　口：啊，好香啊！

珍　　妮：是啊，今天可要美餐一顿。

服务员：二位小姐来了，欢迎，请进！请坐这儿！

山　　口：谢谢！

服务员：二位小姐吃点儿什么？这是菜单。

山　　口：珍妮，你点菜吧！

珍　　妮：好。我们要这个，这个，还有这个。

服务员：好，请稍等，马上就来。

山　　口：呀，怎么是咖啡、面包、冰激凌啊？

珍　　妮：怎么？你不喜欢？

山　　口：喜欢是喜欢，不过我想吃中餐啊！

32

第三十二课 你爱吃什么（二）

Lesson 32 What Is Your Favorite Food (II)

课 文 Text

在课外

（珍妮在门外敲门）

珍　妮：杰克！杰克！
杰　克：谁呀？
珍　妮：是我，珍妮，快起床！
杰　克：现在几点了？
珍　妮：七点一刻了。
杰　克：干吗这么早就来了？我还想睡会儿懒觉呢！
珍　妮：不行。你不是想去赶北京早市吗？再睡懒觉，可就收摊儿了！
杰　克：好吧，你等等。

珍　妮：杰克，你看！这马路边儿一溜儿都是卖小吃的。
杰　克：嗬，真香！都是卖什么的？
珍　妮：这是天津风味小吃"煎饼果子"。师傅，来两份儿煎饼果子。
小　贩：好嘞，两份儿煎饼果子！

珍　妮：杰克，怎么样？

杰　克：嗯，不错。外软里脆，很有特色。

珍　妮：看，这些是油条和炸糕，都是现炸现卖。还有馄饨、豆浆，北京人最爱吃。要不要来碗尝尝？

杰　克：好。这豆浆又香又甜，很好。馄饨味道也不错。

珍　妮：走吧，前边还有小吃呢，什么包子呀，烧饼呀，糖耳朵呀，名堂可多了，也都去尝尝吧。

杰　克：哎，今天不行了，肚子已经吃撑了，改天再来吧。

珍　妮：不吃，也看看啊！

（山口、杰克和珍妮在一家大商场里）

山　口：杰克，听说这个商场里有食品一条街，我已经走饿了，去吃点儿东西吧。

珍　妮：现在中国人做生意，讲究的是效益，越来越灵活，你们看，商场里也有美食街了。

杰　克：说得没错。

山　口：买东西的人很多，看饿了，吃点儿东西，吃了东西，再继续买，两不耽误不是？

杰　克：就像我们现在这样。

山　口：你们看，这里有麦当劳、肯德基，还有很多中式小吃店。

珍　妮：别光顾说了，都快饿死我了！

生词 New Words

1. 干吗　　　　gànmá　　　　why on earth, whatever for
2. 睡懒觉　　　shuì lǎnjiào　　to sleep in, to sleep late

32 你爱吃什么（二）

3.	赶	gǎn	to try to catch up with, to hurry up
4.	早市	zǎoshì	morning market
5.	收摊儿	shōutānr	to shut up shop, to wind up the day's business
6.	一溜儿	yíliùr	in a row, in a line
7.	风味	fēngwèi	special flavor, local flavor
8.	煎饼果子	jiānbingguǒzi	pancake roll with crisp fritter
9.	份儿	fènr	share, part, portion
10.	软	ruǎn	soft
11.	脆	cuì	crisp
12.	油条	yóutiáo	deep-fried twisted dough sticks
13.	炸糕	zhágāo	fried glutinous rice cake
14.	馄饨	húntun	dumpling soup, wonton
15.	豆浆	dòujiāng	soybean milk
16.	碗	wǎn	bowl
17.	尝	cháng	to taste, to try the flavor of
18.	包子	bāozi	steamed stuffed bun
19.	烧饼	shāobing	sesame seed cake
20.	糖	táng	sugar, candy
21.	耳朵	ěrduo	ear
22.	名堂	míngtang	variety, item
23.	撑	chēng	to fill to the point of bursting
24.	改天	gǎitiān	another day, some other day
25.	食品	shípǐn	food
26.	效益	xiàoyì	benefit, profit
27.	灵活	línghuó	flexible, elastic
28.	继续	jìxù	to continue
29.	耽误	dānwu	to delay, to hold up
30.	顾	gù	to pay attention to, to take care of

专　名　Proper Noun

天津　　　　　　Tiānjīn　　　　　Tianjin, a municipality in China

注释 Notes

1 "赶",动词,指加快行动,使不耽误时间。例如:

赶, a verb, means speeding up the action to avoid wasting time. For example:

1. 师傅,请快点儿,我想赶七点的飞机。
2. 我等会儿再跟你说吧,我现在赶着去上班呢。

"赶"也可以指去,到(某处)。例如:

赶 also means going to someplace. For example:

1. 她每天都去赶早市。
2. 过年的时候很多人去赶庙会。

2 "来",动词,表示做某个动作(代替意义更具体的动词)。例如:

来, a verb, means taking a certain action (to replace verbs with more specific meanings). For example:

1. 别来这一套。
2. 来一场篮球比赛吧。
3. 你休息一会儿,让我来。

3 "名堂",名词,意思是"花样,名目"。例如:

名堂, a noun, means "variety" or "item". For example:

1. 你别看都在吆喝"买一送一",名堂可多了!
2. 中国的快餐,名堂多得很,一句两句说不清。
3. 我看不出这里边有什么名堂。

32 你爱吃什么（二）

4 "顾"，动词，意思是"注意，照管"。例如：

顾, a verb, means "to pay attention to" or "to take care of". For example:

1. 事情太多，顾不过来了。
2. 今天太忙了，都顾不上吃饭了。
3. 别光顾着说话，快吃吧。

练 习
Exercises

一、替换练习。
Substitution drills.

A：你为什么这么早起床？
B：我要去赶<u>火车</u>。

| 飞机 |
| 班车 |
| 公共汽车 |
| 早市 |

A：你看，这马路边一溜儿都是卖什么的？
B：都是卖<u>早点摊儿</u>。

| 书 |
| 小吃 |
| 旧货 |
| 水果 |

A：这是<u>天津煎饼</u>，要不要尝尝？
B：好的，来<u>一份儿</u>。
A：味道怎么样？
B：味道<u>不错</u>。

现炸的油条	五根	还行
馄饨	两碗	还可以
新出的汉堡包	两个	很特别
山口做的菜	一点儿	好极了

A：小王，我们一起去北海好吗？
B：现在不行，改天再去吧！

| 长城 |
| 书店 |
| 图书城 |
| 中国银行 |

A：这是书店，怎么会卖食品？
B：这有什么奇怪的？现在做生意越来越灵活，效益好就行。

电影院	小吃
中餐馆	西餐
小吃店	米饭、炒菜
游泳馆	冰淇淋

二、把下面的词组成句子。
Rearrange the following words into sentences.

1. 每天 都 你 懒觉 睡 吗
2. 你 早上 今天 几点 是 的 醒
3. 吃 煎饼果子 你 过 吗
4. 我 风味 喜欢 最 小吃 北京 的
5. 我 尝尝 小吃 可以 吗 这种
6. 他 怕 学习 最 耽误 汉语
7. 耽误 别 了 早市 赶
8. 做 我们 很 经理 生意 灵活
9. 效益 我们 今年 很 的 好 经济

三、用指定的词语完成下面的对话。
Complete the following dialogues with the given words.

A：小王，_____？（忙）
B：干吗？
A：我想请你去看电影。
B：对不起，_____。（时间）

A：杰克，你为什么急急忙忙的？
B：_____。（赶）
A：可现在已经七点五十五分了。
B：_____。（迟到）

A：哎哟……
B：你怎么啦？
A：_____！（吃撑了）
B：你为什么吃这么多？
A：_____！（饿）

四、谈谈你在北京最爱吃什么。

Talk about your favorite food in Beijing.

第三十三课　今年流行什么（一）
Lesson 33　What Is in Vogue This Year (I)

课文　Text

在课上

王老师：你们昨天去看时装发布会了吗？

珍　妮：我们都去了。

王老师：印象如何？

山　口：印象太深了！真是美极了！

珍　妮：品种多，款式新，有中国的时装，也有不少世界名牌。

杰　克：老师，我发现世界流行的款式，发布会上差不多都有。

珍　妮：真的，法国今年刚上市的流行款式，这里就有了，中国市场跟得真快！

杰　克：我听说，在中国的一些高档时装店，一套西服要近万元，一件毛衣近千元，一双皮鞋好几百元，一双袜子都要几十元，买的人还不少。

珍　妮：中国人的消费水平提高了。

山　口：发布会上还有法国时装，特别漂亮，就是太贵了。

珍　妮：你要漂亮，还舍不得花钱？

33 今年流行什么（一）

山　口：可法国时装变化快，去年流行的，今年又不时髦了。要是每年都买，得花多少钱啊？

杰　克：那是，法国时装，领导世界新潮流，谁叫你想赶时髦呢？

山　口：不是赶时髦，是挡不住诱惑！

珍　妮：其实，时装有高档的，也有中低档的；有贵的，也有便宜的。

杰　克：我觉得，高档的都是很贵的，不过名牌倒不一定都是很贵的高档时装。

王老师：嗯，也许杰克说得更准确！

杰　克：比如李维斯公司的牛仔裤，真正的世界名牌，巴黎、伦敦、北京、东京，哪儿都有，有高档的，也有中低档的。

山　口：你这么说，中国的旗袍，也是驰名中外的商品，在世界各地都很流行。

王老师：不错，只可惜还没有一个叫得响的商标。

生词 New Words

1. 流行	liúxíng	popular, fashionable, in vogue
2. 时装	shízhuāng	fashionable dress
3. 发布会	fābùhuì	(fashion) show, launch event
4. 印象	yìnxiàng	impression
5. 如何	rúhé	how, what
6. 深	shēn	deep
7. 品种	pǐnzhǒng	variety, assortment, breed
8. 款式	kuǎnshì	pattern, style, design

9.	名牌	míngpái	famous brand
10.	发现	fāxiàn	to find, to discover
11.	市场	shìchǎng	market
12.	档	dàng	grade, level, class
13.	西服	xīfú	suit
14.	毛衣	máoyī	woolen sweater
15.	皮鞋	píxié	leather shoes
16.	袜子	wàzi	socks, stockings
17.	消费	xiāofèi	consumption; to consume
18.	水平	shuǐpíng	level, standard
19.	舍不得	shěbude	to hate to part with (or use), to be reluctant to
20.	花	huā	to spend
21.	变化	biànhuà	to change
22.	时髦	shímáo	fashionable, in vogue
23.	领导	lǐngdǎo	to lead
24.	潮流	cháoliú	tide, trend
25.	挡	dǎng	to block, to resist
26.	诱惑	yòuhuò	temptation, enticement
27.	其实	qíshí	in fact, as a matter of fact, actually
28.	倒	dào	*adverb implying that it is out of expec-tation, or contrary to reason or fact*
29.	也许	yěxǔ	perhaps, maybe
30.	准确	zhǔnquè	accurate, exact, precise
31.	牛仔裤	niúzǎikù	jeans
32.	旗袍	qípáo	cheongsam, a traditional close-fitting Chinese women's dress with high neck and slit skirt
33.	驰名	chímíng	famous, well-known

33 今年流行什么（一）

34. 可惜	kěxī	it's a pity, unfortunately
35. 响	xiǎng	resounding, loud
36. 商标	shāngbiāo	trademark, brand name

专 名 Proper Nouns

1. 李维斯公司	Lǐwéisī Gōngsī	Levi Strauss and Co., an American clothing company
2. 巴黎	Bālí	Paris
3. 伦敦	Lúndūn	London
4. 东京	Dōngjīng	Tokyo

注 释 Notes

1 "如何"，代词，意思是"怎么""怎么样"，但"如何"多用于书面语，"怎么""怎么样"多用于口语。例如：

如何, a pronoun, means 怎么 (how) or 怎么样 (how about), but 如何 is more often used in written Chinese while 怎么 or 怎么样 in spoken Chinese. For example:

1. 您看今天的工作如何安排？
2. 你的生意做得如何了？
3. 这事我以前没有做过，不知道如何开始。
4. 中国人现在的消费水平如何，到市场看一看就知道了。

2 "倒"，副词，表示出乎意料，跟情理或事实相反。例如：

倒, an adverb, indicates that something is out of expectation or is contrary to reason or fact. For example:

1. 妹妹倒比姐姐高了。
2. 我们是老朋友了，你今天怎么倒客气起来？
3. 已经十月了，天倒比九月热，你说奇怪不奇怪？

也可以表示让步。例如：
It may also express concession. For example:

1. 我倒是见过他，就是不知道他叫什么名字。
2. 货倒是好货，可是太贵了。
3. 我倒是想去，就是没时间。

3 "也许"，副词，表示猜测、估计或不肯定的语气。例如：

也许, an adverb, indicates a tone of guessing, estimation or uncertainty. For example:

1. 今天也许要下雨。
2. 畅销商品也许会变成滞销商品。
3. 这种款式今年夏天也许会流行起来。

也可以表示委婉语气。例如：
It may also express a mild, softened tone. For example:

1. 你说得也许对，但我不想听。
2. 这也许很时髦，但我不喜欢。
3. 这样做也许更好。

练 习
Exercises

一、**替换练习**。
Substitution drills.

A：你对<u>他</u>的印象如何？
B：我觉得<u>他很热情</u>。

天津	天津的小吃很好吃
北京	北京很大
珍妮	珍妮很漂亮
杰克	他是一个很实在的人

33 今年流行什么（一）

A：你来北京以后，有什么发现？
B：我发现<u>北京人很好客</u>。

| 商店的东西很丰富 |
| 网上购物很流行 |
| 好玩儿的地方很多 |
| 饭馆特别多 |

A：你买这<u>套西服</u>花了多少钱？
B：我花了<u>一千元</u>。

件	毛衣	一百三十元
条	牛仔裤	四十五元
台	电视机	两千五百元
辆	小汽车	二十万

A：你舍得离开<u>你爸爸妈妈</u>吗？
B：舍不得，可我<u>已经是个大人了</u>。

你家	想来北京学习
女朋友	不能不工作
北京	应该回国
同学们	得找工作

二、把下面的词组成句子。
Rearrange the following words into sentences.

1. 可惜　已经　他　了　国　回
2. 北京人　我　印象　给　的　极了　好
3. 名牌　法国　畅销　的　北京　在　很
4. 款式　这　上市　新　的　是
5. 今年　很　这　流行　款式　夏天　种
6. 他　了　已经　家　回　也许
7. 他　花　买　钱　东西　舍得
8. 挡不住　杰克　的　诱惑　美食
9. 她　一　很　是　个　的　时髦　女人
10. 他　问题　回答　准确　极了　得

三、完成下面的对话。
Complete the following dialogues.

A：你昨天去哪儿了？
B：_____。
A：_____？
B：中国的名牌产品给我的印象最深。

A：_____？
B：是的，我常常去逛商店。
A：有什么发现吗？
B：_____。

A：今年北京的服装市场如何？
B：_____！
A：你喜欢哪种款式？
B：_____。

A：你喜欢赶时髦吗？
B：_____。
A：为什么？
B：_____。

A：_____？
B：五年前，我来过北京。
A：北京有什么变化吗？
B：_____。

四、用下面的词语造句。
Make sentences with the following words.

1. 挡不住
2. 发现
3. 舍不得
4. 变化
5. 可惜

五、你看过时装发布会吗？给大家介绍一下。
Have you ever seen a fashion show? Talk about it.

第三十四课 今年流行什么（二）
Lesson 34 What Is in Vogue This Year (II)

课文 Text

在课外

山　口：珍妮，今天有中国时装表演，我有票，你和我一起去好吗？

杰　克：嗨，我也去。

珍　妮：看你，山口又没邀请你。

山　口：你着什么急，还能忘了你？给！

珍　妮：山口，时装表演在什么地方？

山　口：在国贸大厦。

杰　克：中国的时装表演怎么样？

山　口：不看不知道，一看吓一跳！

杰　克：吓一跳？那么可怕？我不去了！

珍　妮：亏你还是个男子汉呢！不是可怕，是叫你感到吃惊。

山　口：一看就着迷！

杰　克：真的？有这么好？

珍　妮：我在巴黎看过一回中国的时装表演。

杰　克：那你快介绍介绍，详细点儿！

珍　妮：中国时装，大都是用中国丝绸做的，新潮、鲜亮，

34 今年流行什么（二）

有民族风格，又有时代感。

杰　克：时装模特儿怎么样？

珍　妮：那就更没的说了，个个是东方美人……

杰　克：快走，这个机会可不能错过。

珍　妮：看把你急得，你还让我说详细点儿呢，我的话都没说完……

山　口：杰克，刚才看了时装表演，印象如何？

杰　克：嗯，印象非常深刻，同法国的时装表演一样精彩，毫不逊色！

珍　妮：你是看着那些模特儿着迷吧！

杰　克：你这就不懂了。你不是常想同那模特儿比美吗？

珍　妮：那又怎么样？

杰　克：那你至少也要去买一套她们展示的衣服，穿得同她们一样漂亮，对不？

珍　妮：那是。

杰　克：你看，时装不就有销路了？

珍　妮：嗬，你还挺懂生意经的嘛！

杰　克：那自然。

山　口：算了，别得意了。你们瞧，这街边一溜儿服装店，你们不想去挑几件？说不定，也有流行的时装呢！

珍　妮：我正想去呢。今年夏天特别流行短裙，不知道这儿有没有卖的。

山　口：你们看，那个中国姑娘正在试穿的不就是？

杰　克：珍妮，要不要我给你参谋参谋，把你打扮得跟时装模特儿一样美？

珍　妮：你有那本事？

杰　克：怎么，不相信？今天的时装表演白看了？

生 词
New Words

1.	表演	biǎoyǎn	to perform; performance
2.	票	piào	ticket
3.	邀请	yāoqǐng	to invite
4.	吓	xià	to frighten, to scare
5.	可怕	kěpà	fearful, frightful, terrifying
6.	亏	kuī	*saying the opposite, implying sarcasm*
7.	男子汉	nánzǐhàn	man
8.	感到	gǎndào	to feel, to sense
9.	吃惊	chījīng	to be shocked, to be startled, to be amazed
10.	着迷	zháomí	to be fascinated, to be spellbound
11.	详细	xiángxì	detailed, minute
12.	丝绸	sīchóu	silk
13.	鲜亮	xiānliang	bright, brightly-colored
14.	民族	mínzú	nationality, nation, ethnic group
15.	风格	fēnggé	style
16.	时代	shídài	era, epoch, times
17.	感（觉）	gǎn (jué)	feeling, sense
18.	模特儿	mótèr	model
19.	机会	jīhuì	chance, opportunity
20.	错过	cuòguò	to miss, to let slip
21.	完	wán	to finish, to complete
22.	非常	fēicháng	very, extremely
23.	深刻	shēnkè	deep, profound
24.	精彩	jīngcǎi	wonderful, splendid, brilliant
25.	毫不	háo bù	not at all

34 今年流行什么（二）

26. 逊色	xùnsè	inferior
27. 至少	zhìshǎo	at least
28. 展示	zhǎnshì	to show, to reveal
29. 衣服	yīfu	clothes, clothing
30. 销路	xiāolù	sale, market
31. 挺	tǐng	very, rather, quite
32. 生意经	shēngyijīng	knack of doing business
33. 得意	déyì	proud of oneself, pleased with oneself
34. 短	duǎn	short
35. 裙	qún	skirt
36. 参谋	cānmóu	to give advice
37. 打扮	dǎban	to dress up, to make up
38. 本事	běnshi	skill, ability, capability
39. 白	bái	in vain, for nothing

专 名 Proper Noun

国贸大厦	Guómào Dàshà	China World Trade Center

注 释 Notes

1 "亏"，动词，说反话，表示讥讽，常见的句式是："亏＋你（他）＋动＋得……"和"亏＋你（他）＋还……"。例如：

亏, a verb, indicates that one is talking ironically, showing a satirical tone. The usual patterns are: "亏 + 你(他) + verb + 得……" (how can you/he…?) and "亏 + 你(他) + 还 ……" (how come…and yet you/he…?). For example:

1. 这种事，亏你做得出来！

2. 这种话，亏她说得出口！
3. 你怎么不帮助他，亏你还是他的朋友。
4. 他怎么一句话也听不懂，亏他还学了几年汉语。

2 "一……就……"可以表示后一动作紧跟着前一动作发生。例如：

"一……就……" indicates the second action immediately follows the first. For example:

1. 他一学就会。
2. 他一下课就去食堂。

也可以表示前一动作是条件和原因，后一动作是结果。例如：

It can also indicate that the first action is the condition and reason and the second is the result. For example:

1. 杰克一感冒就咳嗽。
2. 一到周末，爷爷就去公园和人下象棋。

3 "没的说"，指所谈的对象完美无缺，没有可以指责的地方。也指不成问题，没有申说的必要。例如：

没的说 indicates that the subject under discussion is perfect and faultless, with nothing to criticize for. It can also indicate that there is no question about something and hence no need to state reasons. For example:

1. 你问颐和园怎么样，那可是没的说，真是美极了！
2. 你让办的事，没的说，你放心好了。

4 "看把……得"，这个格式表示程度。"得"的前边是动词或形容词，后边省略了补语，有"无法形容"的意味。例如：

The pattern "看把……得" expresses degree. Before 得 is a verb or an adjective. The complement after 得 is omitted. It has a sense of "beyond description". For example:

1. 看把你美得，你不能坐着说吗?
2. 看把你高兴得，这笔生意赚了多少钱?
3. 看把你累得，快坐下休息休息。

34 今年流行什么(二)

练习
Exercises

一、替换练习。
Substitution drills.

A：你邀请了谁来吃晚饭？
B：我邀请了<u>王老师</u>。

做客	一个老朋友
跳舞	安妮
表演	时装模特儿
开会	公司经理

A：谁和你一起去<u>看表演</u>？
B：小张和我一起去。

| 看电影 |
| 听音乐会 |
| 买火车票 |
| 邀请王老师 |

A：<u>时装表演</u>怎么样？
B：没的说，<u>真是美极了</u>。

北京的市场	商品特别多
这个电影	好看极了
你的朋友	他是个大好人
请你帮忙	只要我能办到

A：你为什么喜欢<u>看京剧</u>？
B：<u>京剧太棒了，一看</u>就让人着迷。

听	中国民族音乐
看	电影
跳	现代舞
读	中国小说

A：珍妮，要不要我<u>给你介绍一下</u>？
B：不用，<u>我们早认识了</u>。

帮帮你	我自己能行
陪你去	我自己去
去接你	我知道该怎么走
送你回去	我坐地铁回去

二、把下面的词组成句子。
Rearrange the following words into sentences.

1. 票 看 表演 你 的 有 时装 吗
2. 他 男子汉 是 真正 一个 的
3. 我 他 邀请 没有 吃 去 饭
4. 他 让 吃惊 话 真 我 的
5. 民族 喜欢 中国 服装 我 的
6. 你 中国 一定 穿 旗袍 迷人 很
7. 请 详细 把 话 说 一点儿 得 你
8. 她 展示 一套 新潮 了 服装
9. 这 销路 时装 些 的 好 很
10. 你 不要 机会 可 生意 错过 做 好 的

三、完成下面的对话。
Complete the following dialogues.

A：_____？
B：我已经买了。
A：多少钱一张票？
B：_____。

A：中国的时装表演怎么样？
B：_____。
A：请你介绍得详细点儿。
B：_____。

A：今年北京流行什么服装？
B：_____。
A：你喜欢流行时装的颜色和款式吗？
B：_____。

34 今年流行什么（二）

A：珍妮，你常常去看时装表演吗？
B：_____。
A：怪不得，你很会打扮。
B：_____。

A：你一定要去看看这次的世界名模表演。
B：_____？
A：_____。
B：好吧，我去见识见识。

四、用指定的词语完成句子。
Complete the following sentences with the given words.

1. _____，你朋友会给你来电话的。（着急）
2. 一时半会儿学不好汉语，_____。（着急）
3. 你怎么不知道他病了，_____。（亏）
4. 大栅栏在哪儿你都不知道，_____。（亏）
5. 你的汉语说得这么好，_____。（感到）
6. 你能来看我，_____。（感到）
7. 想赚钱，_____？（本事）
8. _____，没有什么事他不知道。（本事）
9. 你想在中国做生意，_____。（至少）
10. 从这儿到天安门很远，骑自行车_____。（至少）

五、谈谈今年流行的时装。
Talk about the fashionable dresses this year.

第三十五课　互联网+（一）
Lesson 35　Internet + (I)

课文 Text

在课上

王老师：同学们，你们觉得在中国的生活方便吗？

杰　克：我觉得很方便。买东西，不用去商店，在网上就可以买到你想要的任何东西。

珍　妮：我也喜欢网购，网上不仅货品丰富，还可以货比三家。在网上支付以后，他们还会给你送货上门，你看多方便！

山　口：对。现在吃饭也不用去饭馆，在网上就可以点外卖，一般半个小时就能送到。

王老师：那么出门呢？

珍　妮：出门也非常方便，可以坐地铁、坐公共汽车，还可以在网上打车，或者骑共享单车。

王老师：你们说得对。现在人们的生活越来越离不开互联网了，我们进入了一个"互联网+"的时代。

杰　克：我没骑过共享单车，这和互联网有什么关系呢？

珍　妮：如果要骑共享单车，必须用手机扫描二维码，还得在网上支付，当然和互联网有关系啦！

35 互联网+（一）

杰　　克：原来是这样。那么哪些人喜欢用共享单车呢？

山　　口：大学生。比如我就最喜欢骑共享单车。校园太大，从宿舍到食堂，从食堂到教室，都很远，走路太费时间。

杰　　克：要是睡个懒觉，不仅吃不上饭，上课还会迟到。

山　　口：快别提了，说来丢人，我因为睡懒觉，上课迟到过好几次。自从开始骑共享单车以后，再也没有耽误过事。

珍　　妮：我住在一个中国朋友的家里，他家门口没有公共汽车，也没有地铁。没有共享单车以前，我得走二十分钟才能坐上公共汽车。现在有了共享单车，出门方便多了。

杰　　克：看来，共享单车真是适应了社会需求，给大家带来了方便。

山　　口：对啊，一打开手机，就知道周围哪儿有共享单车。还有，很多"早九晚六"的上班族，也像我一样喜欢共享单车。骑车，可以解决最后一公里的问题。

杰　　克：听你们这么说，我觉得共享单车实在是太方便了，下课以后我也去试试。

珍　　妮：中国的互联网技术很先进，再加上精确的定位系统，共享单车以后使用起来会更加方便、快捷。

山　　口：现在还有共享电动车、共享汽车，也许以后还会有共享房子呢！

王老师：山口说得很对，随着互联网技术的发展，以后肯定还会有更加有趣的发明。

生 词
New Words

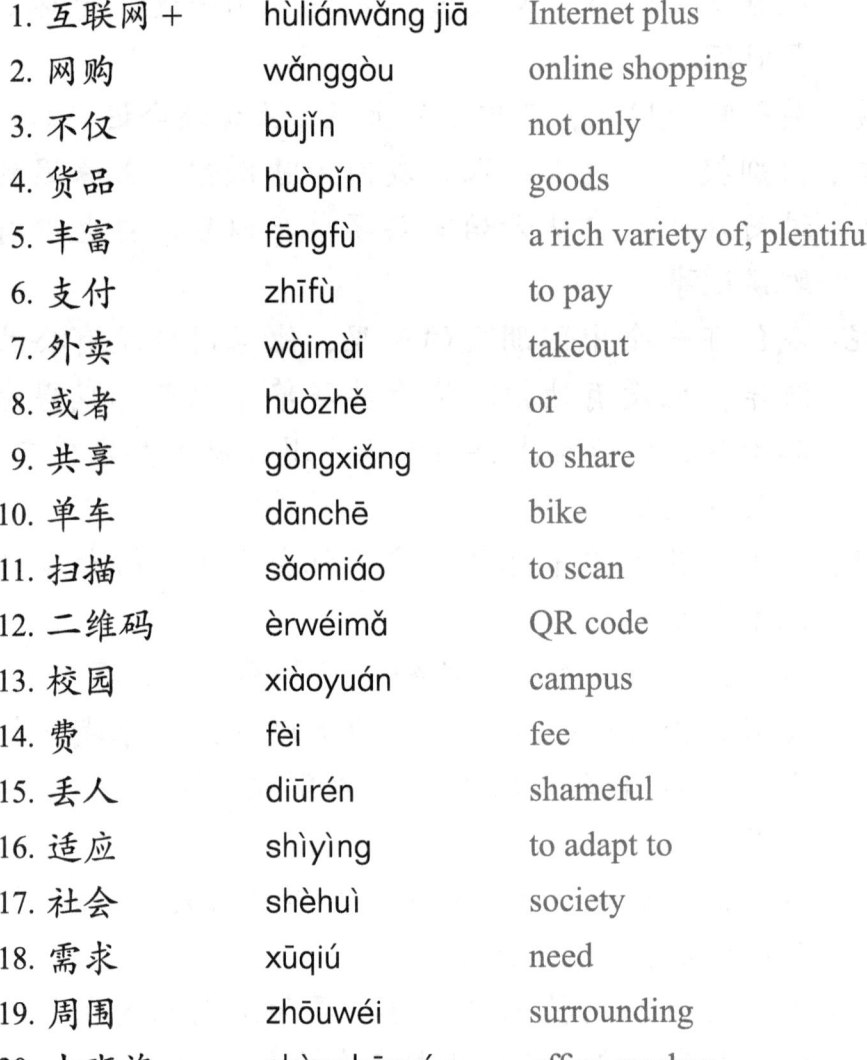

1.	互联网+	hùliánwǎng jiā	Internet plus
2.	网购	wǎnggòu	online shopping
3.	不仅	bùjǐn	not only
4.	货品	huòpǐn	goods
5.	丰富	fēngfù	a rich variety of, plentiful
6.	支付	zhīfù	to pay
7.	外卖	wàimài	takeout
8.	或者	huòzhě	or
9.	共享	gòngxiǎng	to share
10.	单车	dānchē	bike
11.	扫描	sǎomiáo	to scan
12.	二维码	èrwéimǎ	QR code
13.	校园	xiàoyuán	campus
14.	费	fèi	fee
15.	丢人	diūrén	shameful
16.	适应	shìyìng	to adapt to
17.	社会	shèhuì	society
18.	需求	xūqiú	need
19.	周围	zhōuwéi	surrounding
20.	上班族	shàngbānzú	office worker
21.	像	xiàng	like, such as
22.	一样	yíyàng	same, alike
23.	解决	jiějué	to solve
24.	先进	xiānjìn	advanced
25.	精确	jīngquè	accurate
26.	定位	dìngwèi	to position, to locate

35 互联网 + (一)

27. 系统　　　xìtǒng　　　system
28. 使用　　　shǐyòng　　　to use
29. 更加　　　gèngjiā　　　more, -er
30. 发展　　　fāzhǎn　　　to develop
31. 肯定　　　kěndìng　　　surely

注释 Notes

1 "不仅"，连词，常与"而且、也、还"等搭配使用，表示除了所说的之外，还有进一层的意思。例如：

不仅 (not only), a conjunction, is often used together with 而且, 也 or 还 (but also). It indicates that apart from what is said, there is a further meaning. For example:

1. 这事不仅我知道，大家也知道。
2. 北京不仅是中国的首都，也是历史名城。
3. 我来中国，不仅要学习汉语，还要学习经济贸易。

2 "还是"和"或者"的不同用法是：

Both 还是 and 或者 mean "or". Their difference in usage is:

"还是"用于选择问句，"或者"用于陈述句。例如：

还是 is used in alternative questions, while 或者 is used in declarative sentences. For example:

1. A：你喝茶还是喝咖啡？
   B：我喝茶。

2. A：你想去食堂还是点外卖？
   B：我想点外卖。

3. A：你晚上一般做什么？
   B：我一般在家看电视或者玩儿电脑。

3 "看来",动词,根据经验或已知情况做出大概的推断。例如:

看来, a verb, indicates a deduction based on experience or what is known. For example:

1. 他这么晚还没到,看来是发生什么事了。
2. 小王接了电话以后脸色不太好,看来不是什么好消息。
3. 这家饭馆每天都有很多人排队,看来这儿的饭菜应该很好吃。

4 "像……一样",表示比喻或说明情况相似。例如:

"像……一样" indicates an analogy or similarity between situations. For example:

1. 她就像我的姐姐一样。
2. 有很多像山口一样来中国学习汉语的留学生。
3. 我跟他说话,可是他像没听见一样。

练 习
Exercises

一、替换练习。
Substitution drills.

A:你想喝可乐还是咖啡?
B:可乐或者咖啡都行。

买红色的	蓝色的
明天去	后天去
骑共享单车	坐公共汽车
游泳	打球

A:你为什么喜欢骑自行车?
B:骑自行车不仅方便,而且还锻炼身体。

她	漂亮	精明
北京	是首都	是文化中心
旅行	是休息	长见识
青岛啤酒	口感好	价格便宜

35 互联网+（一）

二、把下面的词组成句子。
Rearrange the following words into sentences.

1. 就 买 在 可以 东西 任何 的 要 你 到 网上 想
2. 手机 一 就 哪儿 打 知道 开 共享 有 单车
3. 共享 需求 单车 了 方便 社会 大家 来 了 适应 给 带
4. 进入 "互联网+" 时代 我们 了 一个 的
5. 出门 地铁 非常 网上 坐 方便 打车 或者
6. 和 什么 互联网 关系 共享 单车 有 呢
7. 生活 越来越 了 的 人们 离不开 互联网
8. 食堂 费 走路 离 远 宿舍 太 时间 很
9. 多 方便 以后 了 单车 了 出门 共享 有
10. 车 解决 公里 骑 可以 的 问题 最后 一公里

三、完成下面的对话。
Complete the following dialogues.

A：你骑过共享单车吗？
B：_____。
A：下午我们一起骑车出去，好吗？
B：_____。

A：哪些人最喜欢用共享单车？
B：_____。
A：你喜欢吗？
B：_____。

A：你认为在中国生活方便吗？
B：_____。
A：为什么？
B：_____。

A：你住的地方交通方便不方便？

B：_____。

A：你一般怎么来学校？

B：_____。

四、用指定的词语完成句子。

Complete the following sentences with the given words.

1. 他的汉语特别好，_____。（像……一样）

2. 我喜欢网购，_____。（丰富）

3. 现在的互联网_____。（先进）

4. _____，还特别喜欢中国书法。（不仅）

5. 他今天好像特别开心，_____。（看来）

6. 用手机可以_____。（扫描）

7. 昨天走路的时候摔了一跤，_____。（丢人）

8. 小王特别聪明，_____。（解决）

五、给大家讲一讲，你心中的"互联网+"的生活是什么样的？

Tell everyone what the "Internet +" life is like in your mind.

第三十六课　互联网+（二）
Lesson 36　Internet + (II)

课文 Text

在课外

杰　克：珍妮、山口，这个周末，你们想干什么？

山　口：这周学的生词有些我没记住，得好好儿复习复习。语法也得练习练习，下周就要考试了。

珍　妮：我跟你不一样。学习了一个星期，快累死了。我得好好儿休息，在宿舍睡大觉！

杰　克：你这是消极休息，我有一个建议。

珍　妮：什么建议？

杰　克：周末咱们出去玩儿吧。

山　口：去哪儿？

杰　克：咱们一起骑共享单车逛北京吧，我早就想试试了，一边骑车，一边看风景，感觉一定特别棒！

山　口：北京那么大，骑车一定很累。咱们还是打车去吧，省时省力，还不会迷路。

珍　妮：对。现在在网上打车很方便。一点击预约，你在哪儿，司机在哪儿，离你多远，几分钟能到，马上就可以看到。你再点击一下，还能看到司机的信息：司机叫什么名字，电话号码是多少，车牌是多少，等等。你看这样打车多方便！

杰　　克：方便是方便，就是不环保，不是绿色出行！

珍　　妮：你说得也有道理。我们应该为环保做点儿贡献，骑车既可以减少污染，又可以锻炼身体，我也同意骑车去。

山　　口：好吧！杰克，你说去哪儿？故宫、北海、颐和园，这些有名的地方我们都去过了。

杰　　克：咱们不去那些地方。咱们先沿二环骑，二环沿线风景很美，有小河流水，还有绿树红花。在这条线上可以参观雍和宫、国子监和大观园。然后再从二环骑到三环，这样可以去中央电视塔，登上塔顶的观景台，俯瞰北京全景。总之，好玩儿的地方很多，只要有时间，我们可以玩儿个痛快。

珍　　妮：这个计划听起来不错，而且现在不冷也不热，正是出行的好时候。

杰　　克：我说的这些地方，都是北京市区最美的休闲去处。在河边的林荫道上骑车，空气清新，身心舒畅，一定会让你们满意的！

山　　口：可是，这些地方我们都没去过，如果迷路了怎么办？

杰　　克：好办！只要有网络，就可以在电子地图上定位，马上就知道应该怎么走了。

山　　口：这太好了！那我们周末就骑车去吧，既环保，又锻炼身体，还能欣赏美丽的风景！

珍　　妮：好！咱们就这么说定了。

36 互联网+（二）

生词 New Words

1. 消极　　　xiāojí　　　　negative
2. 建议　　　jiànyì　　　　suggestion
3. 省　　　　shěng　　　　to save (time, money, energy, etc.)
4. 迷路　　　mílù　　　　　to get lost
5. 点击　　　diǎnjī　　　　to click
6. 预约　　　yùyuē　　　　to make an appointment, to reserve
7. 司机　　　sījī　　　　　driver
8. 马上　　　mǎshàng　　　immediately
9. 信息　　　xìnxī　　　　information
10. 车牌　　　chēpái　　　　license plate
11. 环保　　　huánbǎo　　　environment-friendly; environmental protection
12. 出行　　　chūxíng　　　to travel
13. 贡献　　　gòngxiàn　　　contribution
14. 减少　　　jiǎnshǎo　　　to reduce
15. 污染　　　wūrǎn　　　　pollution
16. 同意　　　tóngyì　　　　to agree
17. 沿　　　　yán　　　　　along
18. 沿线　　　yánxiàn　　　along the line
19. 登　　　　dēng　　　　　to climb
20. 观景台　　guānjǐngtái　　observation platform
21. 俯瞰　　　fǔkàn　　　　to overlook, to look down at
22. 总之　　　zǒngzhī　　　in a word
23. 只要　　　zhǐyào　　　　as long as
24. 痛快　　　tòngkuài　　　to one's heart's content
25. 休闲　　　xiūxián　　　relaxed, leisure
26. 林荫道　　línyīndào　　　avenue, boulevard

27. 空气	kōngqì	air
28. 清新	qīngxīn	fresh
29. 身心	shēnxīn	body and mind
30. 舒畅	shūchàng	entirely free from worry
31. 满意	mǎnyì	satisfied
32. 网络	wǎngluò	network, Internet
33. 电子	diànzǐ	electronic

专 名 Proper Nouns

1. 雍和宫	Yōnghé Gōng	Yonghegong Lama Temple
2. 国子监	Guózǐjiàn	Imperial Academy, the national central institution of higher learning in ancient China
3. 大观园	Dàguān Yuán	Grand View Garden
4. 中央电视塔	Zhōngyāng Diànshì Tǎ	China Central Television Tower

注 释 Notes

1 "一边……一边……"表示两种或以上的动作同时进行。例如：

"一边……一边……" indicates that two or more actions are proceeding at the same time. For example:

1. 山口一边听录音，一边读课文。
2. 王老师一边说汉语，一边写汉字。
3. 杰克喜欢一边看电视，一边吃午饭。

2 "A 是 A"，这是一个常见格式。"是"的前后两项相同，表示让步。有"虽然"的意思，后面有"就是、但是、可是"等词相呼应。例如：

A是A is a common structure. The words before and after 是 are the same, which indicates concession, meaning "although". It often echoes with words such as 就是, 但是, or 可是 (but) latter in the sentence. For example:

1. 这电脑贵是贵了点儿，可质量好啊！
2. 这东西我想买是想买，就是现在没钱。
3. 他聪明是聪明，就是不把聪明用在学习上。

3　"既……又……"表示同时具有两个方面的性质或情况。例如：

"既……又……" means that two properties or situations exist at the same time. For example:

1. 她的女儿既聪明又可爱。
2. 骑车既方便，又能锻炼身体。
3. 坐地铁既便宜，又省时省力。

4　"先……然后……"表示连续动作的顺序。例如：

"先……然后……" shows the sequence of successive actions. For example:

1. 我每天先吃早饭，然后去学校。
2. 经理先去上海，然后去广州。
3. 先支付，然后送货。

5　"只要……就……"连接一个条件复句。"只要"后边是一个必要条件，"就"后边是这个条件所产生的结果。例如：

"只要……就……" connects the clauses of a conditional sentence. 只要 is followed by an essential condition and 就 is followed by the result caused by the condition. For example:

1. 只要有地图，就不会迷路。
2. 只要有时间，我就会去书店看看新书。
3. 现在只要有网络，就没有办不了的事情。

练 习
Exercises

一、替换练习。
Substitution drills.

A：骑车出行，环保是环保，就是太累。
B：累点儿不怕，能锻炼身体就好！

坐出租车	方便	太费钱	费点儿钱	省时省力
这个学校	好	学费太贵	贵点儿	学到知识
公园风景	美	游人太多	游人多	玩儿个痛快

A：怎么使用电子地图？
B：先打开网络，然后在地图上定位。

在网上买东西	选好你要的货品	在网上支付
去天安门	坐地铁 2 号线	在复兴门换 1 号线
使用共享单车	扫描二维码	用手机支付

A：你觉得这本书怎么样？
B：既便宜，又实用。

共享单车	方便	快捷
杰克	热情	开朗
她唱歌唱得	动听	感人

二、把下面的词组成句子。
Rearrange the following words into sentences.

1. 考试 我 得 了 好好儿 就要 复习 下周
2. 建议 咱们 吧 玩儿 我 一起 出去 周末
3. 逛 自行车 北京 打算 他们 骑

36 互联网+（二）

4. 可以 既 车 可以 又 骑 污染 锻炼 身体 减少 能

5. 是 方便 就是 方便 开 不 环保 车

6. 时候 正是 的 好 现在 出行

7. 贡献 应该 我们 做 保护 为 点儿 环境

8. 只要 网络 就 定位 地图 有 电子 可以 在 上

三、完成下面的对话。
Complete the following dialogues.

A：周末你打算做什么？
B：_____。
A：我有一个建议，_____。
B：太好了！就这么说定了。

A：你喜欢骑车还是开车？
B：_____。
A：为什么？
B：_____。

A：我的口语不太好，怎么办？
B：_____。
A：这样有用吗？
B：只要_____。

A：现在的网络太方便了！
B：_____。
A：怎么在网上打车呢？
B：_____。

四、完成下面的句子。

Complete the following sentences.

1. 只要打开网络，_____。
2. 只要你努力，_____。
3. 在食堂吃饭方便是方便，_____。
4. 今天暖和是暖和，_____。
5. 我们先学拼音，_____。
6. 杰克想先去大观园，_____。
7. 他一边玩儿手机，_____。
8. 经理一边打电话，_____。

五、你用过共享单车吗？骑共享单车有什么好处？请给大家介绍一下。

Have you ever used shared bikes? What are the advantages of riding shared bikes? Please tell about them.

第三十七课 节日与购物（一）
Lesson 37 Festivals and Shopping (I)

课文 Text

在课上

王老师：同学们，你们来中国多长时间了？

杰　克：我和珍妮来了八个月了。

山　口：我来了快一年了。

王老师：那么你们一定知道很多中国的节日吧？

珍　妮：老师，我知道端午节。端午节是中国农历的五月初五。

杰　克：我还知道端午节要吃粽子，赛龙舟。

王老师：你们喜欢吃粽子吗？

珍　妮：我特别喜欢吃粽子，我还学过包粽子呢。

山　口：我还知道中秋节。中秋节是农历八月十五。这一天人们要和家人团聚，吃月饼。

王老师：你们说得都很对。那你们知道中国最重要的传统节日吗？

珍　妮：我知道，是春节。

山　口：我也听中国朋友说过。春节是全家团圆的日子。春节到来前，家家户户都会忙活起来：为家人买新衣、礼物，为团圆饭准备各种食材，还要把里里外外都打扫得干干净净。

王老师：对。以前电商不发达的时候，大家都要去商店买东西，买完了还要大包小包地往回拿。现在网络购物比以前方便多了，所以准备起来也没有以前那么忙了。

杰　　克：这和我们美国差不多。大家都喜欢在感恩节、圣诞节的时候去买东西。这时商店都在打折，东西特别便宜，所以人们一大早就在商店门口排起了长队。

珍　　妮：杰克说得对，美国的感恩节、圣诞节，既是传统节日，也是购物狂欢节。每年这个时候到处都充满了节日的气氛，人们高高兴兴地去商店挑选物美价廉的商品。不过现在人们也越来越习惯在网上参加购物狂欢节了。

山　　口：老师，中国的购物狂欢节也是传统节日的时候吗？

王老师：中国最大的网络购物狂欢节并不是传统节日的时候，而是每年的11月11日，也叫"双11购物狂欢节"。

杰　　克：可是我听说"双11"原本是"单身节"，怎么变成了购物狂欢节呢？

王老师：单身青年们爱玩儿、爱热闹、肯花钱，他们喜欢接受新事物，还喜欢用网络购物来打发时间。于是聪明的商家就利用单身青年的这种心理，在电商平台上大搞打折促销活动，还加进了许多娱乐元素，制造出狂欢节的气氛，吸引了很多人来参加，所以就变成了现在的"双11购物狂欢节"。

杰　　克：我还听说今年有200多个国家和地区参加了中国的"双11"，最终成交额超过了1000亿元。

37 节日与购物(一)

王老师：对。现在参加这个购物狂欢节的既有年轻人也有中老年人，既有中国人也有外国人，"双 11" 成了真正的购物狂欢节。

生词 New Words

1.	农历	nónglì	lunar calendar
2.	初	chū	beginning
3.	粽子	zòngzi	*zongzi*, Chinese sticky rice dumpling
4.	赛	sài	to race
5.	龙舟	lóngzhōu	dragon boat
6.	包	bāo	to make, to wrap
7.	团聚	tuánjù	to reunite
8.	月饼	yuèbǐng	mooncake
9.	传统	chuántǒng	tradition; traditional
10.	团圆	tuányuán	to reunite
11.	家家户户	jiājiāhùhù	every household
12.	忙活	mánghuo	to be busy
13.	食材	shícái	food material
14.	电商	diànshāng	e-commerce
15.	发达	fādá	developed
16.	比	bǐ	than
17.	狂欢	kuánghuān	carnival
18.	充满	chōngmǎn	to be full of
19.	气氛	qìfēn	atmosphere
20.	挑选	tiāoxuǎn	to choose
21.	物美价廉	wù měi jià lián	high-quality and inexpensive
22.	双	shuāng	double
23.	单身	dānshēn	single (not in a romantic relationship)

24. 肯	kěn	to be willing to
25. 接受	jiēshòu	to accept
26. 打发	dǎfa	to while away
27. 利用	lìyòng	to use, to take advantage of
28. 心理	xīnlǐ	psychology
29. 平台	píngtái	platform
30. 促销	cùxiāo	to promote sales
31. 娱乐	yúlè	entertainment
32. 元素	yuánsù	element
33. 制造	zhìzào	to create
34. 吸引	xīyǐn	to attract
35. 地区	dìqū	region
36. 最终	zuìzhōng	eventually, in the end
37. 成交额	chéngjiāo'é	volume of business
38. 超过	chāoguò	to exceed

专 名 Proper Nouns

1. 端午节	Duānwǔ Jié	Dragon Boat Festival
2. 中秋节	Zhōngqiū Jié	Mid-Autumn Festival
3. 春节	Chūnjié	Spring Festival
4. 感恩节	Gǎn'ēn Jié	Thanksgiving
5. 圣诞节	Shèngdàn Jié	Christmas

注释 Notes

1　时量补语，表达动作或状态持续的时间时用时量补语。时量补语由表示时段的词语充当，如"一会儿、半个小时、一个月"等。例如：

The complement of duration is used to show the duration of an action or a state.

It is often a word or phrase indicating a period of time, such as 一会儿 (a moment), 半个小时 (half an hour), or 一个月 (a month). For example:

1. 他学了一年汉语。
2. 他工作了多长时间？
3. 他走了十五分钟。

如果动词后边有"了"，句末还有语气助词"了"，表示动作仍在进行。例如：

If the verb is followed by 了 and the sentence ends with the modal particle 了, it means that the action is ongoing. For example:

1. 他学了一年汉语。（现在可能已经不学汉语了。）
2. 他学了一年汉语了。（现在还在学汉语。）

2 "起来"，趋向动词，用在动词或形容词后，表示动作或情况开始并且继续。例如：

起来 is a directional verb used after a verb or an adjective to mean that an action or a situation begins and continues. For example:

1. 天气暖和起来了。
2. 他的身体好起来了。
3. 小孩儿摔了一跤，大声哭了起来。

3 "比"，介词，用来比较性状和程度的差别。例如：

比, a preposition, is used to compare the difference in properties and degree. For example:

1. 哥哥比弟弟高。
2. 杰克比珍妮大。
3. 昨天比今天冷。

要表达事物大概的差别时，常用"一点儿、一些"等表达差别不大，用"得多、多了"表达差别很大。例如：

When describing the general differences between things, 一点儿 (a little) or 一些 (somewhat) are often used to show small differences, and 得多 or 多了 (much more) to show big differences. For example:

1. 哥哥比弟弟高得多。
2. 杰克比珍妮大一点儿。
3. 昨天比今天冷多了。

否定形式一般用"没有"。例如：
没有 is used as its negative form. For example:

1. 他没有我跑得快。
2. 苹果没有香蕉便宜。
3. 包子没有饺子好吃。

练 习
Exercises

一、替换练习。
Substitution drills.

A：<u>苹果</u>好吃还是<u>橘子</u>好吃？
B：<u>苹果</u>比<u>橘子</u>好吃。

| 便宜 |
| 大 |
| 甜 |

<u>昨天</u>比<u>今天</u>冷一点儿。

红色的	蓝色的	好看得多
坐车	骑车	快多了
初级的学生	中级的学生	少一些

<u>我</u>没有<u>他</u>跑得快。

弟弟	哥哥	高
火车	飞机	舒服
我写汉字	老师	写得快

37 节日与购物（一）

二、把下面的词组成句子。
Rearrange the following words into sentences.

1. 互联网 大 促销 利用 电商 活动 搞
2. 传统 购物 狂欢节 变成 了 节日
3. 重要 的 最 是 春节 节日 传统 中国
4. 了 起来 了 快 家家户户 忙活 都 到 春节
5. 气氛 了 节日 到处 充满 都 的
6. 喜欢 年轻人 打发 通过 购物 时间 网络
7. 吸引 参加 这个 狂欢节 很 了 人 来 多
8. 珍妮 会 了 粽子 包 学
9. 团圆饭 各种 要 今天 我们 食材 为 准备
10. 高高兴兴 挑选 人们 地 各种 商品

三、完成下面的对话。
Complete the following dialogues.

A：你参加过"双11购物狂欢节"吗？
B：_____。
A：你有什么看法？
B：_____？

A：你知道中国有哪些传统节日？
B：_____。
A：你过过中国的传统节日吗？
B：_____。

A：你昨天写作业了吗？
B：_____。
A：你写了多长时间？
B：_____。

A：你今天学习汉语了吗？

B：_____。

A：你学习了多长时间？

B：_____。

四、选词填空。

Choose the appropriate words to fill in the blanks.

促销　挑选　团圆　狂欢　物美价廉　平台　农历　包　打发　忙活

1. _____五月初五是端午节。
2. 春节是全家_____的日子。
3. 我姐姐的生日快到了，你能陪我一起去商店_____礼物吗？
4. 我妈妈会_____粽子，我不会。
5. "双11"是中国的购物_____节。
6. 下班以后，我喜欢看看小说来_____时间。
7. 别_____了，我坐坐就走。
8. 现在出现了很多电商_____，人们买东西方便多了。
9. 这儿的东西又便宜质量又好，真是_____！
10. 今天商场有打折_____活动，咱们也去看看！

五、说一说你们国家的传统节日和购物狂欢节。

Talk about the traditional festivals and shopping seasons in your country.

第三十八课　节日与购物（二）

Lesson 38　Festivals and Shopping (II)

课文 Text

在课外

杰　克：珍妮、山口，你们参加过购物狂欢节吗？
珍　妮：圣诞节的时候我去商店抢购过。
山　口：感觉怎么样？
珍　妮：人特别多，不过大家都很高兴。因为很多商品平时是不打折的，但在圣诞节的时候折扣力度特别大，所以你得尽早去，否则很可能抢不到心仪的商品。
山　口：那你抢到了吗？
珍　妮：当然！我买了满满三大袋的东西，多得我的汽车都快放不下了！
山　口：你可真够疯狂的！
珍　妮：要不怎么叫购物狂欢节呢！
杰　克：我也是。我喜欢的运动鞋平时要1000美元一双，打折的时候才600美元，便宜多了，我一下子就买了两双。过了这个村，就没有这个店了，谁知道明年还打不打折呢？

山　口：我就参加过一次。有一年商店大促销的时候，我也去抢购了一堆打折的商品回来。

杰　克：结果呢？

山　口：结果我发现有的商品根本没有便宜多少，还有的商品是当时看着特别便宜，但是仔细想想却根本没什么用，现在还放在家里呢。

珍　妮：后来你就很少去了？

山　口：对。我觉得放假的时候与其去抢购一堆不需要的东西，还不如好好儿在家里休息呢。

珍　妮：其实我也跟你一样。只要看到便宜的东西，不管是不是自己需要的，总想着多买一点儿，但是买完了又有点儿后悔。

杰　克：我看，这些商家就是利用了消费者容易冲动的心理，才推出这么多的购物狂欢节。

山　口：没错。有的是你平时嫌贵没买的，现在打折、促销了，当然想买了；有的是根本不需要的东西，但是看到价钱便宜，也顺手买了。这买的人多了，商家可能比平时赚的还多呢！

珍　妮：这些商家可真会做生意。

山　口：对呀。你们看，现在电子商务越来越发达，所以他们又推出了"双11购物狂欢节"，吸引了很多没时间去实体商店的人，听说比实体商店卖得还要多。

杰　克：所以咱们下次去买东西的时候，得先考虑清楚，这些是不是自己真正需要的，千万别被打折、促销冲昏了头脑。

珍　妮：杰克说得对，咱们应该冷静对待购物狂欢节，理性消费，这样才不会在购物的时候毫无节制，买完又觉得后悔。

38 节日与购物（二）

生词
New Words

1.	抢	qiǎng	to rush to (buy), to vie for
2.	力度	lìdù	strength, force
3.	否则	fǒuzé	or else, otherwise
4.	心仪	xīnyí	to admire in the heart
5.	满	mǎn	full
6.	够	gòu	enough, quite
7.	疯狂	fēngkuáng	crazy
8.	要不	yàobu	or, otherwise
9.	运动鞋	yùndòngxié	sports shoes
10.	平时	píngshí	at ordinary times
11.	村	cūn	village
12.	堆	duī	pile
13.	结果	jiéguǒ	result
14.	根本	gēnběn	at all
15.	与其	yǔqí	rather than
16.	需要	xūyào	to need
17.	不如	bùrú	it would be better to
18.	后悔	hòuhuǐ	to regret
19.	消费者	xiāofèizhě	consumer
20.	冲动	chōngdòng	impulsive
21.	推出	tuīchū	to launch, to bring out
22.	嫌	xián	to mind
23.	顺手	shùnshǒu	to do sth. as a natural sequence or in passing
24.	商务	shāngwù	business, commerce
25.	考虑	kǎolù	to consider
26.	千万	qiānwàn	to be sure to
27.	冲	chōng	to wash away, to flush

28. 昏	hūn	muddled
29. 头脑	tóunǎo	mind, brain
30. 冷静	lěngjìng	calm
31. 对待	duìdài	to treat
32. 理性	lǐxìng	rational
33. 毫无	háo wú	not in the least
34. 节制	jiézhì	to control

注释 Notes

1 "否则",连词,意思是"如果不是这样"。例如:

否则, a conjunction, means "or else, otherwise". For example:

1. 他一定有重要的事,否则不会给你打这么多电话。
2. 你快回去吧,否则你父母该着急了。
3. 外面冷,多穿点儿,否则容易着凉。

2 "动词 + 得/不 + 下",表示空间能否容纳。例如:

The structure "verb + 得/不 + 下" means whether there is enough room to hold. For example:

1. 这儿坐得下 20 个人吗?
2. 东西太多了,我的包放不下。
3. 我吃不下了,这些菜打包吧。

3 "够",副词,表示程度高,一般与"的"构成"够……的"结构。例如:

够, an adverb, refers to a high degree and often forms "够……的" with 的. For example:

1. 老王,你儿子够高的!
2. 今天可真够热的!
3. 嗬,这么多人,够热闹的!

38 节日与购物（二）

4 "与其……不如……"用于比较，表示比较以后不选择前者而选择后者。例如：

"与其……不如……" is used for comparison. It means choosing the latter over the former after comparison. For example:

1. 与其抢购一堆不需要的东西，还不如在家好好儿休息。
2. 与其坐出租车，不如坐地铁。
3. 与其在这儿发呆，不如利用这个时间看看书。

练 习
Exercises

一、替换练习。
Substitution drills.

A：人们怎样参加"双11购物狂欢节"？
B：有人很<u>理智</u>，有人很<u>冲动</u>。

毫无节制	精打细算
盲目下单	货比三家
疯狂抢购	细心挑选

A：听说你<u>喜欢吃辣的</u>？
B：谁说的？我根本<u>不喜欢</u>。

打算去上海	没这个打算
买新房子了	没买
昨天去电影院了	没去

A：<u>晚上</u>去<u>食堂</u>吗？
B：与其<u>去食堂</u>，不如<u>自己做饭</u>。

咱们	走路去	骑车去
下午	去游泳	去打篮球
周末	去公园	去爬山

二、把下面的词组成句子。
Rearrange the following words into sentences.

1. 一堆　珍妮　了　商品　购　抢
2. 根本　用　这些　什么　没　东西

3. 推出 狂欢节 很多 了 商家 购物
4. 我 太 做事 今天 后悔 了 冲动 很
5. 今天 特别 大 力度 商家 的 折扣
6. 买 了 心仪 她 商品 的 到
7. 别 冲 头脑 促销 被 了 打折 昏 千万
8. 我们 冷静 狂欢节 应该 购物 对待
9. 利用 心理 了 消费者 商家 冲动 容易 的
10. 的 顺手 拿 你 报纸 是 我 过来 了 这

三、完成下面的对话。
Complete the following dialogues.

A：在你们国家，一般什么时候是购物狂欢节？
B：＿＿＿＿＿＿＿＿＿＿＿＿＿。
A：你喜欢这种购物狂欢节吗？
B：＿＿＿＿＿＿＿＿＿＿＿＿＿。

A：你的运动鞋真不错，在哪儿买的？
B：＿＿＿＿＿＿＿＿＿＿＿＿＿。
A：现在还打折吗？
B：＿＿＿＿＿＿＿＿＿＿＿＿＿。

A：＿＿＿＿＿＿＿＿＿＿＿＿＿！
B：怎么了？
A：＿＿＿＿＿＿＿＿＿＿＿＿＿。
B：买的时候应该考虑清楚，这样买完才不会后悔。

A：我想去书店买本词典，我们一起去吧。
B：与其 ＿＿＿＿＿＿＿＿＿＿＿。
A：网上也有这本词典吗？
B：＿＿＿＿＿＿＿＿＿＿＿＿＿。

38 节日与购物（二）

四、在括号里填上适当的量词。
Fill in the blanks with appropriate measure words.

一（　）书　　一（　）票　　一（　）茶　　一（　）笔
一（　）纸　　一（　）汽车　一（　）杯子　一（　）运动鞋
一（　）衣服　一（　）老师　一（　）手机　一（　）商品
一（　）商店　一（　）啤酒　一（　）水果　一（　）公寓
一（　）面包　一（　）大街　一（　）公司　一（　）牛奶
一（　）同学　一（　）可乐　一（　）电脑　一（　）自行车

五、和朋友讨论一下，怎样才能理性消费？
Discuss with your friend how to spend money wisely.

第三十九课　麦当劳和茶馆（一）
Lesson 39　McDonald's and Teahouse (I)

课文 Text

在课上

王老师：你知道麦当劳卖什么吗？

杰　克：麦当劳卖什么？当然卖汉堡包喽！

王老师：还有呢？

杰　克：各种饮料。

王老师：还有时间、服务、质量。

杰　克：麦当劳卖时间？

珍　妮：哦，我明白了。在麦当劳，40秒钟就能烤好一块牛肉饼，从点饮料、汉堡包到把这些送到顾客面前只要几分钟，确实很快。去那儿用餐，最省时间。

山　口：炸薯条是麦当劳的招牌菜，据说他们对土豆的大小、颜色、含糖量多少都有严格的质量要求。

杰　克：他们的服务态度就更没得说了，周到、热情，从老板到雇员，脸上永远带着微笑。那儿可是一个清洁舒适、轻松愉快的好地方。

珍　妮：价格也很合理，一份套餐，不过二十几块钱，广大消费者都承受得了。

王老师：你们说得对。麦当劳人说，质量、友善、清洁、价值，就是他们的宗旨。

杰　克：我想他们就是靠这个宗旨赢得中国顾客的。

珍　妮：杰克，你去过老舍茶馆吗？

杰　克：去过。

珍　妮：老舍茶馆卖什么？

杰　克：我知道，你要说老舍茶馆不卖茶，是卖时间……

珍　妮：谁说的？老舍茶馆当然卖茶。不过，那可不是普普通通的茶馆。

杰　克：什么意思？

珍　妮：你在喝茶的时候，是不是有人在唱京戏？

杰　克：是呀，还有喝茶的人去唱呢！

珍　妮：一边品茶，一边欣赏京剧，会是什么感觉？

杰　克：嗯，那感觉一定美滋滋的。

山　口：我知道，里边还有魔术表演呢！

杰　克：麦当劳、老舍茶馆、京剧、魔术，既现代，又古老，真有意思，这就是多元化的中国市场，中国特色。

山　口：珍妮，你看，杰克又发高论了！

生词 New Words

1.	茶馆	cháguǎn	teahouse
2.	秒	miǎo	second (1/60 minute)
3.	烤	kǎo	to bake, to roast
4.	牛肉	niúròu	beef
5.	饼	bǐng	round flat cake, pie
6.	确实	quèshí	really, indeed

7.	薯条	shǔtiáo	French fries
8.	据说	jùshuō	it is said that
9.	招牌菜	zhāopáicài	specialty (food), signature dish
10.	土豆	tǔdòu	potato
11.	含	hán	to contain
12.	量	liàng	quantity, amount
13.	严格	yángé	strict, rigorous, rigid
14.	要求	yāoqiú	to demand, to ask, to require
15.	态度	tàidù	attitude, manner
16.	周到	zhōudào	attentive and satisfactory, thoughtful, considerate
17.	热情	rèqíng	warm, enthusiastic
18.	雇员	gùyuán	employee
19.	永远	yǒngyuǎn	always, forever
20.	微笑	wēixiào	smile
21.	清洁	qīngjié	clean
22.	轻松	qīngsōng	light, relaxed
23.	愉快	yúkuài	happy, joyful, cheerful
24.	合理	hélǐ	rational, reasonable
25.	套餐	tàocān	combo meal
26.	广大	guǎngdà	numerous, vast, wide, extensive
27.	承受	chéngshòu	to bear, to endure, to stand
28.	友善	yǒushàn	friendly, amicable
29.	价值	jiàzhí	value, worth
30.	宗旨	zōngzhǐ	aim, purpose
31.	靠	kào	to depend on, to lean on
32.	赢得	yíngdé	to win, to gain
33.	普通	pǔtōng	ordinary, common, plain, average
34.	品	pǐn	to appreciate the taste of, to sample, to savor
35.	欣赏	xīnshǎng	to appreciate, to enjoy, to admire

36. 美滋滋	měizīzī	pleasant, to one's heart's content
37. 魔术	móshù	magic
38. 古老	gǔlǎo	ancient, age-old
39. 多元化	duōyuánhuà	diversified
40. 发（表）	fā(biǎo)	to publish, to voice
41. 高论	gāolùn	brilliant idea (opinion, view, etc.)

专 名　Proper Noun

| 老舍 | Lǎo Shě | Lao She (1899-1966), a Chinese novelist and dramatist |

注释 Notes

1 "招牌"，名词，指挂在商店门前写明商店名称或经销的货物的牌子，是商店的标志。在中国古代，招牌实际上也成为经营者的品牌标识，如"全聚德、六必居、同仁堂"等。不少招牌还蕴含着丰富的人文故事，成为我国特色文化的一部分。另外，"招牌"也比喻某种名义或称号。例如：

招牌 is a noun referring to the signboard that hangs in front of a store to indicate the name of the store or the goods sold and serves as the sign of the store. In ancient China, the signboard actually became the brand of the owner, such as Quanjude, Liubiju and Tong Ren Tang. There are also rich human stories behind many signboards, which becomes part of China's unique culture. In addition, 招牌 also means a certain name or title. For example:

1. 下个月饭店开张，饭店的招牌做好了吗？
2. 这个招牌太旧了，换个新的吧。
3. 前面一定有一家麦当劳，我已经看到它的黄色招牌了。
4. 他的业务能力特别强，是我们公司的金字招牌。

"招牌菜"，名词，指某人或某餐馆等最拿手的菜肴。因可以作为招牌，所以叫招牌菜。例如：

招牌菜 is a noun that refers to the signature dish of a chef or a restaurant. As it can be used as a sign, it is called a "signature dish". For example:

1. 服务员，你们这儿的招牌菜是什么？
2. 尝尝，这可是我的招牌菜，味道怎么样？
3. 我给你介绍一下，这是北京烤鸭，全聚德的招牌菜。
4. 听说这家饭店的招牌菜好吃又不贵，我们去试试吧。

2 "谁说的"，口语中常用的反问句，表示否定。例如：

谁说的 is a rhetorical question often used in spoken Chinese to indicate denial. For example:

1. A：你不喜欢巧克力吗？
   B：谁说的？

2. A：听说经理去上海了？
   B：谁说的？经理一直在北京。

练 习
Exercises

一、替换练习。
Substitution drills.

A：从<u>七月</u>到<u>九月</u>，你在哪儿？
B：我在<u>外地</u>。

2015年	2016年	英国
星期五	星期日	朋友家
上午八点	上午十点	公司
吃完午饭	下午两点	图书馆

A：在这家快餐厅，一份儿<u>小吃</u>多少钱？
B：听说，不过<u>四五</u>块钱。

肉饼	八九
套餐	三十几
炒饭	十几
炒菜	二十几

39 麦当劳和茶馆(一)

A：你靠什么<u>支付学习费用</u>？
B：<u>靠</u>我打工挣的钱。

找到了这份工作　　我出色的翻译水平
做生意　　　　　　热情周到的服务
赢得顾客　　　　　我们的产品质量
取得了成功　　　　我的聪明和努力

二、把下面的词组成句子。
Rearrange the following words into sentences.

1. 这　卖　餐厅　家　的　是　什么
2. 请　有　饮料　问　这儿　什么　都
3. 他　要求　很　的　合理
4. 北京　确实　骑　在　方便　自行车
5. 服务　顾客　赢得　微笑　了　的
6. 这　一　普通　是　茶馆　家
7. 你　习惯　茶　有　吗　喝　的
8. 他　说　普通话　地道　能　很　的
9. 想　我　永远　不　的　雇员　做　公司
10. 他　高论　常常　发表

三、完成下面的对话。
Complete the following dialogues.

A：请问麦当劳在哪儿？
B：_____。
A：_____？
B：我喜欢吃麦当劳的汉堡包。

A：老舍茶馆是一家普通茶馆吗？
B：_____。
A：那么，是一家什么样的茶馆呢？
B：_____。

A：_____？
B：我最喜欢去舒适的饭店用餐。
A：在这种饭店用餐一定得花很多钱吧？
B：_____。

A：_____？
B：别提多有意思了！
A：你为什么觉得有意思？
B：_____。

四、完成下面的句子。

Complete the following sentences.

1. 据说他们对质量的要求_____。
2. 听说在老舍茶馆，可以_____。
3. 他们的经营宗旨是_____。
4. 这家饭馆，既_____又_____。
5. 谁说你_____，你可别误会！

五、你去过老舍茶馆吗？谈谈你的感受。

Have you ever been to Lao She Teahouse? What's your impression?

第四十课　麦当劳和茶馆（二）

Lesson 40　McDonald's and Teahouse (II)

课文 Text

在课外

杰　　克：小姐、先生，你们好！

钱先生：你们好！

杰　　克：我们可以坐这儿跟你们聊聊吗？

钱先生：欢迎，欢迎，请坐吧。服务员，加三碗茶！我们边喝茶边聊吧。

杰　　克：谢谢。请问先生、小姐，你们这是……

钱先生：今天不是"红娘茶会日"吗？

珍　　妮：哦，你们这是在谈情说爱啊！

山　　口：看你嘴快！你看这位小姐的脸都红了。

钱先生：没关系，我们这也是第一次见面，大家都难免有些不好意思。

杰　　克：你们怎么会在这儿见面呢？

钱先生：我们都是单身青年，先到这个茶馆来登记，有了合适的征婚对象，就约好在"红娘茶会日"见面。

杰　　克：现在电视上可以征婚，报纸上也有征婚广告，你们为什么上茶馆来办这事儿？

钱先生：这儿交谈方便，价钱公道呗。
张小姐：登报、上电视，花钱多不说，还丢人现眼，多难为情，我可没那勇气。
钱先生：这儿人少，又安静，约好日子来，坐在一起，品着茶，听着戏，聊聊天儿，多自在，多随便，既是休息，也办了正事，两不耽误。
珍　妮：小姐，你们彼此相中了吗？
张小姐：你问他吧！
钱先生：相中了！相中了！
珍　妮：嘀，这么容易呀，我也来登个记！
杰　克：怎么？你也想找个中国小伙子？
珍　妮：怎么，不行啊？
杰　克：不是不行，就怕你没那个勇气！

珍　妮：经理，你们怎么想起在茶馆办"红娘茶会日"呢？
经　理：哦，中国人喜欢泡茶馆，一泡就是大半天。一边喝茶，一边闲聊，家长里短，都市趣闻，天下大事，什么都聊。来的人又多，茶馆自然就成了信息交流和传播的场所了。
杰　克：老舍茶馆好像没有"红娘茶会日"。
经　理：是的，现在北京有很多茶馆、茶座，每个茶馆、茶座都有自己的特色。老舍茶馆，可以说是文化茶馆。
珍　妮：嗯，你们这里可以叫"红娘茶馆"了？
经　理：是啊。
山　口：那么，还有别的茶馆吗？
经　理：有。比如有一种"公关茶馆"，在那儿，茶客们既可以交流市场行情、供求变化等信息，还可以开展业务洽谈。这类茶馆，有的还安装了电脑，可以随时上网查阅信息！

珍　妮：有人去那儿交流信息，洽谈生意吗？

经　理：当然有，而且成交额还不小，茶馆的生意可兴隆了。

杰　克：看来，办商店最重要的是要办出自己的特色。

生词 New Words

1.	聊（天儿）	liáo(tiānr)	to chat
2.	谈情说爱	tánqíng-shuō'ài	sweet talk, coo, dating
3.	嘴快	zuǐ kuài	to have a loose tongue, to be blunt
4.	青年	qīngnián	youth, young people
5.	登记	dēngjì	to register, to enter one's name
6.	征婚	zhēnghūn	to try to seek a marriage partner
7.	对象	duìxiàng	boy/girlfriend, target
8.	约	yuē	to arrange, to make an appointment
9.	见面	jiànmiàn	to meet, to see
10.	办	bàn	to do, to handle, to manage
11.	交谈	jiāotán	to talk with each other, to chat
12.	公道	gōngdào	fair, reasonable
13.	呗	bei	*modal particle indicating that sth. is obvious*
14.	丢人现眼	diūrén xiànyǎn	to make a fool of oneself
15.	难为情	nánwéiqíng	ashamed, embarrassed, shy
16.	勇气	yǒngqì	courage, nerve
17.	安静	ānjìng	quiet, peaceful

18. 自在	zìzai	comfortable, at ease
19. 随便	suíbiàn	casual, informal
20. 彼此	bǐcǐ	each other, one another
21. 相中	xiāngzhòng	to take a fancy to
22. 小伙子	xiǎohuǒzi	young fellow, young man
23. 泡	pào	to dawdle, to hang about
24. 闲聊	xiánliáo	to chat
25. 家长里短	jiācháng-lǐduǎn	domestic trivia
26. 都市	dūshì	big city, metropolis
27. 趣闻	qùwén	interesting news
28. 传播	chuánbō	to spread, to disseminate
29. 场所	chǎngsuǒ	place, site
30. 公关	gōngguān	public relations
31. 行情	hángqíng	current prices, quotations
32. 供求	gōngqiú	supply and demand
33. 开展	kāizhǎn	to develop, to launch, to carry out
34. 业务	yèwù	business, professional work
35. 洽谈	qiàtán	to discuss, to negotiate
36. 安装	ānzhuāng	to install, to set up
37. 电脑	diànnǎo	computer
38. 额	é	a specified number or amount
39. 兴隆	xīnglóng	thriving, prosperous

专 名 Proper Noun

红娘	Hóngniáng	Hongniang, a character in *Romance of the Western Chamber*—matchmaker

注释 Notes

1 "看",动词,用在表示动作或变化的词或词组前面,表示预见到某种变化趋势,或者提醒对方注意可能发生或将要发生的某种不好的事情或情况。例如:

看, a verb, is used in front of a word or phrase that denotes an action or a change to indicate that a change has been forseen or to remind the other party of something bad that is happening or may happen. For example:

1. 看车,小心点儿!
2. 看饭快凉了,快吃吧。

2 "……不说,还……",这是一个常用格式。前后两个分句,在意思上有递进关系。例如:

"……不说, 还……" is a frequently-used pattern. The two clauses connected by it are progressive in meaning. For example:

1. 我劝他,他不听不说,还骂了我一顿。
2. 他不去不说,还不让我去。
3. 这份工作受累不说,还招人怨。
4. 这个商店质量差、价格高不说,服务态度还不好。

3 "丢人现眼"。"现",指显露、表露在外面,让人可以看见。"丢人现眼",常指丢脸、出丑,也可以单用"现眼"。例如:

In 丢人现眼, 现 means showing or becoming visible so that other people can see. The expression often means losing face or making a spectacle of oneself. One can also simply use 现眼. For example:

1. 你这样做,不怕丢人现眼吗?
2. 今天我可现眼了,当时我恨不得赶快回家!
3. 大学生到饭店去打工,没什么丢人现眼的。
4. 这次当翻译,差点儿现了眼!

4 "泡",动词,指故意消磨时间。例如:

泡, a verb, means idling away the time aimlessly. For example:

1. 他在茶馆里泡了半天。
2. 他没来上班,在家泡病号呢!
3. 她今天在我这儿足足泡了三个小时!
4. 杰克在酒吧里一泡就是一晚上。

练习 Exercises

一、替换练习。

Substitution drills.

A:你们约好在哪儿见面?
B:我们约好在楼前见面。

碰头	公园门口
相亲	茶馆
看货	工厂
洽谈	国贸大厦

A:你为什么上这儿来吃饭?
B:这儿环境好不说,饭菜还便宜。

聊天儿	行人	少
学汉语	老师	好
约会	谈话	方便
做生意	顾客	特别多

A：你怎么想起来中国学习汉语呢？
B：在中国学习汉语有很好的环境。
A：学习汉语最重要的是什么？
B：最重要的是自己要努力。

工作	自己感兴趣
做生意	有顾客
开工厂	产品质量
办公司	有好的雇员

A：你也想唱一支歌？
B：怎么，不行啊？
A：不是不行，就怕你没那个勇气。

开公司	能力
去上海旅行	时间
当老师	学问
当老板	能力

二、把下面的词组成句子。
Rearrange the following words into sentences.

1. 今天　可以　我们　下午　聊聊　吗
2. 生意　难免　做　要　赔钱
3. 请　到　登记　先　服务台　你
4. 你　了　谁　来　请　都　吃饭
5. 他　对象　的　个　合适　是　很
6. 他　很　事　公道　办
7. 她　总是　说话　脸　爱　红
8. 请　随便　吧　坐　你
9. 你　不　正事　可　耽误　要　了
10. 市场　变化　很　行情　快

三、完成下面的对话。
Complete the following dialogues.

A：你们昨天晚上做什么了？
B：_____。
A：都聊些什么呀？
B：_____。

A：你们第一次见面是什么时候？
B：_____。
A：_____？
B：在上海的一家公司。

A：你常看报纸上的征婚广告吗？
B：_____。
A：_____？
B：我想找一个合适的对象。

A：你知道今天是什么日子吗？
B：_____。
A：不，我不是问今天几月几号，我是问今天是什么特别的日子？
B：哦，我明白了，今天是_____。

A：你说，对一个商人来说，_____？
B：最重要的当然是了解市场信息。
A：那么，怎么了解市场信息？
B：_____。

四、选择适当的词语完成句子。

Choose the appropriate words to complete the following sentences.

1. 我要告诉大家一条好_____。（消息　信息）
2. 你们常在一起交流市场_____吗？（消息　信息）
3. 你看，她说话多么_____，一点儿也不紧张。（自在　自然）
4. 你看，她坐在那儿多舒服，多_____。（自在　自然）
5. 我去他的宿舍很_____，谈话也很_____。（随便　方便）
6. 我不能去他的办公室，在那儿谈话也很不_____。（随便　方便）
7. 先生，上午九点，同中方经理有一个业务_____会，请你准时到会。（交谈　洽谈）
8. 晚上，我们还可以同中方经理边进餐边_____。（交谈　洽谈）

五、你认为，要办好一个商店或一家企业，最重要的是什么？

In your opinion, what is most important for running a store or an enterprise well?

第四十一课　味道好极了（一）
Lesson 41　The Taste Is Great (I)

课文 Text

在课上

王老师：同学们，你们知道商标和广告的重要性吗？

杰　克：知道。商标代表商品的质量和信誉。

山　口：商标还是企业的财产和生命。

珍　妮：商标也是商品参加市场竞争的手段。

王老师：你们说得都对，可以举出一两个例子吗？

山　口：松下电器、奔驰汽车、可口可乐，都是世界驰名的，这些商品的商标，就代表了很高的质量、信誉和很强的竞争力。

杰　克：我听说，可口可乐商标价值达七百亿美元，占可口可乐公司财产的四分之三呢！

珍　妮：人们购买商品时，常常先看商标，商标信誉越好，也就越容易赢得顾客。我买东西，就只冲着名牌买。

王老师：这是一种普遍的消费心理。

杰　克：所以激烈的市场竞争中，企业家才大做广告，努力提高自己商品商标的知名度，对吧？

41 味道好极了（一）

王老师：是的。现在，中国市场很活跃，到处都是商品广告。说说你们印象最深的商标和广告，好吗？

山　口：杰克，现在中国流传最广的广告是什么，你知道吗？

杰　克：知道，"嗯，味道好极了！"

珍　妮：看你美得，我这会儿都想来一杯雀巢咖啡了。

山　口：不只喝雀巢咖啡，现在不论男女老少，也不论吃什么，你问他怎么样，只要他感到满意，就都会说："嗯，味道好极了！"

珍　妮：这确实是句极好的广告词。

山　口：好的广告词还多着呢。中国最大的家电生产商——海尔集团，它有一句很响的广告词，叫……

杰　克："海尔，中国造！"

山　口："美的"空调，它的广告词是……

杰　克："原来生活可以更美的。"

山　口：可口可乐？

杰　克："永远的可口可乐，独一无二好味道！"

山　口："万家乐"热水器？

杰　克："万家乐，乐万家！"

山　口：联想电脑？

杰　克："世界因联想更美好。"

山　口：杰克知道得真多！

杰　克：学汉语嘛，能不记住这些绝妙好词儿？

生词 New Words

1.	性	xìng	*suffix attached to a noun, verb or adjective to form an abstract noun or attributive word to denote category, property or characteristic*
2.	代表	dàibiǎo	to represent, to stand for
3.	信誉	xìnyù	prestige, reputation
4.	财产	cáichǎn	property, asset
5.	生命	shēngmìng	life
6.	参加	cānjiā	to join, to take part in
7.	手段	shǒuduàn	means, method, measure
8.	举	jǔ	to raise, to bring up
9.	例子	lìzi	example, instance
10.	达	dá	to reach, to attain, to amount to
11.	占	zhàn	to occupy, to make up, to account for
12.	分	fēn	portion, part
13.	之	zhī	*used between the modifier and the modified*
14.	越	yuè	the more... (the more...)
15.	冲	chòng	aiming at, on the basis of
16.	普遍	pǔbiàn	universal, general, widespread
17.	知名度	zhīmíngdù	popularity
18.	活跃	huóyuè	brisk, active
19.	流传	liúchuán	to spread, to circulate, to hand down
20.	少	shào	young (people)
21.	不论	búlùn	no matter (what, who, how, etc.), whether... or..., regardless of

41 味道好极了（一）

22. 家电	jiādiàn	household appliances
23. 生产商	shēngchǎnshāng	manufacturer
24. 造	zào	to make, to manufacture
25. 空调	kōngtiáo	air conditioner
26. 原来	yuánlái	to turn out to be
27. 生活	shēnghuó	life
28. 更	gèng	more, -er
29. 独一无二	dúyī-wúèr	unique
30. 热水器	rèshuǐqì	water heater
31. 乐	lè	happy, cheerful, joyful
32. 世界	shìjiè	world
33. 绝妙	juémiào	extremely brilliant, excellent, perfect

专　名　Proper Nouns

1. 奔驰	Bēnchí	Mercedes-Benz
2. 海尔集团	Hǎi'ěr Jítuán	Haier Group
3. 美的	Měidì	Midea
4. 万家乐	Wànjiālè	Macro
5. 联想	Liánxiǎng	Lenovo

注释 Notes

1　"越"，可以重叠成"越 A 越 B"式，表示在程度上 B 随 A 的增加而增加，也可以几个"越"字叠用。例如：

越 may take the pattern of 越A越B, indicating that the level of B heightens along with that of A. Sometimes 越 can be reduplicated more than once. For example:

1. 他越想越发愁。
2. 你越问他,他越是不说。
3. 有的商品,广告上越吹,越没有人敢买。
4. 经济越发展,市场越活跃,人民生活也就越方便。

2 "不论",连词,表示在任何条件下结果或结论都不变,后面常有表示任指的疑问代词或表示选择关系的并列词语。下文有"都、也、总"等词相呼应。例如:

不论, a conjunction, expresses that the result or the conclusion remains the same under whatever conditions. It is often followed by an interrogative pronoun that denotes arbitrary reference or by coordinate expressions that indicate alternatives. 都 (all), 也 (still), or 总 (always) is often used in coordination with it in the second clause. For example:

1. 不论顾客的态度如何,她都面带微笑。
2. 不论广告上说些什么,他都只相信自己的眼睛。
3. 他不论多忙,也要抽空给爸爸妈妈写信。
4. 不论买多买少,都是我们欢迎的顾客。

3 "更",副词,表示程度增高。用于比较,多数含有原来也有一定程度的意思。后面可以是形容词,也可以是动词短语。例如:

更, an adverb, indicates an increase in degree. It is used for comparison, often implying the original degree is already high. It can be followed by an adjective or a verb phrase. For example:

1. 下了一夜雪,天气更冷了。
2. 学习是为了更好地工作。
3. 这样做更能解决问题。
4. 我更喜欢这个地方了。

41 味道好极了（一）

练 习
Exercises

一、替换练习。
Substitution drills.

A：你们班的<u>男生</u>占<u>全班人数</u>的几分之几？
B：<u>男生</u>占<u>三分之一</u>。

家	房租	总收入	二分之一
家	旅游消费	总消费	五分之一
公司	广告费	业务费	二分之一

<u>他</u>越<u>跑</u>越<u>快</u>。

衣服	洗	干净
日子	过	红火
钱	挣	多

A：在中国流传最广的<u>广告</u>是什么？
B：是"<u>味道好极了</u>"。

歌曲	《朋友》
书	《红楼梦》
口号	高高兴兴上班去，平平安安回家来。

A：你真的要<u>学汉语</u>吗？
B：是的，无论<u>汉语</u>多么<u>难</u>，我也要<u>学汉语</u>。

去 外地	天气	不好
买 汽车	公共交通	方便
做 生意	市场竞争	激烈

二、把下面的词组成句子。
Rearrange the following words into sentences.

1. 我 代表 是 业务 公司 的
2. 请 认准 您 我们 的 商标 公司 五星牌
3. 请 举例 一下儿 您 说明

4. 怎样 信誉 公司 提高 的 呢
5. 市场 越来越 激烈 竞争
6. 企业家 懂 的 得 应该 消费 顾客 心理
7. 我们 课堂 很 的 活跃
8. 海尔集团 名气 很 的 大
9. 这 不 瞒 事儿 应该 着 他
10. 广告 由 老张 工作 负责

三、完成下面的对话。
Complete the following dialogues.

A：企业家为什么要做广告？
B：_____。
A：_____？
B：广告确实给企业家带来了经济效益。

A：你怎样挑选商品？
B：_____。
A：_____？
B：你应该学会识别商标。

A：你喜欢喝雀巢咖啡吗？
B：_____。
A：_____？
B：嗯，味道好极了。

A：你知道海尔集团的广告词吗？
B：_____。
A：嗬，你记得很清楚嘛！
B：_____！

41 味道好极了（一）

四、用指定的词语完成句子。
Complete the following sentences with the given words.

1. 企业家为了给自己的商品打开市场，_____。（广告）
2. 一个公司，不能光顾赚钱，_____。（信誉）
3. 中国市场变得_____。（越……越……）
4. 认名牌货，买名牌货，_____。（越来越……）
5. _____，我都要买一台电脑。（无论）
6. 我要努力学习，_____。（提高）
7. 一些国际著名的快餐店进入中国市场，_____。（竞争）
8. 比起过去，现在的产品_____。（更）

五、你知道哪些广告词，请说一两例你最喜欢的。
What commercial messages do you know? Give one or two of your favorites.

第四十二课　味道好极了（二）
Lesson 42　The Taste Is Great (II)

课文 Text

在课外

珍　妮：山口，你看这门脸儿上写的字！
山　口："桂香村"，是一家食品店，卖中西糕点、糖果。
珍　妮：这两行字呢？
山　口："名点色香味，云集于一村。"
杰　克：哎，我有点儿饿了，山口，你请客，买半斤点心吃怎么样？看这广告就知道，味道一定好极了。
山　口：半斤点心？一两我也不买！刚出门，怎么见什么都想吃啊？走吧！

珍　妮：山口，你看这是一家饭店。
山　口："笑迎天下客，满意在京城。"
杰　克：进去试试，看看我们满意不满意。
山　口：又来了，走吧。王府井新东安市场，里面不仅可以买东西，还有各种风味小吃，到那儿去解馋吧！
杰　克：好吧！
珍　妮：嗬，好大、好热闹的商场！

42 味道好极了（二）

山　口：你们看这儿，"买一送一"；这儿，"满 200 减 80""清仓大甩卖"；那儿，"开业大吉，七折优惠，欢迎选购"。还有那儿，"有奖销售，当场开奖，祝君好运"。

杰　克："有奖销售"，好，我们去撞撞大运！

珍　妮：杰克，你闻闻，多香，不先解馋了？

杰　克：不急，不急，还是先去撞大运，说不定能抽到一台笔记本电脑呢！

珍　妮：做梦！

珍　妮：唉，今天走了一天，累死我了，可想坐下看会儿电视了。

山　口：我也是。我来开电视吧！

珍　妮：又是广告！看来看去，老是那一套，都看烦了。

山　口：不过，也有许多好的广告，我就喜欢看。你听！"胃，你好吗？""白天服白片不瞌睡，晚上服黑片睡得香。"

珍　妮：你喜欢的怎么都是医药广告呀？

山　口："斯达舒"治胃病，"白加黑"治感冒，我都少不了嘛。

珍　妮：那我也记住了一些。"我只用力士"，还有"巴黎欧莱雅，你值得拥有"。

山　口：你为什么对这些广告感兴趣呢？

珍　妮：这些广告都是中国人喜欢的影星做的，美人用高档化妆品，赏心悦目！

山　口：我可明白了，难怪越来越多的影星、歌星去做广告呢，原来有你这样的观众。

珍　妮：嘿嘿，我本来就喜欢明星，而且我觉得利用明星的魅力推销商品，这才是聪明的做法，你觉得呢？

生词 New Words

1.	糕点	gāodiǎn	cake, pastry
2.	糖果	tángguǒ	sweets, candy
3.	行	háng	line, row
4.	云集	yúnjí	to gather, to converge
5.	于	yú	*(preposition indicating time, place, scope, and other relationship)* in, at
6.	点心	diǎnxin	light refreshments, dessert, pastry
7.	解馋	jiěchán	to satisfy one's craving for delicious food
8.	满	mǎn	to reach the limit or amount
9.	清仓	qīngcāng	to clear out inventory, to destock
10.	开业	kāiyè	to start business
11.	吉	jí	lucky, auspicious
12.	折（扣）	zhé(kòu)	discount
13.	优惠	yōuhuì	preferential, favorable
14.	奖	jiǎng	reward, award, prize
15.	销售	xiāoshòu	to market, to sell
16.	当场	dāngchǎng	on the spot, then and there
17.	祝	zhù	to wish
18.	君	jūn	*(honorific)* you
19.	好运	hǎoyùn	good luck
20.	撞	zhuàng	to try (one's luck), to trust to
21.	抽	chōu	to draw, to take out
22.	做梦	zuòmèng	to dream, to have a dream
23.	累	lèi	tired, fatigued
24.	烦	fán	to be tired of, to be fed up with
25.	胃	wèi	stomach
26.	服	fú	to take (medicine)

27. 片	piàn	pill, tablet
28. 瞌睡	kēshuì	to doze
29. 医药	yīyào	medicine
30. 治	zhì	to treat, to cure
31. 值得	zhídé	to be worth
32. 拥有	yōngyǒu	to own, to have
33. 兴趣	xìngqù	interest
34. 赏心悦目	shǎngxīn-yuèmù	to be pleasing to the eye
35. 难怪	nánguài	no wonder
36. 观众	guānzhòng	spectator, audience
37. 本来	běnlái	of course, truly, naturally
38. 推销	tuīxiāo	to promote sales

专　名　Proper Nouns

1. 桂香村	Guìxiāngcūn	Guixiangcun, name of a food store
2. 新东安市场	Xīndōng'ān Shìchǎng	Xindong'an Market
3. 斯达舒	Sīdáshū	Sidashu, brand name of a stomach medicine (Vitamin U, Belladonna and Aluminium Capsules II)
4. 白加黑	Báijiāhēi	White & Black, a cold medicine
5. 力士	Lìshì	Lux (soap)
6. 欧莱雅	Ōuláiyǎ	L'Oréal

注　释　Notes

1 "看来看去"，这种"A来A去"格式，表示某种动作的多次反复，两个"A"常是同一个动词。例如："飞来飞去、跑来跑去、想来想去、说来说去、变来变去、谈来谈去、讨论来讨论去"等。

看来看去 is an example of the pattern A来A去, which indicates the repetition of an action for many times. Here A and A are frequently the same verb. For example:

1. 想来想去，总算想明白了。
2. 说来说去，还是那么几句话。
3. 你走来走去，想出一个好办法没有？
4. 讨论来讨论去，也没讨论出个名堂来。

2 "难怪"，副词，表示发现了某种情况后，对事情的真相有所了解，因而觉得这种事情的发生是合情合理的。"难怪"还常与"原来"搭配使用。例如：

难怪, an adverb, indicates that after the discovery of a certain condition, one has come to an understanding of the real situation and thus feels that the occurrence of a certain something is fair and reasonable. 难怪 is often used in coordination with 原来 (as a matter of fact). For example:

1. 你没来上课，难怪你不懂。
2. 难怪她生气，谁叫你忘了她的生日。
3. 原来你爸爸是音乐家，难怪你对音乐这么感兴趣。
4. 难怪你今天这么高兴，原来是找到工作了！

3 "本来"，副词，强调"原先、先前"的情况。例如：

本来, an adverb, emphasizes the original or previous condition. For example:

1. 我买东西本来不讨价还价，现在学会了。
2. 她本来就不瘦，现在更胖了。
3. 我们本来不认识，来中国以后才认识的。

"本来"还可以表示按道理就该这样。例如：

本来 can also indicate that it should be like this by reason. For example:

1. 本来嘛，没钱还想买东西？
2. 作业本来就应该当天做完。
3. 你有胃病，本来就不该多吃冰激凌。

"本来"和"原来"，都是副词，但有明显区别。"本来"表示某事物或某情况过去存在,这是说话人知道的,当说话人提到它时,往往是它已经发生了变化。"原来"多表示说话人对某事或某情况以前并不知道,而现在有所发现或醒悟。试比较下面的句子:

Both 本来 and 原来 are adverbs, but there is a marked difference between them. 本来 refers to a thing or situation which existed in the past and which was known to the speaker. When the speaker mentions it, it has often undergone some changes. 原来 often indicates that the speaker did not know about a certain thing or situation, and now has made the discovery or come to realize the truth. Compare the following sentences:

1. A. 我本来就没想去,现在也不想去。
   B. 我原来是不想去,现在觉得应该去。

2. A. 什么七折优惠,本来就卖这个价嘛!
   B. 啊,今天的东西好便宜,原来是打折销售!

练习
Exercises

一、替换练习。
Substitution drills.

A:杰克,你怎么了?
B:走了一天,累死我了。

工作了一天	累
一天没吃饭	饿
昨天没睡觉	困
走路摔了一跤	疼

A:你怎么不去看电视?
B:看来看去,老是那几个节目,有什么好看的!

聊天儿	聊	几句话
买衣服	买	几种款式
逛商店	逛	几个商店
唱歌	唱	几首歌

A：你为什么对广告感兴趣？
B：因为我可以用广告推销商品。

汉语	广交中国朋友
有奖销售	刺激消费
微笑服务	赢得顾客
时装表演	提高名牌知名度

A：你会做生意吗？
B：本来不会，现在会了。

想	登电视广告
会	开车
喜欢	用化妆品
愿意	当时装模特儿

二、把下面的词组成句子。

Rearrange the following words into sentences.

1. 糕点 这儿 卖 有 西式 吗 的
2. 欢迎 来 我 您 餐 用 店
3. 这 饭店 新 是 开业 的 一家
4. 见 你 人家 可 有 就 眼馋 钱 别
5. 祝 做 你 美梦 晚上 个
6. 今天 真 我 事儿 死 这 烦 了
7. 他 一个 很 是 有 的 魅力 男人
8. 中国 越来越 女人 多 化妆 的 喜欢
9. 你 什么 喜欢 最 化妆品 使用
10. 从来 我 不 明星 喜欢 电影

三、完成下面的对话。

Complete the following dialogues.

A：_____。
B：你哪儿是饿了？我看你是嘴馋了。
A：你闻闻，多香，你不馋？不想吃点？
B：_____。

A：嗨，你看这广告，什么是"买一送一"？
B：_____。
A：_____？
B：店主才不会赔本呢！

A：你知道哪儿有"有奖销售"吗？
B：_____。
A：_____？
B：你去吧，祝你中个头奖！

A：_____？
B：我最喜欢看新型汽车广告。
A：为什么？
B：_____。

四、用指定的词语完成句子。
Complete the following sentences with the given words.

1. 啊，有这么多好吃的，_____。（馋）
2. 我想买十箱"力士"洗发水，_____？（优惠）
3. 朋友，_____。（好运）
4. 上学期，我们的学习很紧张，_____。（轻松）
5. _____，原来这里三折优惠。（难怪）
6. 我说是谁在屋里聊天儿呢，_____。（原来）
7. 人们钱多了，就变着法儿花钱，因此_____。（刺激）
8. 你错过了这次好机会，_____。（可惜）
9. 这些食品已经坏了，_____。（本来）
10. 广告是一种竞争手段，_____。（利用）

五、在电视上、报纸上和网上有各种各样的广告，你可以举出几个例子吗？这些广告有什么特点？

There are different kinds of commercials on TV, newspapers, and the Internet. Can you give some examples of them? What features do they have?

第四十三课　永远别说"不"（一）
Lesson 43　Never Say "No" (I)

课文 Text

在课上

山　口：老师，为什么有的售货员跟顾客吵架呢？他们不是说"微笑服务""礼貌待客"吗？

珍　妮：我还听一个顾客说"花钱买气受"，这是什么意思？

杰　克：就是花了钱买东西，但是惹了一肚子气呗！

王老师：是啊，现在还有不少商店服务质量差，顾客不满意，其实，中国商人有很好的服务传统。

杰　克：老师，我知道，中国商人常说"和气生财"。

王老师：对，"生意上门，笑脸相迎""买卖不成，情谊在""留得人情在，下次好相见"嘛。这次没买，下次他还会来的，生意不就有的做了！

山　口：这么说，还是微笑服务、礼貌待客好。回头客越多，生意自然也就越红火。

王老师：那么，你们认为怎样才能搞好"微笑服务"呢？

珍　妮：商店开展微笑服务，最重要的是永远也别对顾客说"不"字。杰克，你说对不对？

杰　克：对。应该这样，因为顾客的要求都是合理的。
珍　妮：那好，现在我是顾客，你是售货员，你不能拒绝我的要求，对我说"不"字，也不准说"没""没有""别"这样的字眼儿。
杰　克：这容易，不信咱们试试。
王老师：杰克，珍妮，你们就表演给大家看看！
杰　克：好！

杰　克：小姐，您好，这些都是今年新款，您进来看看。
珍　妮：这双皮鞋样子不错。
杰　克：这是名牌皮鞋，现在很畅销，小姐真有眼光！
珍　妮：我可以试试吗？
杰　克：当然！给您这只，请……请踩在这个纸盒上，以免弄脏了。
珍　妮：你怎么不说"别"把鞋踩脏了？
杰　克：我相信顾客会爱惜新鞋的。
珍　妮：好，咱们接着来。这双小了点儿，夹脚，给我换……
山　口：喂，杰克！
杰　克：啊，山口，你来啦！
山　口：上次卖的那种上海皮鞋，今天有货了吗？
杰　克：昨天来了，可是一上柜台就抢光了。
珍　妮：先生，你还没给我换鞋呢！
杰　克：你……
珍　妮：你没看见……
杰　克：哦，很抱歉，我这儿有点儿急事，请您等一等。
珍　妮：好嘛，一个"没"字到嘴边又咽了下去。
杰　克：山口，这批货，比你上次看的还好呢。

43 永远别说"不"(一)

山　口：那你怎么不给我留一双？
杰　克：咱俩谁跟谁啊，早给你包好放在这儿了。给！
珍　妮：先生，给我换双鞋……
山　口：杰克，够朋友！晚上我请你看电影。
杰　克：那好啊，什么电影？在什么地方？
山　口：是美国片，首都电影院。
珍　妮：喂，先生，我等了半天了，你们待会儿再闲聊行不行？
杰　克：谁闲聊啦？她也是来买鞋的。
珍　妮：你们不是在谈看电影吗？
杰　克：谁谈看电影啦？你录音啦？
珍　妮：你怎么不讲理啊？
杰　克：你讲理？
珍　妮：你怎么这么说话？怎么这么对待工作？对待顾客？
杰　克：我怎么啦？你说我应该怎么工作？怎么对待顾客？
珍　妮：你们经理在哪儿？我要提意见。
杰　克：提意见？欢迎，欢迎，请提吧，小姐，这是意见簿。吓唬谁啊？
珍　妮：你，你们的服务态度太差了，我要建议经理炒你鱿鱼！
杰　克：我正好想自己开公司，赚大钱去呢！炒就炒，我早就不想干了！
珍　妮：哈哈，你终于说"不"了吧！
杰　克：啊？我说"不"了？！

生词
New Words

1.	受	shòu	to suffer, to be subjected to, to receive
2.	惹	rě	to bring upon oneself (sth. unpleasant), to attract, to cause
3.	和气	héqì	gentle, kind, polite
4.	情谊	qíngyì	friendly feelings
5.	人情	rénqíng	human feelings, favor
6.	回头客	huítóukè	repeat customer
7.	认为	rènwéi	to think, to consider
8.	搞	gǎo	to do, to make, to produce a certain effect (or result)
9.	拒绝	jùjué	to refuse, to reject, to turn down
10.	准（许）	zhǔn(xǔ)	to permit, to allow
11.	字眼	zìyǎn	wording, diction
12.	样子	yàngzi	shape, appearance
13.	眼光	yǎnguāng	sight, vision, insight
14.	踩	cǎi	to step on, to tread, to trample
15.	纸盒	zhǐ hé	cardboard box
16.	以免	yǐmiǎn	so as not to, in order to avoid
17.	弄	nòng	to do, to make, to get sth. into a specific condition
18.	脏	zāng	dirty
19.	鞋	xié	shoes
20.	爱惜	àixī	to cherish, to treasure
21.	接着	jiēzhe	to go on, to follow
22.	夹脚	jiā jiǎo	to pinch (feet)
23.	抱歉	bàoqiàn	to be sorry, to feel apologetic, to regret
24.	咽	yàn	to swallow
25.	批	pī	batch, lot, group

43 永远别说"不"（一）

26.	首都	shǒudū	capital (of a country)
27.	待	dāi	to stay
28.	讲理	jiǎnglǐ	to listen to reason, to be reasonable
29.	意见	yìjiàn	opinion, objection, complaint
30.	簿	bù	notebook
31.	吓唬	xiàhu	to bluff, to scare
32.	炒鱿鱼	chǎo yóuyú	to fire, to sack
33.	终于	zhōngyú	at last, in the end, finally

注释 Notes

1 "回头"，动词，把头转向后方的意思。例如：

回头, a verb, means turning one's head. For example:

1. 你回头看看，是谁来了？
2. 我刚一回头，就看到小王跑过来了。

"回头客"，指对曾经提供过消费服务的商店、饭店、旅馆等产生好感、信任感因而再次光临的顾客。例如：

回头客 refers to customers who come back again to the same shop, restaurant or hotel, etc. that once provided services for them because they have a good opinion of it or have trust in it. For example:

1. 商店的回头客越多越好。
2. 商店的回头客越多，说明商店的信誉越好。
3. 这个饭店的房客80%是回头客。

回头，也可以是副词，意思是"过一段时间以后"。例如：

回头 can also be used as an adverb to mean "later, after a while". For example:

1. 你先吃饭，回头再谈。
2. 我先走了，回头见！
3. 我正忙着呢，回头给你打电话。

2 "谁跟谁",这个格式中的两个"谁"字,指不同的人,且不是任指,而是确切地指说话双方,表示两个人关系亲密,非同一般。例如:

In the pattern 谁跟谁, the two 谁 refer to different persons. They do not refer to just anyone, but precisely to the two parties engaged in the conversation, indicating the extremely close relationship between them. For example:

1. 我们这是谁跟谁呀,还这么客气!
2. 你我谁跟谁呀,还不能帮这点儿忙?

3 "炒就炒",这种"A就A"式,表示容忍或无所谓。例如:

This pattern of 炒就炒 (A就A) expresses tolerance or indifference. For example:

1. 东西丢就丢了,急也没用。
2. 没考好就没考好,我才不在乎呢!
3. 挨骂就挨骂,反正我也习惯了。

练习
Exercises

一、替换练习。
Substitution drills.

A:你不是说没有<u>钱</u>了吗?
B:是没有了,这些<u>钱</u>是我刚从<u>银行取</u>的。

牛奶	小卖部	买
邮票	邮局	买
面包	商店	买
美元	银行	换

A:你说,我怎么就<u>学不好汉语</u>呢?
B:<u>学不好就学不好</u>,着急也没用。

买不到	飞机票
找不到	工作
见不到	老板
做不成	一笔生意

43 永远别说"不"（一）

A：这间屋子怎么样？
B：嗯，挺干净，就是小了点儿。

那本小说	有意思	长
那个售货员	和气	做事慢
小张这个人	懂礼貌	能力差
北京的商场	大	人多

A：喂，杰克，你还去不去商店了？
B：别叫了，你没看他正忙着吗？

上课	病着
旅行	发愁
看女朋友	着急
看电影	穿衣服

A：这种电脑很好，你怎么不给我借一台？
B：咱俩谁跟谁呀，我早给你借来了。

衬衣	漂亮	买	件
面包	甜	带	块
咖啡	香	倒	杯
手机	流行	买	个

二、把下面的词组成句子。

Rearrange the following words into sentences.

1. 你 谁 跟 了 吵架
2. 谁 你 惹 了 生气
3. 顾客 满意 商店 质量 不 服务 的
4. 他 很 和气 人 待
5. 请 来 下次 您 再
6. 请 包 商品 一下 把 你
7. 这 鞋 夹脚 双 点儿 有
8. 我们 说 下去 接着 吧
9. 你 建议 有 好 什么 吗
10. 你 学 讲理 会 终于 了

三、完成下面的对话。

Complete the following dialogues.

A：＿＿＿＿＿＿＿＿＿＿＿＿＿？
B：我不小心踩了她的脚。
A：你也可以好好说嘛，用不着吵架！
B：＿＿＿＿＿＿＿＿＿＿＿＿＿。

A：＿＿＿＿＿＿＿＿＿＿＿＿＿？
B：她们待人礼貌，周到热情。
A：还有什么不满意吗？
B：＿＿＿＿＿＿＿＿＿＿＿＿＿。

A：＿＿＿＿＿＿＿＿＿＿＿＿＿？
B：对不起，今天卖完了。
A：最近会有货吗？
B：＿＿＿＿＿＿＿＿＿＿＿＿＿。

A：喂，看那柜台边的人在做什么？
B：＿＿＿＿＿＿＿＿＿＿＿＿＿。
A：为什么要抢购呢？
B：＿＿＿＿＿＿＿＿＿＿＿＿＿。

A：＿＿＿＿＿＿＿＿＿＿＿＿＿？
B：那工作太没意思了。
A：你想做什么样的工作？
B：＿＿＿＿＿＿＿＿＿＿＿＿＿。

四、用指定的词语完成句子。

Complete the following sentences with the given words.

1. 长城给我的印象太深了，＿＿＿＿＿＿＿＿＿＿。（永远）

43 永远别说"不"（一）

2. 待客热情周到，_____。（传统）
3. 我们在一起学习、生活，_____。（情谊）
4. 开展优质服务，_____。（提高）
5. _____，没几天就把电脑弄坏了。（爱惜）
6. 他刚想说点什么，_____。（咽）
7. 你有急事，你先走吧，_____。（待）
8. 为了推销公司的产品，我跑遍了北京城，_____。（终于）
9. _____，我听你的！（建议）
10. _____，她胆小，会吓坏的。（吓唬）

五、你所在的城市商店、旅馆的服务质量怎么样？你遇到过什么不愉快的事吗？

What is the service like in your city's stores and hotels? Have you ever had any unhappy experiences?

第四十四课　永远别说"不"（二）
Lesson 44　Never Say "No" (II)

课文 Text

在课外

珍　妮：山口，你来看，我多倒霉。

山　口：怎么啦？

珍　妮：这是我昨天买的风衣，你看，背后抽丝了，你说怎么办？

山　口：嗯，是有一点儿抽丝，不过不显眼，没关系。

珍　妮：那穿着也糟心。

山　口：要不就去退了吧！

珍　妮：退货？能退吗？

山　口：应该能退！

珍　妮：可我听说，好多商店都是"商品一经售出，概不退换"。

山　口：咳，那都是过去的事儿了。现在市场竞争越来越激烈，商家也越来越明智了。

珍　妮：现在有了新规定、新做法？

山　口：对。顾客要求退货，总是有原因的。他们现在这样做，说明他们心中有了顾客。

44 永远别说"不"（二）

珍　　妮：就是嘛，谁愿意没事找事，穷折腾，把称心如意的商品退掉？

山　　口：所以，商店让顾客退货，尊重顾客的选择权，才是真正为顾客着想。

珍　　妮：理是这个理，也不知他们认不认这个理？

山　　口：那咱们就去试试！

珍　　妮：好！

珍　　妮：小姐，这是我昨天在这儿买的风衣，有点儿毛病，我想换一件，行吗？

售货员：啊，实在对不起，让您又跑一趟，请给我看看。

山　　口：你看人家服务态度多好！

珍　　妮：先别夸，她还没答应换呢！

售货员：啊，质量是有问题，我给您换一件，请等一等。

山　　口：怎么样？我没说错吧！中国市场很精彩，天天都有新发现！

珍　　妮：她怎么去了这半天还没回来？

山　　口：可能是到库房给你找去了。

售货员：小姐，实在抱歉，您这样的风衣已经卖完了。

珍　　妮：那怎么办？我很喜欢这件衣服，你不能跟厂家联系一下吗？

售货员：我刚才已经联系过了。每种款式工厂都只小批量生产，现在已经转产别的新款式了。您这种风衣已经停产了。

珍　　妮：啊？真的没办法了？看来只能退货了！

售货员：要不给您打点儿折，便宜些卖给您？

珍　　妮：花几百块钱买件次品，心里不舒服啊。

山　　口：不能退吗？我们可以付手续费。

售货员：当然能退，不用付任何费用。我是看小姐很喜欢这件衣服，虽然有点儿毛病，并不显眼，退了也遗憾。

山　　口：我看还是退了吧，以后看见合适的再买件新的，珍妮，你说呢？

珍　　妮：嗯，小姐，还是麻烦你给退了吧。

售货员：好的，请稍等。

生词 New Words

1. 倒霉　　　dǎoméi　　　to have bad luck, to be out of luck
2. 背　　　　bèi　　　　　back
3. 抽丝　　　chōusī　　　(where some stitches have come undone) to run, to ladder
4. 显眼　　　xiǎnyǎn　　　obvious, apparent, noticeable
5. 糟心　　　zāoxīn　　　vexed, annoyed
6. 退　　　　tuì　　　　　to return
7. 一经　　　yìjīng　　　once, as soon as
8. （一）概　(yí)gài　　　without exception, totally
9. 明智　　　míngzhì　　　sensible, wise
10. 规定　　　guīdìng　　　stipulation, provision, regulation
11. 做法　　　zuòfǎ　　　　way, method, practice
12. 原因　　　yuányīn　　　cause, reason
13. 说明　　　shuōmíng　　to explain, to show, to illustrate
14. 穷　　　　qióng　　　　willfully, groundlessly
15. 折腾　　　zhēteng　　　to do sth. over and over again, to cause physical (or mental) suffering
16. 称心如意　chènxīn rúyì　to find sth. satisfactory, to be gratified
17. 权（利）　quán(lì)　　　right(s)
18. 着想　　　zhuóxiǎng　　to consider (the interest of...)

44 永远别说"不"（二）

19. （承）认	(chéng)rèn	to admit, to acknowledge, to recognize
20. 趟	tàng	*measure word referring to the number of trips*
21. 夸	kuā	to praise
22. 库房	kùfáng	storehouse, storeroom
23. 联系	liánxì	to contact
24. 种	zhǒng	kind, sort, type
25. 批量	pīliàng	lot, batch
26. 停产	tíng chǎn	to stop production
27. 次品	cìpǐn	inferior goods
28. 手续费	shǒuxùfèi	service charge
29. 遗憾	yíhàn	to regret, to be a pity

注 释 Notes

1. "一经"，副词，表示只要经过某个步骤或者某种行为（就能产生相应的结果）。例如：

一经, an adverb, means as long as a certain step is made or a certain action is taken (, a corresponding result will appear). For example:

1. 一经批准，马上生效。
2. 一经同意，我们立刻去上海。
3. 新手机一经推出，就受到大家的热烈欢迎。

2. "（一）概"，副词，表示适用于全体，没有例外。例如：

（一）概, an adverb, means that something can be applied to all without exception. For example:

1. 他说的我一概不相信。
2. 这种材料太差，一概不能用。
3. 货物出门，概不退换。

3 "穷"，形容词，意思是"缺少钱"。

穷, an adjective, means "lack of money".

"穷"做副词用，表示在财力、能力方面不够条件却还勉强去做或本来不应该这样做却还要这样做。

穷 can also be used as an adverb to mean doing something despite the lack of money or ability, or doing things which should not be done. For example:

1. 他成天穷忙，也没忙出什么结果来。
2. 你穷折腾什么呀，快睡吧！

练习
Exercises

一、替换练习。
Substitution drills.

A：你<u>看</u>过<u>这本书</u>吗？
B：不知<u>看</u>过多少<u>遍</u>了。

听	支	歌	次
来	个	公园	趟
买	种	化妆品	瓶
逛	个	夜市	回

A：怎么，<u>客人没有接来</u>？
B：唉，别提了，白<u>跑</u>了一<u>趟</u>！

手续	办完	忙	阵
自行车	修好	折腾	回
货	卖完	吆喝	场
老板	答应	去	趟

44 永远别说"不"（二）

A：经理，你说顾客会上门吗？
B：只要我们的推销广告好，顾客总是会上门的。

购买	商品质量
光顾	购物环境
再来	信誉
满意	服务态度

A：你不能跟他说一下吗？
B：我刚才已经跟他说过了，不过没有说通。

学	会
谈	成
联系	上
讨论	出结果

二、把下面的词组成句子。
Rearrange the following words into sentences.

1. 我 一件 遇到 昨天 事 倒霉
2. 商店 广告 把 的 显眼 写 地方 在
3. 可以 要求 我 吗 一个 提
4. 答应 换 给 件 她 售货员 一
5. 已经 我 过 跟 了 商场 联系
6. 这 权利 是 的 你
7. 售货员 态度 好 不 承认
8. 答应 帮助 他 来 我 明天
9. 请 跟 联系 总服务台 你 一下
10. 这 件 事 是 遗憾 非常 的

三、完成下面的对话。
Complete the following dialogues.

A：你今天怎么不高兴？
B：_____。
A：是真够倒霉的！你可以去退货呀。
B：_____。

A：你说，顾客为什么要求退货？
B：_____。
A：_____？
B：应该不问原因，一概退换。

A：提高服务质量的关键是什么？
B：_____。
A：可是有些服务员态度不好。
B：_____。

A：请问，经理在吗？
B：_____。
A：_____。
B：实在对不起，那就麻烦您再跑一趟了。

四、选择适当的词语完成句子。

Choose the appropriate words to complete the following sentences.

概不退换　　概不负责　　概不收费
概不接待　　概不回答　　概不承认

1. 如果你提出无理要求，_____。
2. 明天星期六，公司休息，_____。
3. 本店售出的商品，如果不是质量问题，_____。
4. 我店开展售后服务，终身保修，_____。
5. 这家商店的商品质量很差，我给他们一个一个指出来，可他们_____。
6. 这种问题，我们_____。

五、你们国家旅馆、商店的服务质量如何？哪些地方让人满意？哪些地方让人不满意？

What is the service like in the stores and hotels of your country? Which aspects are satisfying and which are not?

第四十五课　承诺以后（一）

Lesson 45　After Making a Promise (I)

课文 Text

在课上

珍　妮：王老师，我常常看见商场的墙上写着"本商场郑重承诺……"，这是什么意思？

山　口：我有时候也听见顾客对售货员说"你们有承诺，应该兑现"。

王老师：是的，现在很多商场都对顾客做出了承诺。你们查一下字典，看看"承诺"是什么意思。

杰　克：啊，我明白了。商场的"承诺"就是向服务对象保证提供什么样的商品和服务。

王老师：理解得很对。你能举一个例子吗？

杰　克：在网上买东西，有一种退换服务，是不是一种承诺？

山　口："买空调，免费安装"，也是一种承诺吧？

珍　妮：还有"正常使用，出现故障，一年包换"什么的。

王老师：对，看来你们知道得真不少。

珍　妮：王老师，这些承诺都能兑现吗？

45 承诺以后(一)

王老师：大部分的承诺都能兑现。

杰　克：对，比如刚才我说的退换服务。网店承诺，七天内可以免费退换。

珍　妮：要是不退换呢？

杰　克：如果不退换，就要罚款。

珍　妮：罚谁？

杰　克：当然是罚网店啰！

珍　妮：真是太好了！这样我以后在网上买东西就不会犹豫了，想买什么买什么，反正不喜欢的话还可以免费退换。

杰　克：不过你也得看清楚再买，因为有些商品是不能退换的，比如食品什么的。

山　口：对，虽然商家做出了承诺，不过顾客也应该想好了再买，免得造成麻烦。

珍　妮：如果实体商店不兑现承诺怎么办？

山　口：如果商店不能兑现承诺，你可以去投诉。

珍　妮：向谁投诉？

王老师：向各地的消费者协会和有关部门投诉。现在，各方面都在加强监管，规范市场秩序，商家一旦做出承诺，就必须要兑现。

珍　妮：还是有承诺好！

杰　克：当然，这样顾客可以根据承诺跟商家讲理，如果商家找出各种理由不兑现承诺，那就有可能被投诉，或者被罚款。

王老师：现在是买方市场，承诺是激烈竞争逼出来的。商家要吸引更多的顾客，就必须诚实守信，提高经营和服务质量，才能赢得顾客的信任。

杰　克：顾客按承诺来监督商家，对商家是一种促进。

山　口：承诺对顾客的权利也是一种保障。以后咱们买东西、办事情，都要先看清承诺。

生词 New Words

1.	承诺	chéngnuò	to promise
2.	墙	qiáng	wall
3.	郑重	zhèngzhòng	solemn
4.	兑现	duìxiàn	to fulfill
5.	保证	bǎozhèng	to guarantee
6.	理解	lǐjiě	to understand
7.	正常	zhèngcháng	normal
8.	出现	chūxiàn	to appear
9.	故障	gùzhàng	malfunction, breakdown
10.	什么的	shénmede	and the like, and so on
11.	网店	wǎngdiàn	online shop
12.	内	nèi	within
13.	罚	fá	to punish, to penalize
14.	款	kuǎn	sum of money
15.	犹豫	yóuyù	to hesitate
16.	反正	fǎnzhèng	anyway
17.	投诉	tóusù	to complain
18.	协会	xiéhuì	association
19.	有关	yǒuguān	relevant
20.	部门	bùmén	department, sector

45 承诺以后（一）

21. 加强	jiāqiáng	to strengthen
22. 监管	jiānguǎn	to supervise, to regulate
23. 规范	guīfàn	standard, norm
24. 秩序	zhìxù	order
25. 一旦	yídàn	once, in case of
26. 根据	gēnjù	according to
27. 理由	lǐyóu	reason, excuse
28. 激烈	jīliè	fierce
29. 竞争	jìngzhēng	competition
30. 逼	bī	to force, to push
31. 诚实	chéngshí	honest
32. 守信	shǒuxìn	faithful
33. 经营	jīngyíng	to manage, to run
34. 信任	xìnrèn	trust
35. 促进	cùjìn	to promote
36. 保障	bǎozhàng	to guarantee

注 释 Notes

1 "什么的"，助词，用在一个成分或并列的几个成分后，相当于"等等"，多用于口语。例如：

什么的, a particle, follows one item or several coordinate items, equivalent to 等等 (and so on). It is often used in spoken Chinese. For example:

1. 他不喜欢游泳什么的，就爱打篮球。
2. 款式什么的没关系，质量是最重要的。
3. 桌子上放着一本书，还有笔、本子什么的。

2 两个"什么"连用,前后照应,表示由前者决定后者。"什么"也可以换成"谁、哪儿"等。例如:

When two 什么 are used together corresponding with each other, it means that the former one decides the latter one. The same is with 谁, 哪儿, and so on. For example:

1. 今天我请客,你别客气,想吃什么吃什么。
2. 这又不是我说的,谁说的你找谁去。
3. 我跟着你走吧,你往哪儿走我就往哪儿走。

3 "反正",副词,表示情况虽然不同,但结果并没有区别。例如:

反正, an adverb, shows that despite the different situations, the results are the same. For example:

1. 不管你怎么说,反正他不会答应。
2. 别人去不去我不管,反正我要去。

"反正"还可以表示坚决肯定的语气。例如:
反正 can also express a strong affirmation. For example:

1. 你别着急,反正不是什么贵重的东西。
2. 出来了就多玩儿一会儿吧,反正回去也没什么事。

4 "一旦",副词,指不确定的时间。用于未然时,表示"要是有一天"。例如:

一旦, an adverb, refers to an uncertain time. It is used to indicate the future, meaning "once, in case of". For example:

1. 一旦你做出了承诺,就必须要兑现。
2. 科学实验必须仔细,一旦出错整个实验就会失败。
3. 这儿放的都是珍贵的书籍,一旦着火就会造成很大的损失。

45 承诺以后（一）

练习
Exercises

一、替换练习。
Substitution drills.

A：你买东西先看商品还是先看承诺？
B：当然是先看承诺后看商品。

品牌	质量
颜色	质量
样式	价格

A：你打算去哪儿？
B：哪儿好玩儿就去哪儿。

做什么工作	什么赚钱	做什么
几点回家	几点做完	几点回家
买哪件	哪件漂亮	买哪件

二、把下面的词组成句子。
Rearrange the following words into sentences.

1. 我们 免费 承诺 退换 郑重
2. 承诺 你们 兑现 无 应该 条件 的
3. 我 故障 的 出 电脑 今天 点儿 了
4. 吸引 必须 要 顾客 守信 就 诚实
5. 免费 可以 要是 喜欢 你 退换 不
6. 你 我 应该 认为 吗 投诉
7. 承诺 顾客 商家 要求 是 监督 兑现 一种 的 对
8. 消费者 顾客 是 向 的 投诉 权利 协会
9. 监督 对 市场 规范 顾客 秩序 的 对 好处 有
10. 赢得 诚实 才能 顾客 商家 信任 守信 的

三、完成下面的对话。

Complete the following dialogues.

A：_____？
B：当然是先看商家的承诺。
A：为什么？
B：_____。

A：你怎么了？为什么不高兴？
B：_____。
A：你可以去投诉。
B：_____。

A：_____？
B：不会。
A：_____？
B：杰克会安装。

A：小王这个人怎么样？
B：_____。
A：怪不得大家都喜欢跟他做朋友。
B：_____。

四、用指定的词语完成句子。

Complete the following sentences with the given words.

1. 本商场_____，买到假冒伪劣商品，假一罚十。（郑重）
2. 我们的承诺，_____。（兑现）
3. 房间里放着很多东西，_____。（什么的）
4. 不管他喜不喜欢，_____。（反正）

45 承诺以后（一）

5. 我们承诺，_____。（免费）
6. 要是商店不退货，_____（投诉）
7. _____，想买就买吧！（犹豫）
8. 春节过完了，今天大家又开始_____了。（正常）
9. 请问，_____？（理解）
10. 现在是买方市场，_____（竞争）

五、举例说说你知道的"承诺"和"兑现承诺"的情况。
Give examples of "promising" and "fulfilling a promise".

第四十六课　承诺以后（二）

Lesson 46　After Making a Promise (II)

课文　Text

在课外

杰　　克：二位，假期真的不回国，准备去旅行吗？

山　　口：当然，这是了解中国、学习汉语的最好机会，多难得啊！

珍　　妮：杰克，你跟我们一块儿去吧！

杰　　克：怎么，想找劳动力啊？

珍　　妮：按劳付酬，行不行？

杰　　克：好！这样吧，我给你们扛行李，你们包我全部的旅行费用。

珍　　妮：你想得倒美！你那点儿劳动值那么多钱吗？

杰　　克：我还可以为二位小姐提供别的服务啊，比如做旅游计划，预订车票，安排住宿，到了旅游景点买门票，当导游做讲解，等等。

山　　口：好了，说正经的吧，你到底去不去啊？

杰　　克：当然去。不过，你们想去哪儿？

珍　　妮：去上海，上海是世界著名的国际大都市，商业发达，是购物的天堂。

46 承诺以后（二）

山　口：我还想去苏州、杭州，听珍妮说风景可美了！
杰　克：可我想去云南的西双版纳，那儿的少数民族风情太吸引我了。
山　口：要不咱们都去吧。
珍　妮：好，就这么决定了！
山　口：那怎么安排旅行才能既省钱又省事呢？
杰　克：咱们就自助旅游吧，你们只管玩儿，其余一切事务，我都包了。
珍　妮：这是你说的，到时候别不兑现自己的承诺！
杰　克：那哪儿能啊！

（两天后）

杰　克：山口、珍妮，我已经做好了旅游计划，你们要是同意，我们马上就可以出发。
珍　妮：你还真是说话算数！
杰　克：那当然！咱们先去上海。从北京坐高铁去上海，大概四五个小时就能到。
珍　妮：这样是不是早上出发，下午就能到了？
杰　克：对。酒店我也在网上订好了，是一家四星级酒店，离外滩不远。下午到了之后我们休息一下，晚上就可以去欣赏美丽的外滩夜景了。
珍　妮：这个安排太棒了！
杰　克：然后咱们再坐火车去苏州、杭州。
山　口：苏州园林、杭州西湖，是中国最有名的风景名胜，我一定要多拍几张照片！
杰　克：没问题，到时候我给你当摄影师！
珍　妮：那从杭州怎么去西双版纳？也坐火车吗？
杰　克：杭州离西双版纳很远，所以咱们坐飞机去。

山　　口：西双版纳那边有什么好玩儿的？

杰　　克：西双版纳的风景也很美。在那儿可以欣赏到跟苏州、杭州不一样的热带风情，还可以参加一些互动环节，亲身去体验呢。

珍　　妮：有意思！

山　　口：我听说那儿还有大象表演，我们也能跟大象互动吗？

杰　　克：当然可以！

山　　口：这太好玩儿了！

珍　　妮：杰克，看来你真的做了很多准备工作，值得信任！

杰　　克：那当然！做了承诺，就要兑现，你说是不是？

生词 New Words

1.	劳动力	láodònglì	labor force
2.	按劳付酬	àn láo fù chóu	cash-for-work
3.	扛	káng	to carry (on the shoulder)
4.	行李	xíngli	luggage
5.	包	bāo	to undertake the whole thing, to cover
6.	全部	quánbù	all, whole
7.	费用	fèiyong	fee
8.	提供	tígōng	to provide
9.	服务	fúwù	service
10.	安排	ānpái	to arrange
11.	住宿	zhùsù	accommodation
12.	景点	jǐngdiǎn	scenic spot

46 承诺以后（二）

13. 门票	ménpiào	entrance ticket
14. 导游	dǎoyóu	tour guide
15. 讲解	jiǎngjiě	to explain, to commentate
16. 正经	zhèngjing	proper, serious
17. 国际	guójì	international
18. 少数民族	shǎoshù mínzú	ethnic minority
19. 风情	fēngqíng	lifestyle, local customs
20. 自助	zìzhù	self-service
21. 其余	qíyú	other, the rest
22. 出发	chūfā	to start off, to depart
23. 夜景	yèjǐng	night scene
24. 园林	yuánlín	garden
25. 摄影师	shèyǐngshī	photographer
26. 热带	rèdài	the tropics; tropical
27. 互动	hùdòng	interaction
28. 环节	huánjié	session
29. 亲身	qīnshēn	personally, by oneself
30. 体验	tǐyàn	to experience
31. 大象	dàxiàng	elephant

专　名　Proper Nouns

1. 云南	Yúnnán	Yunnan Province
2. 西双版纳	Xīshuāngbǎnnà	Xishuangbanna, a prefecture in Yunnan
3. 外滩	Wàitān	the Bund
4. 西湖	Xīhú	West Lake

注释 Notes

1 "包",动词,意思是"容纳在里头、总括在一起"。例如:

包, a verb, means "to include" or "to cover". For example:

1. 你们尽管吃,今天的餐费我全包了。

2. A:您好,参加旅行团的费用一共是5000元。
   B:食宿费已经包在里边了吗?
   A:是的,5000元是包食宿的价格,但是不包门票。

"包"也可以是"担保"的意思。例如:

包 also means "to assure". For example:

1. A:我头疼,好像有点儿感冒了。
   B:没关系,回去多喝水,吃点儿感冒药,今天早点儿休息,包你明天就好。

2. A:这个饭店怎么样?
   B:我去过,又便宜又好吃,包你满意。

2 "正经",形容词,意思是"正式的、正当的"。例如:

正经, an adjective, means "serious" or "appropriate". For example:

1. 你的钱要花在正经地方。
2. 你什么时候做过一点儿正经事?
3. 你们别闲聊了,说点儿正经的吧!
4. 我们在说正经的,你别开玩笑了!

"正经人",指正派人,即道德高尚、作风严肃、行为规矩的人。例如:

正经人 refers to an honest and decent person, who has moral integrity, upright character and honorable behavior. For example:

1. 他可是个正经人,不喜欢吹牛拍马那一套。
2. 我们都是正经的商人,不搞不正当竞争。

3. 他算什么正经人？假正经！
4. 是正经人就不会干出这种事！

3 "西双版纳"，在中国云南省的南部，中国少数民族傣族聚居的地方，浓郁的民族风情、秀丽的风光和热带雨林原始生态环境，成为中外旅游者向往的地方，是中国著名的旅游风景区。

西双版纳 (Xishuangbanna) is located in the south of Yunnan Province, a place where the Dai ethnic group inhabits. With its rich ethnic manners and customs, beautiful scenery and primitive ecological environment of the tropical rainforest, it is a famous tourist resort in China, attracting numerous tourists, both Chinese and foreigners.

4 "其"，代词，可以指代任何人、物、事。根据上下文，可翻译成现代汉语的"那个、他（她、它）、他的（她的、它的）"等。

"其"构成的合成词，如"其他、其中、其余、其次"等都是常用词。例如：

其 is a pronoun which can be used to denote any person, thing or matter. According to the context, it can be translated into the equivalent of "that one", "he (she, it)", "his (her, its)", etc.

Compound words with 其 such as 其他 (other, else), 其中 (among them, in it), 其余 (the rest) and 其次 (next, secondly) are all frequently used. For example:

1. 首先，你得努力。其次，你也得有一定的运气。这样你才能成功。
   （"其次"，次序较后、第二。）
2. 今天就谈到这儿吧，其余的事以后再谈。
   （"其余"，剩下的。）
3. 承诺了又不兑现，其中的原因究竟是什么呢？
   （"其中"，那里面。）
4. 我的话已经说完了，其他人还有什么意见？
   （"其他"，别的。）

练习
Exercises

一、替换练习。
Substitution drills.

A：郑重承诺以后，你是兑现还是不兑现？
B：当然应该兑现。

放假	去旅行	打工
大学毕业	工作	考研究生
挣钱	先买房	先买车

A：你为什么想去西双版纳？
B：那儿的少数民族风情太吸引我了。

上海	国际大都市风情
苏杭	美丽风景
秀水街	特色商品

A：咱们怎么去天津？
B：天津离北京很近，咱们坐汽车去。

大观园	学校	比较远	坐地铁
海南	北京	很远	坐飞机
北京大学	这儿	很近	走路

二、把下面的词组成句子。
Rearrange the following words into sentences.

1. 谁 门票 钱 买 花 景区
2. 门票 预订 也 在 景区 网上 可以
3. 你 劳动力 求职 过 吗 去 市场
4. 我们 一起 旅行 去 打算
5. 你 能 点儿 说 正经 吗 事
6. 杰克 信任 兑现 了 值得 承诺
7. 这个 得 不错 计划 安排 旅游
8. 我们 英语 说 汉语 导游 会 和 需要 一个 的

9. 这个 我 不 决定 假期 回国 了
10. 上海 著名 大 国际 的 都市 是

三、完成下面的对话。
Complete the following dialogues.

A：_____？
B：当然，按劳付酬。
A：_____？
B：一小时二十块。

A：杰克，我们一起去吃饭吧！
B：_____？
A：我请客，你去吗？
B：_____。

A：_____？
B：我早就决定要去了。
A：_____？
B：这是学习汉语的好机会，多难得啊！

A：听说，_____？
B：是，我们决定一起去旅行。
A：_____？_____？
B：放假以后就出发，去西双版纳。

四、选择适当的词语完成句子。
Choose the appropriate words to complete the following sentences.

1. 我_____，他一定会兑现他的承诺。（信任　相信）
2. 他的努力赢得了大家的_____。（信任　相信）
3. 这双鞋_____500块钱。（值　值得）

4. 他成功的经验_____我们好好儿学习。（值　值得）
5. 这个国家自然森林公园的_____真美。（风情　风景）
6. 这个咖啡馆的异国_____吸引了大量顾客。（风情　风景）
7. 我跟老板说了半天好话，他就是不_____。（答应　承诺）
8. 我们的_____是郑重严肃的，请你相信我们。（答应　承诺）
9. 他们从北京_____，经过天津、济南，到达上海。（上路　出发）
10. 他刚开始工作，还没_____呢，你别要求太高。（上路　出发）

五、你在中国参加过结伴自助旅行吗？谈谈旅行的过程和体验。

Have you ever taken a self-guided tour with others in China? Talk about your experience and feelings.

第四十七课　公关工作（一）
Lesson 47　A Career in Public Relations (I)

课文　Text

在课上

王老师：同学们，你们知道公关工作主要做什么吗？
杰　克：知道，就是拉关系嘛。
山　口：杰克，你说什么呀？
杰　克：在家靠父母，出门靠朋友，办事靠关系，见面讲交情。有了关系、人情，什么都好办。这在哪个国家都一样。
山　口：我看不见得。
杰　克：不见得？你在某公司工作，有进口电子产品，很走俏。我送你两瓶好酒，请你吃顿大餐，再套套近乎，然后请你帮我弄一批货，你好意思拒绝？
山　口：是不大好意思拒绝。
杰　克：那就费心费心，拜托拜托了！
珍　妮：事情就这么成了？
杰　克：那当然。再说，吃了人家的嘴软，拿了人家的手短，你能不给人家办事？
王老师：杰克，你说的这种现象属于不正之风，不是真正的公关工作。

山　　口：老师，什么是真正的公关工作呢？

王老师：你们有很丰富的经历，还是你们自己讨论吧。

珍　　妮：我看过一本关于公关工作的书，书中说，公关工作就是负责接待客商，比如迎来送往呀，安排吃住呀，陪同观光娱乐呀，为客人送香槟鲜花呀……

山　　口：这些看起来都是小事，但是要把这些小事做得礼貌、得体，对事业成功起好作用，也不简单。

杰　　克：是的，比如宴请吧，主人热情、周到和幽默的谈吐，都可以给严肃的谈判带来轻松愉快的气氛，增进双方感情交流，使商务谈判进展顺利。

山　　口：不过，在我们日本商人看来，交情归交情，生意归生意，货好客求主，货次主求客。在宴请的时候，如果你过分殷勤，对方会认为你是故意讨好，一定是你有求于他。这笔生意还做不做，就要好好儿想想了。

珍　　妮：那么买卖就吹了？

山　　口：很可能。

杰　　克：所以公关工作最重要的是要了解对方、尊重对方。

珍　　妮：这恐怕也是公关工作最困难的地方了。不同国家有不同的文化、不同的风俗，哪能都了解？

杰　　克：所以，我们就得多学习、多了解。比如，有的国家送礼物不能送双数，有的国家不喜欢单数。

珍　　妮：我还听说有的国家不喜欢白色，还有的国家不喜欢黑色。国家不同，喜好也不一样。

杰　　克：可见，了解对方、尊重对方是多么重要。如果因

47 公关工作(一)

为一点儿小事,引起对方反感,甚至伤害了对方感情,生意还能谈成吗?

山　口:这么说,通过礼貌得体的接待和友好往来,使双方建立起真诚的友谊和良好的合作伙伴关系,才是真正的公关工作。

生词 New Words

1.	拉关系	lā guānxi	to try to establish a relationship with
2.	父母	fùmǔ	father and mother, parents
3.	交情	jiāoqing	friendship, friendly relations
4.	某	mǒu	certain, some
5.	走俏	zǒuqiào	to be in great demand
6.	套近乎	tào jìnhu	to try to be friendly with, to cotton up to
7.	费心	fèixīn	to make extra efforts, to take a lot of trouble
8.	拜托	bàituō	to request sb. to do sth.
9.	现象	xiànxiàng	phenomenon
10.	属于	shǔyú	to belong to, to be part of
11.	真正	zhēnzhèng	genuine, true, real
12.	经历	jīnglì	experience
13.	关于	guānyú	about, on, regarding
14.	接待	jiēdài	to receive (guests, customers, etc.)
15.	陪同	péitóng	to accompany, to keep company
16.	观光	guānguāng	to go sightseeing, to tour
17.	香槟	xiāngbīn	champagne
18.	事业	shìyè	cause, undertaking

19. 作用	zuòyòng	effect, function
20. 宴请	yànqǐng	to entertain at a banquet
21. 幽默	yōumò	humorous
22. 谈吐	tántǔ	style of conversation
23. 严肃	yánsù	serious, solemn, earnest
24. 增进	zēngjìn	to enhance, to promote, to further
25. 感情	gǎnqíng	emotion, feeling, sentiment
26. 进展	jìnzhǎn	to progress, to advance
27. 归	guī	*used between two identical words, indicating what's mentioned has not brought about the corresponding result*
28. 过分	guòfèn	excessive, undue, over-
29. 殷勤	yīnqín	eagerly attentive, solicitous
30. 对方	duìfāng	the other side, the other party
31. 讨好	tǎohǎo	to try to win the favor of
32. 吹	chuī	to fail, to fall through
33. 尊重	zūnzhòng	to respect, to esteem
34. 困难	kùnnan	difficult
35. 风俗	fēngsú	custom
36. 引起	yǐnqǐ	to cause, to lead to, to give rise to
37. 反感	fǎngǎn	resentment, discontent
38. 甚至	shènzhì	even to the extent that, so much so that
39. 伤害	shānghài	to harm, to hurt, to injure
40. 通过	tōngguò	by means of, through
41. 建立	jiànlì	to build, to establish, to set up
42. 真诚	zhēnchéng	true, sincere, genuine
43. 良好	liánghǎo	good, well
44. 合作	hézuò	to cooperate; cooperation

47 公关工作（一）

注 释
Notes

1 "不见得"，意思是"不一定"，表示一种主观的估计，语气比较委婉，句中常用"我看、看样子"一类词语。例如：

不见得 has the meaning of "not necessarily" or "not likely". It expresses a subjective estimation, with a mild and roundabout tone. Expressions like 我看 (I think) or 看样子 (it seems) are often used in such a sentence. For example:

1. 今天不见得会下雨。
2. 钱多了不见得就幸福。
3. 你可以去套近乎，可人家不见得就领情。
4. 你去找他借钱，他不见得会拒绝你。

2 "关于"，介词，引出关联、涉及的事物，组成介词结构，可做状语和定语。例如：

关于, a preposition, introduces the thing that is concerned or involved, forming a prepositional phrase which functions as an attributive or adverbial. For example:

1. 关于走后门的问题，我们已经讨论过多次。
2. 关于公关工作，我知道得不多。
3. 关于市场经济，有许多问题还要研究。
4. 我们参观了一个关于中国经济发展的展览。

3 "归"，介词，意思是"由（谁负责）"。例如：

归, a preposition, means "in sb.'s charge, by". For example:

1. 这事归我管。
2. 接待来宾的事归公关部门负责。

也可以是动词，用在相同的动词、形容词或名词之间，表示尽管如此，但并未引起相应的结果。例如：

It can also serve as a verb. Used between the same verbs, adjectives, or nouns, it means that no corresponding result appears despite all this. For example:

1. 说归说，做归做。
2. 人情归人情，咱们还得按规矩办事。

4 "甚至"，连词，在并列两项或多项的句子中，用在后面一项表示强调，有进一层的意思。例如：

甚至, a conjunction, is used in a sentence that has two or more coordinate items in order to stress the latter item, meaning "to go a step further". For example:

1. 参加晚会的人很多，甚至很多老人也来了。
2. 学生、老师，甚至学校校长都报名参加运动会。
3. 贸易谈判中，业务员的知识、谈吐甚至一个小小的动作，都可能关系到谈判的成败。
4. 在我们这儿，不仅大人会游泳，甚至六七岁的小孩儿也会。

5 "通过"，做介词时，引进动作的媒介和手段。例如：

通过, when used as a preposition, introduces the medium or means of an action. For example:

1. 我们通过翻译交谈了一个小时。
2. 通过大做广告提高产品的知名度。
3. 我们通过新闻媒介了解市场信息。
4. 通过一个朋友的介绍，我们认识了公司的老板。

练 习
Exercises

一、替换练习。
　　Substitution drills.

A：你看他会<u>高兴</u>吗？
B：我看他不见得会<u>高兴</u>。

| 生气 |
| 满意 |
| 同意 |

148

47 公关工作（一）

A：你在看什么？
B：我在看一本关于公关工作的书。

部	英国历史	电影
份	市场调查	报告
份	开发新产品	计划书

A：公关工作最重要的是了解对方、尊重对方。
B：这恐怕也是公关工作最困难的地方了。

学习汉语	掌握汉语语法
开办公司	有足够的资金
网络购物	理性消费

A：你是怎样找到贸易伙伴的？
B：我是通过友好交往找到贸易伙伴的。

取得事业成功	多年努力
认识王总经理	同事介绍
了解市场信息	阅读新闻

二、把下面的词组成句子。

Rearrange the following words into sentences.

1. 你 什么 生活 靠 中国 在
2. 的 你 和 他 深 交情 吗
3. 走俏 这 吗 商品 些 是
4. 为什么 你 套近乎 他 跟 呢
5. 请 我 不要 建议 拒绝 的 你
6. 这 拜托 就 事 了 你
7. 刮风 是 下雨 一种 现象 自然
8. 她 非常 什么 认真 都 事 做
9. 从来 我 讨好 他人 愿意 不
10. 他 谈吐 幽默 的 很

三、完成下面的对话。

Complete the following dialogues.

A：你能帮我买一台电脑吗？
B：_____。
A：_____！
B：不用客气，就等我回复吧。

A：你觉得公关工作要做些什么？
B：_____。
A：听起来真不简单。
B：_____。

A：_____？
B：一台机器一万五。
A：_____？
B：交情归交情，生意归生意。

A：_____？
B：这是送给王总经理的生日礼物。
A：你们不是生意场上的竞争对手吗？
B：是的。不过，_____，_____。

四、用指定的词语完成句子。

Complete the following sentences with the given words.

1. 一个人要想事业成功，_____。（靠）
2. 我知道办成这事非常困难，_____。（费心）
3. 这家公司的一切财产_____。（属于）
4. 如果产品质量有问题，_____。（负责）
5. 大家的要求都是合理的，_____。（过分）

6. _____，我们表示深深的感谢。（接待）
7. 别开玩笑了，_____。（严肃）
8. 他提出的问题 _____。（引起）
9. 通过双方努力，_____。（建立）
10. 每一个人都应该_____。（尊重）

五、试谈一两个公关工作做得得体或不得体的例子。

Give one or two examples of appropriate or inappropriate handling of public relations.

第四十八课 公关工作（二）
Lesson 48 A Career in Public Relations (II)

课文 Text

在课外

山　口：祝你生日快乐！
杰　克：祝你生日快乐！
珍　妮：谢谢，谢谢。
山　口：请寿星珍妮吹蜡烛，切生日蛋糕！
杰　克：听！好像有人敲门。
珍　妮：请进！
服务员：小姐，有人给你送来一束鲜花。
山　口：哇！这么大一束花，真漂亮！是你男朋友送的？
珍　妮：他在法国，怎么给我送花来？
山　口：兴许是在网上的花店给你订购的。
杰　克：别猜了，看看花上的贺卡就知道了。
山　口：对，给我们念念。
珍　妮："珍妮小姐，祝你生日快乐。愿你永远像鲜花一样美丽、迷人！又，明晚七点，在我店举行饮食文化节开幕式，欢迎你和你的朋友光临。你的朋友刘京京敬赠。"

48 公关工作（二）

山　口：啊，多漂亮的鲜花，多温馨的话语！
杰　克：刘京京是谁？
山　口：你怎么忘了？迎宾饭店的公关经理。
珍　妮：是她，可我从来没对她提起过我的生日，她怎么知道的？真叫人感动！
杰　克：这就是公关经理的本事啦！
山　口：你明天去不去参加饮食文化节开幕式？
珍　妮：当然去，明天一定要当面谢谢她。你们也去吧，她也邀请了你们。

刘京京：珍妮，山口，欢迎，欢迎！
珍　妮：你好，刘小姐，谢谢你昨天送的鲜花和生日贺卡，你的盛情让我终生难忘！
山　口：我们都被深深感动了，谢谢你的盛情邀请。
刘京京：你们都不用客气，快请进吧。嘿，杰克先生，欢迎你的光临。
杰　克：嗨！刘小姐，你还记得我？
刘京京：哪能不记得？美国来的高才生！我们见过两次面，你是个非常乐观幽默的人。
杰　克：听你这么说，我真高兴。谢谢。
刘京京：你们请随便吧，过会儿见。我去招待别的客人了。

杰　克：珍妮，我们同刘小姐是什么时候见过的？
山　口：至少有半年了吧。
珍　妮：那会儿我们刚到北京，人生地不熟，她主动热情地帮助过我们。
杰　克：她说见过我们两次。
珍　妮：是两次，一次在她们饭店的卡拉OK厅，一次在惠侨饭店附近。

杰　克：你们看，一见面，她就立即说出了我们的名字、性格，她的记性真好！

山　口：你们注意听，刘小姐能说出每一位来宾的名字、职务、工作单位，还提到一些愉快的往事。

杰　克：这可不容易，你们有什么感受？

珍　妮：我心里感到热乎乎的，好像回到了家里一样。

山　口：我也是，她一叫我，我就感到了自己在主人心目中的地位，好亲切，好高兴。

杰　克：是的，一见面，她就能准确叫出你的名字，然后亲切攀谈起来，这就有了一种宾至如归的气氛，谁能不被感动？谁又能不对这儿产生特殊的好感？

珍　妮：京京真是一位出色的公关经理！

刘京京：先生们！女士们！欢迎诸位光临今晚的盛会。现在，我宣布饮食文化节正式开幕！祝大家今晚过得愉快！

生 词

New Words

1.	快乐	kuàilè	happy, joyful, cheerful
2.	寿星	shòuxing	God of Longevity; person who is celebrating his/her birthday
3.	蜡烛	làzhú	candle
4.	切	qiē	to cut
5.	敲门	qiāo mén	to knock at the door
6.	鲜花	xiānhuā	(fresh) flower

48 公关工作（二）

7.	兴许	xīngxǔ	perhaps, maybe
8.	订购	dìnggòu	to order (goods)
9.	猜	cāi	to guess, to speculate, to conjecture
10.	贺卡	hèkǎ	greeting card
11.	念	niàn	to read aloud, to read out loud
12.	美丽	měilì	beautiful
13.	迷人	mírén	charming, fascinating, enchanting
14.	举行	jǔxíng	to hold (a meeting, an event, etc.)
15.	节	jié	festival, holiday
16.	开幕式	kāimùshì	opening ceremony
17.	敬	jìng	to respect, to offer politely
18.	赠	zèng	to give as a present
19.	温馨	wēnxīn	warm and sweet
20.	从来	cónglái	at all times, all along, from the past to the present
21.	感动	gǎndòng	moved, touched
22.	当面	dāngmiàn	to sb.'s face, in sb.'s presence
23.	盛情	shèngqíng	great kindness
24.	终生	zhōngshēng	lifelong, all one's life
25.	被	bèi	*(in passive sentences)* by
26.	高才生	gāocáishēng	outstanding student
27.	乐观	lèguān	optimistic
28.	招待	zhāodài	to receive, to entertain, to serve
29.	生	shēng	unfamiliar, strange
30.	主动	zhǔdòng	on one's own initiative, active, voluntary
31.	性格	xìnggé	nature, character, personality
32.	记性	jìxing	memory

33.	注意	zhùyì	to pay attention to, to take notice of
34.	来宾	láibīn	guest, visitor
35.	职务	zhíwù	job, post, position
36.	单位	dānwèi	workplace
37.	往事	wǎngshì	past event, the past
38.	感受	gǎnshòu	feeling
39.	热乎乎	rèhūhū	warm
40.	地位	dìwèi	position, standing, status
41.	亲切	qīnqiè	cordial, kind
42.	攀谈	pāntán	to engage in small talk, to chit-chat
43.	宾至如归	bīnzhì-rúguī	guests feel at home
44.	产生	chǎnshēng	to produce, to form, to generate
45.	特殊	tèshū	special, exceptional
46.	好感	hǎogǎn	good opinion, favorable impression
47.	出色	chūsè	splendid, outstanding
48.	女士	nǚshì	lady, madam
49.	诸	zhū	all, various
50.	盛会	shènghuì	grand meeting, distinguished gathering
51.	宣布	xuānbù	to announce, to declare, to proclaim
52.	正式	zhèngshì	formal, official

专　名　Proper Nouns

1.	刘京京	Liú Jīngjīng	Liu Jingjing, name of a person
2.	迎宾饭店	Yíngbīn Fàndiàn	Yingbin Hotel
3.	惠侨饭店	Huìqiáo Fàndiàn	Huiqiao Hotel

48 公关工作(二)

注释 Notes

1 "兴许",副词,表示猜测、估计或不能肯定的语气。跟"也许"的第一种用法相同(参见第三十三课),多见于北方人的口语中。例如:

兴许, an adverb, expresses a tone of guessing, estimation or uncertainty. Its usage is the same as the first meaning of 也许 (see Lesson 33). It is often used in northerners' colloquial Chinese. For example:

1. 她身边的那位先生兴许就是她的男朋友。
2. 你兴许是太紧张了,周末去海边轻松轻松吧!
3. 市场变化很快,转眼间畅销品兴许就变成了滞销品。
4. 她这个人见了什么人都是那么热乎乎的,兴许你会对她产生好感。

2 "从来",副词,意思是"从过去到现在",多用于否定式。例如:

从来, an adverb, means "from the past to the present", mostly used in negative sentences. For example:

1. 他从来没去过上海。
2. 我从来没说过这样的话。
3. 他是一个真正的商人,从来不惧怕竞争。

用于肯定句时,后边一般要跟"就、都"。例如:

When used in affirmative sentences, it is usually followed by 就 or 都. For example:

1. 他对工作从来都很负责。
2. 这家商店的服务质量从来都很好。
3. 山口的房间从来就很干净,她每天都要打扫。

3 "被",动词,引出动作的施动者,"被"字前面的主语是动作的受动者,动词后面常有表示完成或结果的词语。例如:

被, a verb, introduces the agent of an action. The grammatical subject preceding 被 is the patient of the action. Following the verb are often expressions indicating completion or result. For example:

1. 我刚睡着就被人叫醒了。
2. 他被老板炒了鱿鱼。
3. 一笔大买卖被他搞砸了。
4. 我的话可能被误解了。

练 习
Exercises

一、替换练习。
　　Substitution drills.

A：<u>生日晚会</u>在什么地方举行？
B：在<u>珍妮的宿舍</u>。

运动会	学校操场
招待会	北京饭店
开幕式	公司新楼
讨论会	会议室

A：你对他提起过<u>王先生</u>吗？
B：我从来没对他提起过<u>王先生</u>。

| 我（你）的职务 |
| 我们的老师 |
| 学校文化节 |
| 公司业务情况 |

A：你的<u>手机</u>呢？
B：我的<u>手机</u>被<u>小张</u><u>弄坏</u>了。

自行车	金正和	骑走
照相机	马丽	借走
电影票	同屋	拿走
钱包	小偷	偷走

A：他那么<u>热情</u>地接待你，你有什么感受？
B：我感到很<u>不好意思</u>。

隆重	高兴
亲切	舒服
严肃	紧张
无礼	吃惊

48 公关工作（二）

二、把下面的词组成句子。
Rearrange the following words into sentences.

1. 我们　送　一个　珍妮　蛋糕　生日
2. 花篮　这　送　刘京京　是　的
3. 他　幽默　非常　说话
4. 他　一个　是　人　亲切　的　非常
5. 这　书　感动　我　本　深深　了　被
6. 他　本事　有　的　经商
7. 请　喝　大家　随便　吧　什么　点儿
8. 请　注意　诸位　时间　开幕式　地点　的　和
9. 你　她　是不是　好感　对　产生　了
10. 经理　宣布　大家　一件　事情　向　重要　了

三、完成下面的对话。
Complete the following dialogues.

A：_____？
B：是的，这是上星期订购的。
A：在哪儿订购的呢？
B：_____。

A：你手里拿的什么？
B：_____！
A：我猜不出来。
B：_____。

A：_____。
B：我代表我们公司热烈祝贺贵店开业！
A：欢迎您明天光临我们的开业典礼。
B：_____。

A：_____？

B：听说过，但不认识。

A：我跟她很熟，要不要给你介绍一下？

B：_____。

A：你知道她在哪个单位工作吗？

B：_____。

A：_____？

B：我跟她见过几面。

四、用指定词语完成句子。

Complete the following sentences with the given words.

1. 他答应要来的，可现在还没来，_____。（兴许）
2. 这事能不能办成，_____。（本事）
3. 你们在这儿，就像在自己家里，_____。（随便）
4. 今天是星期天，_____。（邀请）
5. 我每次去王老师家_____。（招待）
6. 今天的招待会开得很好，_____。（气氛）
7. 今天新店开业，营业额_____。（至少）
8. 刘京京是位出色的公关经理，_____。（好感）
9. 上街要小心，过马路的时候，_____。（注意）
10. 人们说，中国是一个非常迷人的国家，我来中国以后，_____。（感受）

五、把下面的句子改写成"被"字句。

Rewrite the following sentences using 被.

1. 他弄坏了我的自行车。
2. 他的热情招待深深地感动了大家。
3. 许多往事，他都忘了。

4. 他解决了这个问题。

5. 老板把女秘书叫走了。

六、你认识从事公关工作的人吗？熟悉他们的生活吗？请你介绍一位从事公关工作的人的一两件事。

Do you know anyone working in public relations? Are you familiar with their lives? Tell something about a person in public relations with one or two examples.

第四十九课 选准"上帝"(一)
Lesson 49 Choose the Right "God" (I)

课文 Text

在课上

王老师：外国有句名言："顾客就是上帝。"这句话在中国也很流行。你们说，这话有道理吗？

山　口：顾客就是"上帝"，如果他不爱你，商店就要关门，企业就要倒闭。

杰　克：所以美国的希尔顿饭店，就是以微笑服务名满天下的。

山　口：没错，亲切的服务态度才会让顾客有宾至如归的感觉，才能吸引更多的顾客前来消费。

珍　妮：顾客确实是"上帝"，而且是个很不好伺候的"上帝"。

山　口：珍妮说得对。顾客千千万万，有男有女，有老有少，有人很富，有人很穷。

珍　妮：还有不同国家民族，有不同的文化；不同的人，受过不同教育，也有不同的爱好。

山　口：总之，有各种各样的顾客，就有各种各样的需求，商店和企业要满足他们，可不容易！

49 选准"上帝"（一）

杰　　克：这大概就是中国人说的"众口难调"了，萝卜白菜，各有所爱嘛！这么看来，我们没办法迎合所有"上帝"的口味，只能把一部分顾客当作自己的"上帝"。

王老师：所以，每一个企业、商店都要选择自己的"上帝"，而且要选准"上帝"。选准了"上帝"，就选准了企业的经营方向，企业才会兴旺发达。

珍　　妮：杰克，对怎样选择"上帝"，你有什么高见？

杰　　克：自然是搞市场调查喽。

山　　口：不光是调查，更要研究。

杰　　克：对，搞市场调研。我听说，肯德基快餐店在北京开业以前，就进行过大规模的市场调研。

山　　口：他们是怎么做的？

杰　　克：他们首先注意到，北京当时有三大难题，就是住房难、吃饭难、交通难。因此断定，肯德基快餐在北京有广大市场。

山　　口：嗯，能了解这一点很重要，如果没有市场，别的就都谈不上了。

杰　　克：接着，他们几乎吃遍了北京大大小小的饭店，了解饭店经营的品种、北京人的口味，以及消费者的文化教育、经济收入，等等。

山　　口：又得出什么结论呢？

珍　　妮：你先别问结论，看看他们下一步又是怎么做的。

杰　　克：他们根据了解的情况，立即做出了适合中国国情的肯德基快餐样品，免费请不同层次的人品尝，征求意见。

山　　口：都问了什么问题？

杰　　克：味道怎么样呀，什么样的价格才是普通中国人所能承受的呀，材料选择和色彩搭配如何呀，对用餐时间和环境有什么要求呀……

山　口：调研真够深入的。好了，调研结果就不用谈了。我想，我已经明白怎样选择"上帝"了。

注释 Notes

1.	上帝	Shàngdì	God
2.	关门	guānmén	to close, to close down
3.	倒闭	dǎobì	to close down, to go bankrupt
4.	以	yǐ	with, by, through
5.	伺候	cìhou	to wait upon, to look after
6.	富（裕）	fù(yù)	rich, wealthy
7.	教育	jiàoyù	education
8.	爱好	àihào	hobby, interest
9.	众口难调	zhòngkǒu-nántiáo	it is difficult to cater to all tastes
10.	萝卜	luóbo	turnip
11.	白菜	báicài	Chinese cabbage
12.	所	suǒ	*used before a verb to form a noun phrase*
13.	迎合	yínghé	to cater to
14.	所有	suǒyǒu	all
15.	部分	bùfen	part, section, portion
16.	当作	dàngzuò	to regard as, to take as, to treat as
17.	方向	fāngxiàng	direction, orientation
18.	兴旺	xīngwàng	prosperous, flourishing, thriving
19.	高见	gāojiàn	(your) brilliant idea, (your) opinion

49 选准 "上帝" （一）

20. 调查	diàochá	to investigate, to inquire into, to survey
21. 不光	bùguāng	not only
22. 研究	yánjiū	to study, to research
23. 进行	jìnxíng	to carry on, to carry out
24. 规模	guīmó	scale, scope
25. 首先	shǒuxiān	first, first of all, above all
26. 当时	dāngshí	that time, then
27. 难题	nántí	difficult problem
28. 断定	duàndìng	to conclude, to determine, to figure out
29. 几乎	jīhū	nearly, almost
30. 遍	biàn	all over, all around
31. 收入	shōurù	income, earnings
32. 结论	jiélùn	conclusion
33. 步	bù	step, stage
34. 样品	yàngpǐn	sample, specimen
35. 层次	céngcì	stratum, layer, level
36. 品尝	pǐncháng	to taste, to sample, to savor
37. 征求	zhēngqiú	to solicit, to seek, to ask for
38. 材料	cáiliào	material
39. 色彩	sècǎi	color, hue, tint
40. 搭配	dāpèi	to match, to go with
41. 深入	shēnrù	deep, thorough

专　名　Proper Noun

希尔顿饭店	Xī'ěrdùn Fàndiàn	Hilton Hotel

注释 Notes

1 "所", 助词, 用在及物动词前, 构成名词性短语。例如:

所, a particle, is used before a transitive verb to form a noun phrase. For example:

1. 我所知道的就是这些了。
2. 据我所知, 他已经回国了。
3. 我们所讨论的, 都写在这上面了。
4. 他去找你, 总是有所求吧!

2 "不光", 副词, 表示超出某个数量或范围。例如:

不光, an adverb, means exceeding a certain number or range. For example:

1. 来参加的不光是老人。
2. 这家商店不光卖水果。

也可以是连词, 意思是"不但"。例如:

It can also serve as a conjunction to mean "not only". For example:

1. 这双鞋不光款式好, 质量也不错。
2. 我不光会画画儿, 还会唱歌。

3 "进行", 动词, 从事(某种活动), 后面可带动词宾语。例如:

进行, a verb, means being engaged in a certain activity and can be followed by a verb as the object. For example:

1. 我们对中国市场进行了详细的调查。
2. 事情进行得很顺利。
3. 昨天杰克和珍妮对保护环境的问题进行了讨论。

"进行"总是用来表示持续性的和正式、严肃的行为, 短暂性的和日常生活中的行为不用"进行"。例如不说"进行午睡"等。

进行 is always used with persistent, formal, and serious behaviors instead of transient and everyday activities. For example, you cannot say 进行午睡 (to have a nap after lunch).

49 选准"上帝"（一）

4 "遍"，副词，普遍，全面。可以用在动词后做结果补语。例如：

遍, an adverb, means "all over, all around". It is used as a complement of result after verbs. For example:

1. 这条街上的小吃我都吃遍了。
2. 我这次一定要把好玩儿的都玩儿个遍。
3. 我找遍了整个房间，也没找到钥匙。

练 习
Exercises

一、替换练习。
Substitution drills.

顾客确实是"上帝"，而且是个很不好伺候的"上帝"。

坐出租车	不划算	容易堵车
这儿的东西	很多	价钱很便宜
苹果	很好吃	营养丰富

A：你们昨天做什么了？
B：我们对环保问题进行了讨论。

产品质量	调查
提高服务水平	讨论
公关工作	研究

A：你们公司的经营方向是什么？
B：我们打算做中式快餐。

| 经营电脑 |
| 提供互联网服务 |
| 做服装贸易 |

A：这家商店怎么样？

B：不光东西少，价格也很贵。

商场	服务好	东西质量也很好
饭馆	味道好	价钱也不贵
饭店	房间舒适	而且去机场很方便

二、把下面的词组成句子。

Rearrange the following words into sentences.

1. 企业 方向 的 要 选 准 经营
2. 深入 了 进行 他们 的 调查
3. 这 公司 倒闭 了 家
4. 他 教育 受 高等 过 吗
5. 我们 尽力 满足 应该 的 他们 需求 不同
6. 你 迎合 要 随便 不 他 意见 的
7. 你们 市场 进行 的 调研 怎么样 得 了
8. 你们 的 规模 生产 工厂 多 有 大
9. 他 你 意见 向 征求 吗 了
10. 色彩 搭配 非常 得 合适

三、完成下面的对话。

Complete the following dialogues.

A：你知道怎么搞市场调查吗？

B：_____。

A：还有什么方法呢？

B：_____。

49 选准"上帝"（一）

A：中国普通家庭的消费水平怎么样？
B：_____。
A：他们一般喜欢买什么样的商品？
B：_____。

A：要开办一家企业，首先应该做什么？
B：_____。
A：怎样才能选准经营方向呢？
B：_____。

A：_____？
B：经营各种糖果糕点。
A：可以先尝后买吗？
B：_____。

A：_____？
B：我对市民的收入情况进行了非常深入的调查。
A：得出了什么结论？
B：_____。

四、用指定词语完成句子。
Complete the following sentences with the given words.

1. 我必须一边工作一边学习，因为_____。（富裕）
2. 我们是好朋友，_____。（爱好）
3. 他的要求太多了，_____！（满足）
4. 这是我做的蛋糕，_____。（品尝）
5. 他是一个受过良好教育、有丰富经验的人，_____我最好的伙伴。（当作）
6. 他们公司的经营情况怎么样，_____。（调查）
7. 我们了解的市场信息已经很不少了，_____。（研究）

8. 根据北京市人口情况，_____大有市场。（断定）

9. 节假日的时候，北京市的很多公园_____。（免费）

10. 如果你想了解中国人的生活，_____交朋友。（普通）

五、什么叫"众口难调"？请你举例说明。

What is meant by "it is difficult to cater to all tastes"? Explain it with examples.

50

第五十课 选准"上帝"(二)
Lesson 50　Choose the Right "God" (II)

课文 Text

在课外

珍　妮：山口，我发现你对肯德基的市场调研相当感兴趣，为什么？

杰　克：你是不是将来也想在北京开发餐饮业市场？

山　口：你们猜对了，我是有这个打算。我们今天就进城去转转，了解一下北京餐饮业市场的情况，好吗？

珍　妮：好，走吧。

山　口：哎，我们走了半天，你们注意到没有，什么食品受欢迎？

珍　妮：我发现北京人爱吃面食。你们看这条街上，有很多面馆儿、包子铺什么的。

山　口：嗯。看，这里就有一家拉面馆儿，咱们进去找顾客聊聊。

山　口：先生，您好！请问，您常来这儿用餐吗？

顾　客：是。

山　口：这条街上有好几家面馆儿，都很经济实惠，您为什么会来这家呢？
顾　客：我觉得这儿的用餐环境更好一些。
山　口：您很看重用餐环境吗？
顾　客：那当然。
珍　妮：那么，肯德基和麦当劳，您也常去喽？
顾　客：也经常去，但我还是更喜欢吃面条儿。
山　口：为什么呢？
顾　客：因为我不喜欢喝冷饮，还是吃有汤有水、热乎乎的面条儿舒服。
珍　妮：谢谢您。

山　口：杰克，你听了刚才这位顾客的话，有什么感想？
杰　克：现在，大大小小的饭店遍布北京城，特别是快餐业发展迅速。
山　口：那你认为在中国开发餐饮业市场的前景如何？
杰　克：我看前景并不妙！
山　口：我的看法与你相反。
杰　克：哦，是吗？
山　口：是的。现在虽然相当多的外国快餐打入了中国市场，但并不完全适合中国人的口味。中国有悠久的饮食文化，人人都是美食家，中国人是不会丢掉自己的饮食传统的。
杰　克：你说得很对，这点我倒没想到。外国人在中国开发餐饮业市场，应该充分考虑到这一点。
山　口：所以，我认为，在中国开发餐饮业还是很有前景的。不过，必须走出一条适合中国国情的大众化快餐食品新路。
珍　妮：这个想法很好，快说说什么新路？
山　口：外国快餐的质量和速度，中国饮食的传统和口味，普通群众能够接受的价格。

珍　妮：好主意！山口，真有你的！

杰　克：这说起来容易，做起来就难了。这事恐怕只能让中国人自己去做了。

山　口：我们也可以试试嘛！不然，怎么能在中国市场站稳脚跟？

珍　妮：不过，中式快餐也正在兴起，像"永和豆浆""老家肉饼"就都是中式快餐店。

山　口：这不怕，我就喜欢竞争，没有竞争就没有发展嘛！

生词
New Words

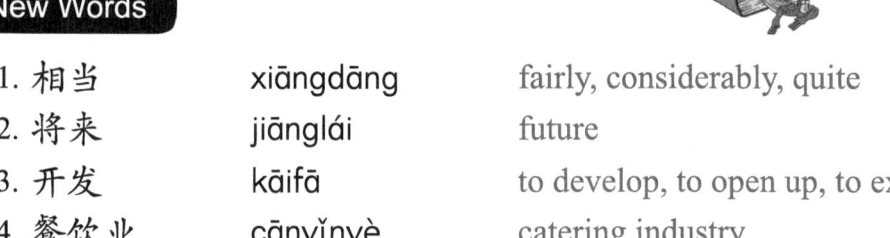

1.	相当	xiāngdāng	fairly, considerably, quite
2.	将来	jiānglái	future
3.	开发	kāifā	to develop, to open up, to exploit
4.	餐饮业	cānyǐnyè	catering industry
5.	铺	pù	shop
6.	拉面	lāmiàn	hand-pulled noodles
7.	实惠	shíhuì	affordable, cost-effective
8.	环境	huánjìng	environment
9.	看重	kànzhòng	to regard as important, to value, to set store by
10.	冷饮	lěngyǐn	cold drink
11.	感想	gǎnxiǎng	reflections, thoughts, opinions
12.	遍布	biànbù	to spread all over, to be found everywhere
13.	迅速	xùnsù	fast, rapid, speedy
14.	前景	qiánjǐng	prospect, vista
15.	妙	miào	excellent, splendid, wonderful
16.	看法	kànfǎ	view, opinion

17. 与	yǔ	and, with
18. 相反	xiāngfǎn	opposite, contrary
19. 虽然	suīrán	though, although
20. 打入	dǎ rù	to enter
21. 悠久	yōujiǔ	long, long-standing, age-old
22. 充分	chōngfèn	full, ample, sufficient
23. 必须	bìxū	must, to have to
24. 大众化	dàzhònghuà	popular, in a popular style
25. 群众	qúnzhòng	the masses, people
26. 不然	bùrán	otherwise, if not, or else
27. 能（够）	néng(gòu)	can, to be able to
28. 站稳	zhànwěn	to stand firm
29. 兴起	xīngqǐ	to rise, to spring up

专 名 Proper Nouns

1. 永和豆浆	Yǒnghé Dòujiāng	Yonho soybean milk
2. 老家肉饼	Lǎojiā Ròubǐng	Laojia meat pie

注 释 Notes

1 "虽然"，连词，用来表示让步。意思是承认甲事是事实，但乙事并不因此而不成立。在下句常有"可是、但是"相呼应。例如：

虽然, a conjunction, expresses concession. The meaning is that while admitting that A is a fact, B is not untrue nevertheless. Echoing with it, 可是 or 但是 is often used in the second clause. For example:

1. 虽然我手中的钱多了，但是还说不上富裕。
2. 我虽然爱吃面条儿，可也不能顿顿吃。
3. 他虽然听了我的意见，可就是不改。
4. 这事还是做错了，虽然我考虑了很久。

50 选准"上帝"（二）

2. "真有你的"，表赞叹的短语，意思是称赞对方有思想、有本领、有主意、有办法等。例如：

真有你的 (you really have the skill / you know your stuff) is an expression to show admiration. It is used to praise the other party for his/her ideas, skills, plans, measures, etc. For example:

1. 这事干得漂亮，真有你的！
2. 这么难的问题都能解决，真有你的！

"真有你的"也可表达吓唬对方的口气，表示将有严重后果。例如：

真有你的 can also be used to express a tone of intimidation, indicating that there will be a serious consequence. For example:

1. 真有你的！这事不算完，咱们走着瞧！
2. 好小子，真有你的，看我以后再教训你！

练 习
Exercises

一、替换练习。
Substitution drills.

A：我发现你对<u>她</u>相当感兴趣。
B：因为我<u>想了解她</u>。

中国民歌	爱好音乐
京剧	学习中国文化
经济学	想做生意
中国少数民族	研究中国民俗

A：这儿的<u>环境</u>怎么样？
B：这儿的<u>环境</u>比较<u>清静</u>。

口味	地道
价格	合理
服务员	亲切
服务	周到

A：你明天有什么打算？
B：我明天打算买东西。

星期天	睡一天觉
寒假	去南方旅行
毕业以后	去中国留学
结婚以后	留在中国工作

A：我认为现在开办公司的前景不太好。
B：我的看法与你相反。

在网上买东西并不划算	相反
骑共享单车可以保护环境	相同
中国人喜欢吃麦当劳	相反
高档时装质量一定很好	相同

A：你认为拉面好吃吗？
B：我认为还算好吃。

在中国旅行方便	不太方便
在麦当劳用餐经济实惠	是贵了点
外国快餐在中国站稳脚跟了	没站稳脚跟
北京的交通问题已经解决了	没有完全解决

二、把下面的词组成句子。

Rearrange the following words into sentences.

1. 我 发现 市场 最近 你 调研 兴趣 感
2. 将来 想 什么 做 你 工作
3. 你 学习 在 中国 打算 年 几
4. 我 看重 情谊 很 朋友 的
5. 什么 有 感想 你
6. 这 问题 难 解决 不 个
7. 知道 原因 你 是 什么 吗
8. 你 考虑 应该 充分 的 建议 我
9. 悠久 文化 的 中国 饮食 有
10. 一些 这儿 环境 的 用餐 好 更

50 选准"上帝"（二）

三、完成下面的对话。
Complete the following dialogues.

A：_____？
B：我对时装表演相当感兴趣。
A：听说最近老舍茶馆有时装表演，我们什么时候去看看？
B：_____。

A：_____？
B：没办法，我一见烤鸭就胃口大开！
A：可是烤鸭太油腻了。
B：不怕，_____！

A：顾客最看重商店的什么？
B：_____。
A：_____？
B：当然是无条件退货！

A：_____？
B：不，我的看法与他相反。
A：为什么？
B：_____。

四、选词填空
Choose the appropriate words to fill in the blanks.

口味　　相当　　站稳　　餐饮业　　群众　　速度

　　山口对肯德基的市场调研_____感兴趣，因为她打算将来在北京开发_____市场。她觉得应该用外国快餐的质量和_____，中国饮食的传统和_____，普通_____能够接受的价格在中国市场_____脚跟。

五、请做一项社会调查，然后谈谈调查结果和建议。（可谈住房、交通、环境、教育等热门话题）

Do a social survey and talk about your findings and suggestions. (The survey can be about hot topics such as housing, transportation, environment, and education.)

第五十一课　巧用推销术（一）
Lesson 51　Skillful Salesmanship (I)

课文 Text

在课上

王老师：一种商品要占领市场，除了质量和价格优势外，还要靠什么？

珍　妮：靠广告。

山　口：靠售后服务。

杰　克：靠出色的推销。赚钱的机遇，随时都会碰到，就看你能不能抓住它，利用各种手段，大做推销、促销工作。

山　口：杰克说得很对。我们日本的汽车、手表和家用电器，都是经过艰苦的推销工作，才畅销世界的。

杰　克：而且商品越丰富，竞争越激烈，推销工作就越是成败的关键。

王老师：那么，怎样才能做好推销、促销的工作呢？

珍　妮：我想，最重要的是要善于研究顾客的心理，然后针对顾客心理，巧用推销术。

杰　克：怪不得北京许多商店，现在都雇用导购小姐呢！谁见过导购先生？

山　口：你这话是什么意思？
杰　克：这还不懂？女人善解人意，容易抓住"上帝"的心。
珍　妮：哦，你也承认男人不通情达理呀，哈哈……
山　口：我们在说正经的，你们又开玩笑！
杰　克：说真的，我很佩服女推销员，很多商品，就是用女推销员更好。
珍　妮：那是自然嘛。比如化妆品，女推销员可以亲自做示范，展示出一种理想的化妆效果，也可以免费为她的女顾客化妆，这不比男推销员拿着化妆品讲解如何如何要好吗？
杰　克：你说得很对。不过，有时候男推销员也有男推销员的优点。
珍　妮：是吗？
杰　克：比如说男士的衣服、裤子、用品等，这些由男推销员去推销，效果不是更好吗？
山　口：这样说也对。
杰　克：以前有一种牛仔服，是用女模特儿做的广告，但是广告播出以后，衣服的销量不是很好。
珍　妮：后来呢？
杰　克：牛仔服公司通过调查发现，购买这种牛仔服的大多数都是男士，所以后来公司做了另一个广告：一个目光深沉、皮肤粗糙、袖子高卷、一身野性的男人穿着牛仔服。就是照片上这样，你们看，怎么样？
山　口：真够帅的！
杰　克：就是嘛。广告播出以后，牛仔服的销量上升了百分之六十，这家公司也变成了一家大公司。
山　口：其实你们说得都很对，不同的商品，要用不同的推销方法。

杰　克：这我懂。戏法人人会变，巧妙各有不同，这就要看推销员的本事了。

生词 New Words

1.	术	shù	skill, technique
2.	占领	zhànlǐng	to capture, to occupy, to seize
3.	除了	chúle	except, besides, apart from
4.	优势	yōushì	superiority, dominant position
5.	机遇	jīyù	opportunity, favorable circumstances
6.	随时	suíshí	at any time, at all times, whenever necessary
7.	抓	zhuā	to seize, to grab, to catch
8.	经过	jīngguò	to go through
9.	艰苦	jiānkǔ	arduous, difficult, hard, tough
10.	成败	chéngbài	success or failure
11.	关键	guānjiàn	key, crux
12.	善于	shànyú	to be good at, to be adept in
13.	针对	zhēnduì	to aim at, to direct at
14.	雇用	gùyòng	to employ, to hire
15.	导购	dǎogòu	shopping guide; to guide shoppers
16.	善解人意	shàn jiě rényì	understanding, considerate
17.	通情达理	tōngqíng-dálǐ	showing good sense, reasonable
18.	佩服	pèifú	to admire
19.	化妆品	huàzhuāngpǐn	make-up, cosmetics
20.	亲自	qīnzì	personally, in person

21. 示范	shìfàn	to set an example, to demonstrate
22. 理想	lǐxiǎng	ideal
23. 化妆	huàzhuāng	to put on makeup
24. 效果	xiàoguǒ	effect, result
25. 优点	yōudiǎn	advantage, merit
26. 男士	nánshì	male, man
27. 用品	yòngpǐn	article for use
28. 由	yóu	by, through
29. 播出	bōchū	to broadcast, to be on air
30. 购买	gòumǎi	to buy
31. 另（外）	lìng(wài)	other; in addition
32. 目光	mùguāng	look, gaze, sight, vision
33. 深沉	shēnchén	deep, dark, reserved
34. 皮肤	pífū	skin
35. 粗糙	cūcāo	rough, coarse
36. 袖子	xiùzi	sleeve
37. 卷	juǎn	to roll up
38. 野性	yěxìng	unruliness, wild nature
39. 照片	zhàopiàn	photo
40. 帅	shuài	handsome, cute
41. 戏法	xìfǎ	conjuring trick, magic
42. 巧妙	qiǎomiào	clever, ingenious

注释 Notes

1 "除了"，介词，表示所说的不计算在内。可以写成"除了……外（以外、之外）"的格式。例如：

51 巧用推销术（一）

除了, a preposition, indicates that what's mentioned is not included. It can also be written as "除了……外 (or 以外/之外)". For example:

1. 这事儿除了王英，谁都知道。
2. 除了旧一点儿外，这辆车还算不错。
3. 这个商场，除了东西价格有点儿贵以外，别的都很好。

2 "经过"，动词，表示从某处通过或时间的延续。例如：

经过, a verb, means passing through a place or the continuation of time. For example:

1. 从北京坐火车去上海，要经过天津。
2. 我经过他宿舍时，见他还没关灯。
3. 经过几十年，公司才发展到现在的规模。
4. 经过半年多，我们的产品才打入北京市场。

经过，也可表示经历某种活动或事件。例如：
经过 can also mean experiencing some activity or event. For example:

1. 经过协商，我们解决了难题。
2. 经过大规模推销工作，我们占领了市场。
3. 经过调查，我们找到了成败的关键。

3 "由"，介词，引进施动者，表示受动者的名词可以放在句子前面做主语，或者放在动词后面做宾语。例如：

由, a preposition, introduces the doer. The noun indicating the patient of the action can be placed at the beginning of the sentence as the subject, or after the verb as the object. For example:

1. 这个问题由经理代表公司回答。
2. 现在，由秘书介绍会议内容。
3. 销售方面的问题由销售部负责。
4. 今天是你的生日，想做什么由你决定。

练 习
Exercises

一、替换练习。
Substitution drills.

A：要做一个成功的企业家，除了<u>机遇</u>以外，还要有什么？
B：还要<u>有真本事</u>。

实干	懂经济学
自己努力	有好的合作伙伴
熟悉市场行情	善于抓住机遇

A：我什么时候可以<u>上班</u>？
B：你随时可以来<u>上班</u>。

买票
退房
办手续

A：我觉得<u>女推销员</u>比<u>男推销员</u>更好。
B：你说得很对。不过，<u>男推销员</u>也有<u>男推销员</u>的优点。

坐飞机	坐火车	舒服
杰克	小王	热情
在外边租房子	住学生宿舍	方便

A：<u>这种产品</u>由谁<u>推销给顾客</u>？
B：应该由<u>销售部</u><u>推销给顾客</u>。

今天的会议	安排	经理
总经理	担任	钱先生
质量方面的问题	解决	公司

二、把下面的词组成句子。
Rearrange the following words into sentences.

1. 他 竞争 占 在 中 优势 吗
2. 问题 有 来 随时 可以 我 找
3. 推销 是 艰苦 的 工作 很
4. 成败 的 是 这 关键
5. 你 说 这些 针对 的 是 吧 我
6. 我们 说 的 正经 吧
7. 善于 要 推销员 心理 研究 的 顾客
8. 这 事 亲自 要 件 我 办理 去
9. 说话 注意 要 效果 做事 都
10. 我们 机遇 的 赚钱 要 抓住

三、完成下面的对话。
Complete the following dialogues.

A：_____？
B：有三分之一的市场。
A：是怎样占领这些市场的呢？
B：_____。

A：你们公司靠什么参加市场竞争？
B：_____。
A：_____？
B：还靠推销工作和售后服务。

A：_____？
B：效果非常理想。
A：会赢得女士们的喜爱吗？
B：_____。

A：你觉得你的老板通情达理吗？

B：＿＿＿＿＿＿＿＿＿＿＿＿＿＿。

A：为什么？

B：＿＿＿＿＿＿＿＿＿＿＿＿＿＿。

A：你看这广告怎么样？

B：＿＿＿＿＿＿＿＿＿＿＿＿＿＿。

A：你为什么这么说？

B：＿＿＿＿＿＿＿＿＿＿＿＿＿＿。

四、选择适当的词语完成句子。

Choose the appropriate words to complete the following sentences.

1. ＿＿＿＿＿＿＿＿＿＿＿＿，我认识了王经理。（通过　经过）

2. 从今年一月到六月，＿＿＿＿＿＿＿＿＿＿我们公司终于开业了。（通过　经过）

3. ＿＿＿＿＿＿＿＿＿＿电视广告，提高公司商品的知名度。（通过　经过）

4. 今天的讨论＿＿＿＿＿＿＿＿＿＿？（效果　结果　果然）

5. 新的牛仔服广告，产生了＿＿＿＿＿＿＿＿＿＿。（效果　结果　果然）

6. 你猜得很对，＿＿＿＿＿＿＿＿＿＿。（效果　结果　果然）

7. 在展览会上，＿＿＿＿＿＿＿＿＿＿最新产品。（示范　展示）

8. 怎么使用这种电脑，＿＿＿＿＿＿＿＿＿＿。（示范　展示）

五、推销手段是多种多样的，请举一两个例子说明。

There are various means to promote sales. Explain one or two kinds with examples.

第五十二课 巧用推销术（二）
Lesson 52 Skillful Salesmanship (II)

课文 Text

在课外

经　理：小罗，这是留学生杰克，他来这儿实习，就交给你了。

小　罗：欢迎，欢迎！你有什么问题只管问。

杰　克：谢谢。您照常接待顾客吧，我先站在一边看，有什么问题再向您请教。

小　罗：小姐您好，您想买点儿什么？

女青年：我想买一个手机，要最新款的。

小　罗：小姐，您看，这款手机是最新产品，刚投放市场，小巧时尚，功能多样。

女青年：有屏幕大点儿的吗？价钱贵点儿没关系。

小　罗：这边几款手机的屏幕都比较大，您可以看看。您比较喜欢哪些功能呢？

女青年：我平时特别喜欢出去旅行，所以最好是拍照效果好一点儿的。

小　罗：那这款手机特别适合您用，前后摄像头的像素都很高，不管是拍人物还是拍风景，都特别出色，还有各种美化照片的功能。

女青年：听音乐、看视频的效果怎么样？

小　罗：这款手机是立体声音效，而且屏幕的分辨率很高，画质清晰。有了它，您随时随地都可以得到最好的享受。

女青年：待机时间长吗？

小　罗：要是只打电话和拍照片的话，用两天都没问题。

女青年：我能试一下吗？

小　罗：当然可以。

女青年：挺好的，用起来又灵敏又流畅，就买这款了。麻烦您给我开张发票。

小　罗：好的。

老大爷：小伙子，你好啊！

小　罗：大爷，您好！您想买什么？

老大爷：我想买台电脑。

小　罗：您买电脑想做什么用呢？

老大爷：我就想上网，在网上买买东西，和孩子们聊聊天儿。

小　罗：那您为什么不买一个能上网的智能手机呢？现在的智能手机既能打电话，又能上网，可方便了。

老大爷：手机上的字太小了，我年纪大，看着费劲，还是买台电脑好用。

小　罗：您说得没错。那您看看这种电脑，屏幕大，颜色好。

老大爷：这个字能调大一点儿吗？

小　罗：当然可以，现在的字是中号的，我给您换成大号的，您看怎么样？

老大爷：不错不错，看得很清楚。等买回去，我还得学学怎

52 巧用推销术（二）

么用，可不能让电脑变成商店里的样品——摆设了。

小　罗：没关系，您用几天就熟悉了，现在电脑的操作都特别简单。

老大爷：不知道这电脑的质量怎么样？要是三天两头儿地出问题，我可受不了。

小　罗：这种牌子的电脑质量挺好，而且保修三年，您放心吧！

老大爷：价钱贵吗？

小　罗：不贵，才三千多。

老大爷：那好，给我拿一台吧。

杰　克：小罗，刚才第一位小姐来买东西，你主动给她介绍了一款高档手机；老大爷买电脑，你却推荐了一款低价位的，这是为什么？

小　罗：哦，不同的顾客，有不同的生活环境和需求，所以要给他们介绍的商品也不一样。那位小姐喜欢功能多、屏幕大的，当然推荐新款手机最好；老大爷的要求不高，所以就给他介绍了一款物美价廉的电脑。

杰　克：就是说，推销商品应该看对象？

小　罗：当然，按照顾客的需求给他们推荐商品才能真正让顾客满意，顾客满意了，生意才会越来越好。

杰　克：嗯，看来做推销也要因人而异。

生词 New Words

1. 实习　　　shíxí　　　to do an internship

2.	只管	zhǐguǎn	don't hesitate to
3.	照常	zhàocháng	as usual
4.	请教	qǐngjiào	to ask, to consult
5.	投放	tóufàng	to launch, to put (on the market)
6.	小巧	xiǎoqiǎo	small, compact
7.	时尚	shíshàng	fashionable
8.	功能	gōngnéng	function
9.	多样	duōyàng	multiple, various
10.	屏幕	píngmù	screen
11.	拍照	pāizhào	to take a photo
12.	摄像头	shèxiàngtóu	camera
13.	像素	xiàngsù	pixel
14.	人物	rénwù	person, figure
15.	美化	měihuà	to beautify
16.	视频	shìpín	video
17.	立体声	lìtǐshēng	stereo sound
18.	音效	yīnxiào	sound effect
19.	分辨率	fēnbiànlǜ	resolution ratio
20.	画质	huàzhì	image quality
21.	清晰	qīngxī	clear, distinct
22.	随地	suídì	anywhere
23.	待机	dàijī	standby
24.	灵敏	língmǐn	sensitive, quick
25.	流畅	liúchàng	smooth
26.	发票	fāpiào	invoice, receipt
27.	智能	zhìnéng	smart
28.	年纪	niánjì	age
29.	费劲	fèijìn	difficult, painstaking
30.	调	tiáo	to change, to adjust
31.	号	hào	size

32. 摆设	bǎishè	ornament, sth. purely ornamental
33. 操作	cāozuò	to operate, to handle
34. 三天两头儿	sāntiān-liǎngtóur	every two or three days
35. 保修	bǎoxiū	to be guaranteed, to be under warranty
36. 价位	jiàwèi	price
37. 因人而异	yīnrén'éryì	to vary from person to person

注 释 Notes

1 "只管",副词,表示没有条件限制,可以放心去做。后面的动词一般不用否定式。例如:

只管, an adverb, indicates that there are no restrictions, and you can do as you like. The verb after it is normally not in the negative form. For example:

1. 你只管躺着,我们坐一会儿就走。
2. 你有什么困难只管对我说,我一定帮助你。
3. 你只管来住吧,这儿就是你的家。
4. 你有什么事儿,只管说出来,不要瞒着我。

2 "商店里的样品——摆设。"汉语中像这样由两个部分组成的一句话叫"歇后语"。歇后语前一部分像谜面,后一部分像谜底,通常用于口语。人们在说话时常常只说前一部分,而本意在后一部分。例如:

"Samples in the store—furnishings." In Chinese, a sentence consisting of two parts like this is called "allegorical saying", with the former part being like a riddle, and the latter part being the answer. It is usually used in spoken Chinese. People often say only the first part, but the real intention is indicated in the latter one. For example:

1. 我们俩人的关系是小葱拌豆腐——一清二白。

Our relationship is just like a dish of white bean curd and green scallions—being perfectly pure (homophonic in Chinese).

2. 我这些货,是皇帝的女儿——不愁嫁。

These goods of ours are the Emperor's daughters—they do not have to worry about getting married.

3. 我是文学专业的，对物理、化学那是擀面杖吹火——一窍不通啊！

I major in literature. To me, physics and chemistry are like trying to blow the fire with a rolling pin—I know nothing about them.

4. 我很少相信广告里的话，那是王婆卖瓜——自卖自夸，没几句真话。

I seldom believe the messages in ads. It's like Old Lady Wang praising her own melons while selling them—praising her own work or wares. Very little is true.

练 习
Exercises

一、替换练习。
Substitution drills.

A：我能问你一个问题吗？
B：当然可以，你只管问。

尝尝这个小吃	尝
看看这本书	看
试试这款手机	试

A：您觉得这个手机怎么样？
B：有屏幕大点儿的吗？价钱贵点儿没关系。

台	电脑	便宜点儿的	质量差点儿
种	汽车	别的牌子的	国产的也
双	运动鞋	白色的	别的款式也

A：这种牌子的电脑质量好吗？
B：质量特别好，您放心吧！

手机	待机时间	长
手机	拍照效果	出色
电脑	画质	清晰

52 巧用推销术（二）

二、把下面的词组成句子。
Rearrange the following words into sentences.

1. 您 向 我 请教 问题 一个 吗 好
2. 效果 拍照 款 一点儿 这 好 手机 的
3. 照常 放假 不 今天 上课
4. 随时随地 用 上网 现在 手机 可以
5. 发票 您 一张 开 我 发票 给
6. 智能 为什么 您 一个 买 手机 呢 不
7. 请 哪儿 问 修 可以 电脑
8. 常常 我 视频 看 手机 用
9. 一款 老大爷 高档 了 买 电脑
10. 推销 商品 应该 因人而异

三、完成下面的对话。
Complete the following dialogues.

A：_____？
B：不用客气，请讲吧。
A："王婆卖瓜"是什么意思？
B：_____。

A：您好，请问这电视机能保修吗？
B：_____。
A：_____？
B：保修五年。

A：_____？
B：刚投放市场。
A：质量怎么样？
B：_____。

A：_____？

B：不大懂，不过我正在学习。

A：你觉得向顾客推销商品难吗？

B：_____。

四、选词填空。

Choose the appropriate words to fill in the blanks.

待机　屏幕　实习　发票　视频　请教　小巧　三天两头儿　年纪　功能

1. 今天我们班来了一位_____老师。
2. 您好，我可以向您_____一个问题吗？
3. 坐出租车记得向司机要_____。
4. 爷爷虽然_____大了，但是每天都坚持锻炼，现在身体依然不错。
5. 这种电脑的_____太小了，我喜欢大一点儿的。
6. 爸爸工作特别忙，_____地出差，一个月在家待不了几天。
7. 我的手机用了两年了，现在_____时间越来越短，我想换个新的。
8. 越来越多的年轻人喜欢在手机上看_____。
9. 您看，这款手机虽然_____，但是_____却很齐全，很适合您这样经常出差的人使用。

五、请你讲一两个推销商品中的趣事。

Give one or two interesting episodes in promoting sales.

第五十三课　快递与外卖（一）
Lesson 53　Express Delivery and Takeout (I)

课文 Text

在课上

王老师：同学们，你们用过快递吗？

山　口：当然用过。我在网上买的书、衣服和电脑，都是用快递给我送过来的。

王老师：那你们和快递小哥打过交道吗？

珍　妮：老师，您说的"快递小哥"，是指快递员吗？

王老师：对，一般大家亲切地把送快递的小伙子称为"快递小哥"。你们觉得他们的工作忙不忙？

杰　克：特别忙。他们得争分夺秒地把货送到，然后又得赶紧去送下一个快递，而且一年到头都是风里来雨里去的，好像从来没见过他们休息。

王老师：杰克说得对。快递快递，最重要的是一个"快"字，要把货物快速、安全、完好无损地送到客户手里。你们知道今年"双11购物狂欢节"的第一单快递，是什么时候送到的吗？

山　口：不知道。

珍　妮：我知道。我在网上看到了，是一位小姐买的一款手机，晚上12点才下的单，20分钟后她的手机就送到了。当时，她正和朋友在一家餐厅吃夜宵呢！

山　口：中国的快递确实很快，常常上午下单，下午就到了。要是从外地发的货，最快三天就能到。

杰　克：我还看到很多中国学生放假回家的时候，只背一个小包，大件行李都用快递，人到家了，快递也到了。可见，快递给我们的生活带来了多大的方便！

珍　妮：我听说，现在世界上很多国家和地区都有中国的快递业务。因为快递越来越方便，我的朋友也开始在中国的网站上买东西了。

山　口：老师，中国的快递员一天要送多少货物？

王老师：快递员平时每天大概要送一百多件快递。但是逢年过节，尤其是"双11"的时候，快递业务要比平时多得多。"双11"以后，接着又是"双12"、圣诞节、元旦和春节，所以一年中这几个月是他们最忙的时候，平均每人每天要送三百多件快递。

山　口：怪不得我没见过女快递员呢，这么大的劳动强度，女性确实吃不消。

珍　妮：老师，快递员每天早出晚归，甚至吃饭都不能歇一歇，他们不觉得累吗？

王老师：有人问过他们，他们说，累是累点儿，但是快递工作很有意义："快"的是货物，"递"的是真情。

杰　克：说得太好了。快递员给我们带来了舒适、便捷的生活。下次我收快递的时候，应该好好儿地感谢他们。

53 快递与外卖（一）

生 词
New Words

1.	快递	kuàidì	express delivery
2.	打交道	dǎ jiāodao	to deal with, to come into contact with
3.	指	zhǐ	to refer to
4.	快递员	kuàidìyuán	courier, mailman
5.	称为	chēng wéi	to call, to refer to as
6.	争分夺秒	zhēngfēn-duómiǎo	to race against time
7.	赶紧	gǎnjǐn	to rush to, to hasten
8.	一年到头	yìnián-dàotóu	all the year round
9.	货物	huòwù	goods
10.	快速	kuàisù	fast
11.	完好无损	wánhǎo wúsǔn	intact
12.	客户	kèhù	customer
13.	单	dān	*measure word for business deals*
14.	夜宵	yèxiāo	midnight snack
15.	网站	wǎngzhàn	website
16.	逢年过节	féngnián-guòjié	at New Year and every festival
17.	尤其	yóuqí	especially
18.	平均	píngjūn	average
19.	强度	qiángdù	intensity
20.	女性	nǚxìng	female, woman
21.	吃不消	chībuxiāo	cannot bear
22.	早出晚归	zǎochū-wǎnguī	to go out early and come back late
23.	歇	xiē	to rest
24.	意义	yìyì	meaning, significance
25.	真情	zhēnqíng	true feelings
26.	便捷	biànjié	convenient
27.	感谢	gǎnxiè	to thank

注释 Notes

1 "赶紧",副词,表示抓紧时间、毫不拖延。例如:

赶紧, an adverb, means seizing the time without delay. For example:

1. 我吃完饭就赶紧上班去了。
2. 听说商店打折,我赶紧去买了几件衣服。
3. 要下雨了,我们赶紧走!
4. 商店明天就要开业了,我们得赶紧做好准备工作。

2 "尤其",副词,表示在全体中或与其他事物比较时特别突出。例如:

尤其, an adverb, means standing out among all things or when compared with other things. For example:

1. 开车时要注意安全,尤其是天气不好的时候。
2. 珍妮的汉语不错,尤其是口语,发音特别标准。
3. 这些礼物我都很喜欢,尤其是这幅画儿,太漂亮了!

3 "平均",动词,指把总数按份儿均匀计算。例如:

平均, a verb, means calculating the average or mean. For example:

1. 十个包子一共六块钱,平均一个六毛钱。
2. 因为工作的原因,他平均每个月都要去一次上海。
3. 平均每年有十几万人来这儿参观。

4 "吃不消",动词,表示支持不住,受不了。反义词是"吃得消"。例如:

吃不消, a verb, means being unable to stand or "can't bear". The antonym is 吃得消. For example:

1. 他年纪大了,爬这么高的山恐怕吃不消。
2. 每天工作18个小时,你吃得消吗?
3. 他的行为真让人吃不消。
4. 你每天这么晚睡,怎么能吃得消?

53 快递与外卖（一）

一、替换练习。
Substitution drills.

A：我喜欢吃<u>中餐</u>，尤其是<u>四川菜</u>。
B：我也喜欢吃<u>四川菜</u>，就是<u>有点儿辣</u>。

唱歌	汉语歌	会的歌不多
看电影	看爱情片	好看的爱情片太少
坐火车	坐高铁	出差的机会太少
运动	打篮球	打得不太好

A：你赶紧<u>去银行</u>，<u>就要关门了</u>！
B：我这就<u>去</u>。

歇歇	你今天的劳动强度太大了	休息
吃夜宵	一会儿就凉了	去吃
告诉山口	她要的书卖完了	打电话
去洗手	太脏了	去洗

二、把下面的词组成句子。
Rearrange the following words into sentences.

1. 夜宵 有 吃 吗 你 习惯 的
2. 我 经常 打交道 顾客 和
3. 快递员 很 工作 劳动 大 的 强度
4. 款 网上 山口 手机 一 了 在 购买
5. 意义 工作 快递 有 很 的 是
6. 国家 都 中国 快递 有 业务 很多 的
7. 快速 地 客户 要 他们 货物 到 手 把 里 送
8. 带 便捷 快递员 了 的 舒适 生活 我们 来 给

199

9. 平均 你们 多少 天 送 货物 一 要

10. 女性 吃不消 这么 劳动 确实 的 大 强度

三、完成下面的对话。
Complete the following dialogues.

A：你想去体验一下快递员的工作吗？
B：_____。
A：为什么？
B：_____。

A：快递员送快递的要求是什么？
B：_____。
A：你觉得容易做到吗？
B：_____。

A：你常和快递员打交道吗？
B：_____。
A：他们的工作让你满意吗？
B：_____。

A："快递小哥"这个词挺有意思的，你还知道别的词吗？
B：_____。
A：这个词是什么意思？
B：_____。

四、选词填空。
Choose the appropriate words to fill in the blanks.

一年到头　赶紧　歇　逢年过节　吃不消　打交道　夜宵　早出晚归　平均　亲切

53 快递与外卖（一）

1. 我和他_____过几次_____。
2. 看，绿灯亮了，我们_____过去。
3. 没想到在这儿能看到家乡的特产，感觉特别_____。
4. 爸爸最近经常加班，我有点儿担心他的身体_____。
5. _____每天有上千名游客来这儿旅行。
6. 在中国，_____的时候大家都喜欢去亲戚朋友家聚一聚，热闹热闹。
7. 快过来，我给你准备了_____。
8. 小王，你最近_____的，在忙什么呢？
9. 谢谢你们帮我搬家，先喝口水，_____一_____吧。
10. 听说快递员_____都难得休息一下。

五、你了解快递员的工作吗？你对他们的工作有什么样的看法？

Do you know about the job of couriers? What is your opinion of their job?

第五十四课　快递与外卖（二）

Lesson 54　Express Delivery and Takeout (II)

课文 Text

在课外

山　口：珍妮、杰克，中午去食堂吃饭吗？

珍　妮：不去，我想吃汉堡了。杰克，你想吃汉堡吗？

杰　克：我一连几天都吃汉堡，有点儿吃腻了。

山　口：那咱们吃什么？

杰　克：学校附近新开了一家四川特色风味小吃，听说特别地道，还能送外卖，我想尝尝。

珍　妮：那儿有什么招牌菜？给我们介绍介绍吧。

杰　克：水煮鱼、酸辣粉、麻辣香锅……

山　口：这些菜，我连听都没听过，你这样介绍，我们还是不知道是什么菜啊。

杰　克：没关系，咱们在网上看看他们的菜品介绍，你们就知道这些菜什么样了。

山　口：这些菜看起来都挺辣的。

杰　克：对，四川菜是以麻辣闻名的。

珍　妮：太好了，我特别喜欢吃辣的。

54 快递与外卖（二）

杰　克：那你今天有口福了。

珍　妮：嗬，这就是你刚才介绍的水煮鱼吗？看起来真辣！

杰　克：怎么，不敢吃了？

珍　妮：谁说的？来一份水煮鱼！

杰　克：山口想吃什么？

山　口：我想吃面条儿。

杰　克：你看这个"担担面"怎么样？

山　口：看起来不错，也不太辣的样子，那我就吃担担面吧。

杰　克：我再来一个麻婆豆腐。好，下单了。你们看，这儿显示已经接单，待会儿就会有外卖小哥给咱们送过来了。

山　口：还是点外卖方便。不用出门，饭菜就给咱们送到家了。一般多长时间能送到呢？

杰　克：一般是半个小时左右。不过也说不好，因为现在正是送餐的高峰时段，也是餐厅客人最多的时候。

珍　妮：对，现在生活节奏快，很多上班的白领中午休息时间短，所以大部分都会选择在网上订外卖。点餐的时间基本上集中在每天中午12点前后，所以外卖送过来的时间也就不能保证了。

杰　克：外卖小哥也想每一份订单都能准时送到。这说起来简单，要做到却不容易。要是赶上刮风下雨，就难免会超时。

珍　妮：我昨天还看到一个新闻。一个大楼电梯维修，所以外卖小哥只好爬上12层去送餐。

山　口：外卖小哥也真不容易，所以我们都应该宽容一点儿，互相理解才对。

杰　克：等外卖送到了，咱们给外卖小哥写个好评吧！

生词
New Words

1.	一连	yìlián	in a row, in succession
2.	腻	nì	tired of
3.	特色	tèsè	characteristic, special
4.	地道	dìdao	authentic
5.	煮	zhǔ	to boil
6.	鱼	yú	fish
7.	酸	suān	sour
8.	辣	là	hot, spicy
9.	粉	fěn	noodles made from flour, bean or sweet potato starch
10.	麻	má	tongue-numbing
11.	锅	guō	pot
12.	连	lián	even
13.	菜品	càipǐn	variety of dishes
14.	闻名	wénmíng	famous
15.	口福	kǒufú	luck to get sth. nice to eat
16.	敢	gǎn	to dare
17.	担	dàn	carrying pole
18.	婆	pó	old woman
19.	豆腐	dòufu	tofu, bean curd
20.	显示	xiǎnshì	to show, to indicate
21.	高峰	gāofēng	peak
22.	时段	shíduàn	time period
23.	节奏	jiézòu	pace, tempo
24.	基本上	jīběn shang	basically
25.	集中	jízhōng	to concentrate, to focus
26.	赶上	gǎnshàng	to encounter, to come across
27.	难免	nánmiǎn	inevitable

28. 超	chāo	to exceed, to surpass
29. 电梯	diàntī	elevator
30. 维修	wéixiū	to maintain, to repair
31. 宽容	kuānróng	tolerant
32. 好评	hǎopíng	good comment

专 名 Proper Noun

四川	Sìchuān	Sichuan Province

注 释 Notes

1 "一连",副词,表示动作连续不断或情况连续发生,强调数量多或时间长。例如:

一连, an adverb, indicates that an action or a situation happens continuously, emphasizing the large number or long time. For example:

1. 一连下了三天雨。
2. 今天一连参加了好几个会议。
3. 他太饿了,一连吃了十个包子。

2 "腻",形容词,表示因过多而厌烦。例如:

腻, an adjective, means being tired of something because it is too much. For example:

1. 他那些话我都听腻了。
2. 这个电影看了好几遍了,我已经看腻了。
3. 吃腻了大鱼大肉,来点儿清粥小菜吧。

3 "连",介词,有"甚至"的意思,常跟"也、都"等搭配用,组成"连……也/都……"的格式,用来表示强调。例如:

连, a preposition, means "even". It is often used together with 也 or 都 in the form of "连……也/都……" to indicate emphasis. For example:

1. 连我都不怕，难道你怕？
2. 我连做梦也没有想过会成为百万富翁。
3. 现在，我真的成功了。在这以前，我连想都不敢想。

4 "赶上"，动词，遇到。例如：

赶上, a verb, means encountering something. For example:

1. 我们赶上了互联网发展得最迅速的时候。
2. 今天去超市，正好赶上打折。

也可以是"来得及"的意思。例如：

It also means "there's still time". For example:

1. 快点儿走，也许还能赶上末班车。
2. 离开车只有十分钟了，恐怕赶不上了。

练 习
Exercises

一、替换练习。

Substitution drills.

<u>四川菜</u>以<u>麻辣</u>闻名。

杭州	优美的风景
这家饭馆	价格实惠
全聚德	北京烤鸭

A：你最近忙不忙？
B：<u>很忙</u>，一连<u>工作了好几天</u>。

累不累	很累	加了十天的班
忙不忙	不忙	休息了五天
想不想吃西餐	不想	吃了七八天了

54 快递与外卖（二）

A：在大城市里，如果想去远一点儿的地方，应该提前出门，免得耽误事儿。

B：对，我上周三就是赶上了<u>堵车</u>，所以<u>上班迟到了</u>。

> 天气不好　　上课迟到了
> 高峰时段　　耽误了坐火车
> 交通事故　　考试迟到了

二、把下面的词组成句子。
Rearrange the following words into sentences.

1. 听说　地道　饭馆　四川菜　的　很　家　那
2. 高峰　堵车　时段　容易　出行　最
3. 外卖　适应　上班族　了　需求　的
4. 答案　的　连　小孩儿　问题　知道　这个　都
5. 杰克　了　吃　已经　每天　汉堡　腻　吃
6. 难免　困难　中　各种　遇到　工作
7. 越来越　了　节奏　现在　的　生活　快
8. 基本上　了　懂　今天　的　我　课文　听
9. 吧　维修　正在　我们　楼梯　电梯　走
10. 一点儿　互相　宽容　我们　应该　理解

三、完成下面的对话。
Complete the following dialogues.

A：你常常叫外卖吗？
B：_____。
A：一般什么时候叫外卖？
B：_____。

A：你在接到外卖小哥送来的外卖时会说什么？
B：_____。
A：为什么？
B：_____。

A：你会给外卖小哥好评还是差评？
B：_____。
A：为什么？
B：_____。

A：我太生气了！
B：_____？
A：_____。
B：别生气了，大家应该相互理解。

四、选词填空。

Choose the appropriate words to fill in the blanks.

  腻 风味 连 好评 口福 招牌菜 基本上 闻名 维修 难免

1. 他的服务太周到了，给他写个_____吧。
2. 这首歌我早就听_____了。
3. 哇，这么多好吃的！我今天有_____了。
4. 空调坏了，请李师傅来_____一下吧。
5. 麻烦你给我介绍一下这儿的_____吧。
6. _____大人都搬不动，更不用说小孩儿了。
7. 尝尝，这是天津的_____小吃，好吃吗？
8. 这个会议的准备工作_____已经做完了。
9. 这句话有点儿过分，他听到_____会生气。
10. 西湖的风景特别漂亮，远近_____。

五、说一说你点外卖的经历。

Talk about your experiences of ordering takeouts.

英 译 课 文

English Translation of the Texts

Lesson 29 Travel by High-Speed Rail (I)

(In class)

Professor Wang: Guys, do you want to travel during the holiday?

Jenny: Yes, all of us plan to.

Professor Wang: How will you travel?

Jack: By bike! China is the kingdom of bikes. I will have many fellow travelers.

Jenny: There are many cycling enthusiasts in China. I also like to ride a bike to places nearby for physical exercise. But it would be tiring to ride to places far away.

Jack: Then you can take a plane. When traveling in the U.S., we either drive a car or take a plane.

Jenny: Why don't you take a train?

Jack: It is inconvenient because there are only a few railways there.

Jenny: When traveling in Europe, people either drive their own cars or take trains instead of taking planes.

Yamaguchi: Countries in Europe are quite near to each other. Due to the short journey and convenient railways, people can drive or take trains. It is similar in Japan.

Professor Wang: Countries differ from each other in terms of this. How about China?

Jenny: I heard from my Chinese friend that Chinese people used to travel by train, which was time-consuming and tiring.

Yamaguchi: But now private cars are quite popular in China. With the increasing number of expressways, many families love to drive to travel.

Jack:	Now the speed of high-speed trains can reach 200-300 km/h. The increased speed and cheap price make high-speed rail travel convenient and fast.
Professor Wang:	Yes, you are right! Traveling in China by private car, high-speed rail, or plane are all good options. You can talk about your plan of traveling in China after class.

Lesson 30   Travel by High-Speed Rail (II)

(After class)

Jack:	Yamaguchi, you have come back!
Yamaguchi:	Yes. When did you come back?
Jack:	I came back yesterday. Where have you been? Did you have a good time?
Yamaguchi:	I went to Dunhuang. I love ancient Chinese culture. Dunhuang grottos and frescos have a history of over one thousand years. That is really great!
Jack:	How did you get there?
Yamaguchi:	I took the high-speed rail to Lanzhou first and traveled along the way to Dunhuang.
Jenny:	I also love ancient Chinese culture like you.
Jack:	Where have you been?
Jenny:	I went to Yangtze River Delta. Wuzhen in Zhejiang and Zhouzhuang in Jiangsu have many old houses and streets of ancient China. Wupeng boats come and go in the net of rivers where girls sing melodies. Wooden buildings stand along the river bank. Water flows beneath little bridges. The peach trees are in bloom and the willows are turning green. It is really fascinating!
Yamaguchi:	Are they that beautiful?
Jenny:	Of course. You must go there if you have a chance. "Up above there is Paradise, down here there are Suzhou and Hangzhou."

Yamaguchi:	I want to go there now after hearing your words. By the way, how did you get there?
Jenny:	By high-speed rail, of course. China's high-speed rail is great because it is fast, safe, smooth, and comfortable. How about you, Jack? Where did you go?
Jack:	I went to Hainan.
Yamaguchi:	Did you take the high-speed rail, too?
Jack:	No, it is so far that I can only take the plane.
Yamaguchi:	Air tickets are very expensive and you cannot enjoy the scenery on the way. I prefer the high-speed rail.
Jenny:	I think plane and high-speed rail both have their own advantages. Did you have fun in Hainan, Jack?
Jack:	It is very beautiful there. I enjoyed the sea, sunshine and sand beach very much. I swam and surfed in the water and drank cola and listened to music on the beach. It was really a wonderful experience.
Yamaguchi:	Are there many foreigners there?
Jack:	There are many foreigners as well as Chinese. With the convenient transportation, many people take a holiday there in winter.
Jenny:	Let's travel there together next winter!

Lesson 31 What Is Your Favorite Food (I)

(In class)

Professor Wang:	Everybody, are you used to Chinese food now?
Yamaguchi:	Yes, I'm quite used to it.
Jenny:	I like eating Chinese food too.
Jack:	Come on, you bought a hamburger at McDonald's when you were at Wangfujing yesterday.
Jenny:	It was twelve o'clock and I was hungry.
Professor Wang:	Is Chinese food more delicious or Western food?
Jenny:	Both are delicious.

Jack:	Professor, I know there are McDonald's and KFC everywhere in Beijing. Their business is extremely booming. Does it mean that the Chinese also like Western food?
Professor Wang:	Yes, many people do.
Jack:	Why?
Professor Wang:	Let me ask you this question first. Aren't there many Chinese restaurants in your country?
Jack:	Yes, each city at least has several of them, and some may have as many as dozens.
Professor Wang:	How's their business then?
Jenny:	Quite thriving too.
Professor Wang:	Good. Now you can tell me why Westerners like Chinese food.
Jenny:	Yamaguchi, you're from the Orient and are more familiar with the dietary habits of the Oriental people. Will you be the first to answer the professor's question?
Yamaguchi:	Chinese cuisine pays special attention to the color, fragrance, taste and shape.
Jack:	What do you mean by the color, fragrance, taste and shape?
Yamaguchi:	They refer to the color, fragrance, taste and design of the dishes.
Jack:	Is there anything special?
Yamaguchi:	Let me put it this way. As soon as you take your seat and start choosing your dishes from the menu, you will smell a fragrance. As soon as the dish is placed on your table, the color will prompt you to use the chopsticks and have a bite. Oh, the taste, ah...
Jenny:	Just like the ad for Nescafé: "The taste is great!" Isn't it?
Jack:	When you put it this way, I wish I could go and have a good meal right now. Oh, and what about the shape?
Yamaguchi:	Oh, it looks just like a work of art.
Jenny:	But Yamaguchi was referring to the regular meals with rice

	and fried dishes. I like Beijing snacks better.
Jack:	What is so special about Beijing snacks?
Jenny:	I don't know how to put it. But tomorrow I can take you to try it by yourself.
Jack:	Much as we have said, how can we answer the professor's question then?
Yamaguchi:	I think for the Chinese to like Western food and the Westerners to enjoy Chinese food, it is also probably a form of cultural exchange.
Jenny:	It is to satisfy their curiosity, and everybody has curiosity.

Lesson 32 What Is Your Favorite Food (II)

(After class)

(Jenny knocks on the door.)

Jenny:	Jack! Jack!
Jack:	Who's that?
Jenny:	It's me, Jenny. Please get up quickly.
Jack:	What time is it now?
Jenny:	A quarter past seven.
Jack:	Why so early? I want to get more sleep.
Jenny:	That won't do. Didn't you want to go to the morning market? If you get up late, it will wind up business for the day.
Jack:	OK. Just a minute.
Jenny:	Jack, look! Along this street there's a whole row of snack stands.
Jack:	Oh, what a good smell! What do they sell?
Jenny:	This is a Tianjin-style snack, "pancake roll with crisp fritter". *Shifu* (address for a skilled man), I would like two pancake rolls.
Peddler:	OK. Two pancake rolls.

Jenny:	Jack, how do you like it?
Jack:	Mm, not bad. Soft outside and crisp inside. It's really special.
Jenny:	Look, here are deep-fried twisted dough sticks and fried glutinous rice cakes. They are all newly fried. And there are wontons and soybean milk, which are Beijingers' favorites. Do you want to have a taste of them?
Jack:	OK. The soybean milk smells and tastes sweet, very good indeed. And the wontons taste good too.
Jenny:	Let's walk on. Ahead of us there are snacks, such as stuffed buns, sesame seed cakes, and fried sugar cakes, an extremely large variety indeed. Let's go and have a taste of them all.
Jack:	Oh, I can't eat any more today. I have eaten so much that I'm bursting at the seams. We can come again some other day.
Jenny:	We can have a look even if we don't want to eat any more.

(Yamaguchi, Jack and Jenny are in a shopping mall.)

Yamaguchi:	Jack, I hear that there is a food court in this shopping mall. I feel hungry after so much walking. Let's go have something to eat.
Jenny:	In doing business, the Chinese now pay special attention to the profits. And they are now much more flexible than ever before. Look, there is a food court in the shopping mall.
Jack:	You are right.
Yamaguchi:	Lots of people have come shopping. When they are hungry, they can have something to eat. After eating, they can go on shopping. Neither need is neglected.
Jack:	Just like what we are doing now.
Yamaguchi:	Look, there are McDonald's, KFC and many Chinese snack bars.
Jenny:	Hey, don't just talk. I'm starving!

Lesson 33   What is in Vogue This Year (I)

(In class)

Professor Wang: Did you go to the fashion show yesterday?

Jenny: We all did.

Professor Wang: What is your impression?

Yamaguchi: It is very impressive and really beautiful!

Jenny: With a great variety and new styles, it has both Chinese fashionable dresses and many world-famous brands.

Jack: Sir, I found almost all the world's most popular styles in the show.

Jenny: Yes. The popular styles appearing on the market in France this year are seen there. The Chinese market keeps pace with the fashion trend!

Jack: I have heard that in some high-end fashion boutiques in China, a suit costs nearly 10,000 *yuan*, a sweater is nearly a thousand *yuan*, a pair of shoes is several hundred *yuan*, and even a pair of socks costs nearly a hundred *yuan*, and there are many buyers.

Jenny: Chinese people's consumption level has risen.

Yamaguchi: There are French fashionable dresses in the show too. They are beautiful but too expensive.

Jenny: You want to look pretty and yet you are reluctant to spend money?

Yamaguchi: But French fashions change too fast. What was popular last year is no longer in vogue this year. To buy them every year costs too much money.

Jack: That's true. French fashions lead world trends. That's what you pay for keeping abreast with the trends.

Yamaguchi: I'm not keeping abreast with the trends. I simply can't resist the temptation.

Jenny: In fact, there are middle- and low-grade fashionable dresses as well as top-grade ones. There are inexpensive ones as well as expensive ones.

Jack:	I think top-grade dresses are all expensive, but famous brands are not necessarily expensive dresses of the top grade.
Professor Wang:	Mm, maybe what Jack said is more accurate.
Jack:	For instance, Levi Strauss and Co. is a genuine world-famous brand. Its jeans are available everywhere, whether in Paris, London, Beijing or Tokyo. But there are middle- and low-grade ones as well as top-grade ones.
Yamaguchi:	From this point of view, the Chinese cheongsam is also a world-famous commodity. It is very popular in many places in the world.
Professor Wang:	That's true. Unfortunately, it doesn't have a resounding trademark.

Lesson 34 What is in Vogue This Year (II)

(After class)

Yamaguchi:	Jenny, I've got tickets for today's Chinese fashion show. Would you like to go with me?
Jack:	Hey, I'd like to go too.
Jenny:	Look here. Yamaguchi didn't invite you.
Yamaguchi:	What's the hurry? How could I forget you? Here you are!
Jenny:	Yamaguchi, where is the show?
Yamaguchi:	At China World Trade Center.
Jack:	What is a Chinese fashion show like?
Yamaguchi:	You won't know until you see it. Once you see it, you'll be given a fright.
Jack:	A fright? That's scary. I won't go then.
Jenny:	You're a complete outsider again! It's not scary; it's amazing.
Yamaguchi:	You would be fascinated as soon as you see it.
Jack:	Really? Is it that good?
Jenny:	I once saw a Chinese fashion show in Paris.

Jack:	Tell us about it. In detail, please.
Jenny:	Chinese fashionable dresses are mostly made of Chinese silk. They are trendy, bright, with a national style and a feel of the times too.
Jack:	What about the models?
Jenny:	They are perfect. Each and everyone is an Oriental beauty...
Jack:	Be quick. We can't miss the chance.
Jenny:	Look how anxious you are! You asked me to explain to you in detail, and I haven't finished yet...
Yamaguchi:	Jack, what do you think of the fashion show we just watched?
Jack:	I am very impressed. It is by no means inferior to the French fashion shows.
Jenny:	Hold it! You were fascinated by the models.
Jack:	That you don't understand. Haven't you always wanted to compete with the models to see who is more beautiful?
Jenny:	So what?
Jack:	Then you have to go and buy a dress that they are displaying, dressing up as beautifully as they do. Is that right?
Jenny:	That's right.
Jack:	You see, in this way fashionable dresses get a good market.
Jenny:	Oh, you know quite a lot about the knack of doing business.
Jack:	Naturally.
Yamaguchi:	Forget it. Don't be too proud of yourself. Look, there is a whole row of fashion shops along this street. Don't you want to go and make your choice? There may be some fashionable dresses too.
Jenny:	That's just what I want to do. This summer miniskirts are in vogue. I don't know whether they sell them here.
Yamaguchi:	Look, isn't that what the Chinese girl is trying on?
Jack:	Jenny, do you want me to help you choose, so you can dress

	up as beautifully as the models do?
Jenny:	Are you capable of that?
Jack:	What? You don't believe me? Do you think I have watched today's fashion show for nothing?

Lesson 35   Internet + (I)

(In class)

Professor Wang:	Do you think life in China is convenient?
Jack:	I find it convenient. You do not have to buy things in stores but can get anything you want online.
Jenny:	I also like online shopping. There are a rich variety of goods available online for you to compare and choose from. After paying, the goods will be delivered to you. It is so convenient!
Yamaguchi:	Right. You also don't need to go to restaurants for meals now. The takeaway ordered online can usually be delivered within half an hour.
Professor Wang:	So how about going out?
Jenny:	It is also very convenient to go out. You can take the subway or the bus, call a taxi online, or ride a shared bike.
Professor Wang:	You are right. Now people's lives are increasingly inseparable from the Internet, and we have entered an era of "Internet +".
Jack:	I have never ridden a shared bike. What does it have to do with the Internet?
Jenny:	If you want to ride a shared bike, you have to scan the QR code with your mobile phone and pay online. Of course it is connected with the Internet!
Jack:	So it is. So what kind of people like to ride shared bikes?
Yamaguchi:	College students, for example me. I like to ride a shared bike. The campus is too large. It is far from the dormitory to the canteen and from the canteen to the classroom. Walking

	is too time-consuming.
Jack:	If you sleep in, you may not have time to eat and even be late for class.
Yamaguchi:	Don't mention it. I even feel ashamed. I was late for class several times because I got up too late. After I start to ride a shared bike, I've never delayed things.
Jenny:	I live at a Chinese friend's place. There is no bus or subway nearby. Before the appearance of shared bikes, I had to walk twenty minutes to the bus stop. Now with the shared bikes, it is much more convenient to go out.
Jack:	It seems that shared bikes really meet the needs of society and bring convenience to everyone.
Yamaguchi:	Yes, you can know where there are shared bikes from the phone. Also, a lot of office workers who work from 9:00 a.m. to 6:00 p.m. love shared bikes like me. They can finish the last kilometer by bike.
Jack:	Hearing what you said, I think shared bikes are really convenient. After class, I will also have a try.
Jenny:	China's Internet technology is very advanced. Coupled with a precise positioning system, it will be more convenient and faster to use shared bikes.
Yamaguchi:	There are also shared electric bikes and cars. Maybe there will be shared houses too in the future!
Professor Wang:	Yamaguchi is right. With the development of Internet technology, there will certainly be more interesting inventions.

Lesson 36   Internet + (II)

(After class)

Jack:	Jenny, Yamaguchi, what do you want to do this weekend?
Yamaguchi:	I do not remember some of the words learned this week and need to review them. I also need to practice my grammar

	because the exam is coming up next week.
Jenny:	I'm not like you. I'm almost exhausted after studying for a week. I'm going to have a good rest and sleep in the dorm!
Jack:	It is a negative kind of rest. I have a suggestion.
Jenny:	What?
Jack:	Let's go out for fun on the weekend.
Yamaguchi:	Where to go?
Jack:	Let's ride shared bikes all around Beijing together. I've long thought of having a try. It must be great riding a bike while watching the scenery.
Yamaguchi:	Beijing is so big and riding a bike must be very tiring. Let's take a taxi to save time and effort and avoid getting lost.
Jenny:	Yes. It is very convenient to call a taxi online now. Click "taxi-hailing" and you will immediately see where you are, where the driver is, how far away he is from you, and how long it takes to pick you up. Click again and you can see the driver's information such as his name, phone number, license plate number, and so on. Taking a taxi is so convenient!
Jack:	Nevertheless, it is not environment-friendly, not a green trip!
Jenny:	You're right. We should make a little contribution to environmental protection. Riding a bike can reduce pollution as well as help build up the body. I also agree to ride a bike.
Yamaguchi:	OK! Jack, where are we going? We have been to famous places such as the Forbidden City, Beihai, and the Summer Palace.
Jack:	We will not go to these places. Let's ride along the second ring, which has beautiful sceneries such as water flowing in a small river and green trees and red flowers. We can also visit the Yonghegong Lama Temple, the Imperial Academy

	and the Grand View Garden. Then we can go from the second ring to the third ring, reaching the observation platform of the China Central Television Tower to have a bird's-eye view of Beijing. In short, there are a lot of interesting places and we will have great fun.
Jenny:	The plan sounds good. Now the weather is neither cold nor hot, and it's a good time to travel.
Jack:	The places I mentioned are the most beautiful recreation areas in Beijing. Biking in the avenue along the riverside in fresh air will make you comfortable both in body and in mind. You will certainly be satisfied!
Yamaguchi:	However, we have never been to these places. What if we get lost?
Jack:	That is easy to handle! As long as there is network, we can locate on the phone's electronic map and immediately know where to go.
Yamaguchi:	This is great! Then let's ride bikes on the weekend. We can build up our bodies, enjoy the beautiful scenery while protecting the environment.
Jenny:	Great! That's a deal!

Lesson 37 Festivals and Shopping (I)

(In class)

Professor Wang:	How long have you been in China?
Jack:	Jenny and I have been here for eight months.
Yamaguchi:	I've been here for almost a year.
Professor Wang:	Then you must have known a lot about Chinese festivals, right?
Jenny:	Sir, I know the Dragon Boat Festival, which falls on the fifth day of May in Chinese lunar calendar.
Jack:	I also know that people eat *zongzi* and race dragon boats on that day.

Professor Wang:	Do you like *zongzi*?
Jenny:	I love it very much. I also learned to make *zongzi*.
Yamaguchi:	I also know Mid-Autumn Festival on lunar August 15th. People reunite with their families and eat mooncakes on that day.
Professor Wang:	All of you are right. Do you know which is the most important traditional festival in China?
Jenny:	I know. It is the Spring Festival.
Yamaguchi:	I also heard about it from my Chinese friends. It is the day for family reunion. Before the Spring Festival, every household would get busy, buying new clothes and gifts for the family, preparing all kinds of food materials for the reunion dinner, and cleaning both inside and outside of the house.
Professor Wang:	Yes. In the past when e-commerce was underdeveloped, everybody had to go to stores to buy things and brought a lot of shopping bags back home. Now online shopping is quite convenient, and it is not as busy as before to prepare for the festival.
Jack:	It's about the same in the U.S. Everyone likes to buy things on Thanksgiving and Christmas when stores have special offers and things are particularly cheap. People would queue up in front of the shops in the early morning.
Jenny:	Jack is right. Thanksgiving and Christmas in the United States are both traditional festivals and shopping carnivals. The festival atmosphere is everywhere during these occasions every year, and people go happily to stores to select cheap products of good quality. But now they are getting used to online shopping carnivals too.
Yamaguchi:	Sir, are the shopping carnivals in China also during the traditional festivals?
Professor Wang:	China's grandest online shopping carnival is not during

	the traditional festivals, but on November 11th every year, which is also known as the "Double 11th Shopping Carnival".
Jack:	But I heard that "Double 11th" was originally "Singles' Day". How did it become a shopping carnival?
Professor Wang:	Single young people love to play, enjoy crowds, and are willing to spend money. They are ready to accept new things and like to kill time by shopping online. Therefore, clever businessmen took advantage of this psychology and started large-scale promotion on the e-commerce platform while adding fun and creating a carnival atmosphere, thus attracting a lot of people and creating the "Double 11th Shopping Carnival" now.
Jack:	I also heard that more than 200 countries and regions have participated in China's "Double 11th" this year and eventually the transaction volume has exceeded 100 billion *yuan*.
Professor Wang:	Yes. Now young people and old people, and Chinese and foreigners alike participate in the shopping carnival. "Double 11th" has become a real shopping carnival.

Lesson 38 Festivals and Shopping (II)

(After class)

Jack:	Jenny, Yamaguchi, have you ever participated in any shopping carnivals?
Jenny:	I rushed to buy things in stores at Christmas.
Yamaguchi:	How did you feel?
Jenny:	There were a lot of people, but everyone was happy. As many products with no discount at ordinary times are remarkably discounted during Christmas, you need to queue up early. Otherwise you may not get your favorite products.

Yamaguchi:	Then did you get them?
Jenny:	Of course! I bought three full bags of things and there was even not enough room for them in my car!
Yamaguchi:	That was really crazy!
Jenny:	Otherwise it would not be called a shopping carnival!
Jack:	Me, too. The sports shoes I wanted were $1000 at ordinary times but only $600 on sale. I bought two pairs at the sight of the low price. It was the only chance. Who knows whether there will be any discount next year?
Yamaguchi:	I have participated only once. I bought many discounted goods during a big sales promotion one year.
Jack:	And then?
Yamaguchi:	Then I found that some products were only a bit cheaper and some others seemed to be cheap at the time but useless after I thought it over. They are still at my home now.
Jenny:	So you rarely participate later.
Yamaguchi:	Right. I think it's better to rest at home instead of buying a bunch of unwanted things on holidays.
Jenny:	Actually, I am just like you. When seeing cheap things, I always think of buying a little more whether I need them or not. But I often come to regret it later.
Jack:	I think the businessmen are taking advantage of consumers' impulse spending and bringing so many shopping carnivals.
Yamaguchi:	Yes. Some products you find too expensive in normal times are on sale and you certainly want to buy them; some are not needed at all but you will also buy them due to the low price. With so many buyers, the businessmen may make more money than usual!
Jenny:	The businessmen are really good at doing business.
Yamaguchi:	Yes. You see, e-commerce is now more and more developed, and thus the "Double 11th Shopping Carnival" appears, which attracts many people who do not have time to go to physical stores. I heard that it sold more than

physical stores.

Jack: So when we go shopping next time, we must first think about whether we really need the things to avoid being dazzled by discounts.

Jenny: Jack is right. We should treat the shopping carnivals calmly and spend rationally so as not to be out of control when shopping and regret after purchase.

Lesson 39   McDonald's and Teahouse (I)

(In class)

Professor Wang: Do you know what McDonald's sells?

Jack: What does McDonald's sell? It sells hamburgers of course.

Professor Wang: What else?

Jack: Beverages.

Professor Wang: And time, service, and quality as well.

Jack: McDonald's sells time?

Jenny: Oh, I see. At McDonald's, it takes only 40 seconds to prepare a hamburger patty. And it is only a few minutes between the time one orders drinks and hamburgers and the time when they are placed before the customer. It is really fast. It's most time-saving to eat there.

Yamaguchi: French fries are the specialty of McDonald's. It is said that they have strict quality requirements on the size, color and sugar content of the potatoes.

Jack: And their services are impeccable, always considerate and warm. From the boss to the employees, they all wear a smile on their faces. It is indeed a nice, clean, relaxing and comfortable place.

Jenny: The prices there are very reasonable too. A combo meal costs only twenty-something. Regular customers can all afford it.

Professor Wang:	You are right. People working at McDonald's say that they aim for quality, friendliness, cleanliness and value.
Jack:	I think they have relied on such aims in winning Chinese customers.
Jenny:	Jack, have you ever been to Lao She Teahouse?
Jack:	Yes, I have.
Jenny:	What does Lao She Teahouse sell?
Jack:	I know you are going to say that Lao She Teahouse does not sell tea, but it sells time...
Jenny:	Who says that? Lao She Teahouse of course sells tea. But it is not an ordinary teahouse.
Jack:	What does that mean?
Jenny:	Was there someone singing a Beijing opera while you were drinking your tea?
Jack:	Yes, and some customers also went up the stage to sing.
Jenny:	Appreciating Beijing opera while sipping tea and appraising its flavor. How does it feel?
Jack:	Mm, that must be a wonderful feeling.
Yamaguchi:	I know there are magic performances too.
Jack:	McDonald's, Lao She Teahouse, Beijing opera, and magic, they are modern and classical at the same time. How interesting! This is the diversified Chinese market, full of Chinese characteristics.
Yamaguchi:	Jenny, look, Jack is voicing his brilliant ideas again.

Lesson 40   McDonald's and Teahouse (II)

(After class)

Jack:	Good afternoon, Mister and Miss.
Mr. Qian:	Good afternoon.
Jack:	May we sit here and chat with you?
Mr. Qian:	Welcome. Please sit down. Waiter, another three bowls of

	tea, please. Let's have a chat over the tea.
Jack:	Thank you. May I ask, Mister and Miss, you are...
Mr. Qian:	Isn't today the day for Hongniang's (matchmaker) Tea Gathering?
Jenny:	Oh, you are dating here.
Yamaguchi:	Look, you do have a loose tongue. The young lady is blushing.
Mr. Qian:	It's all right. This is our first meeting anyway and both of us are a bit ill at ease.
Jack:	How come you have arranged to meet here?
Mr. Qian:	We are both single and older than the average age for marriage. So we came to this teahouse to register. When they have found us a suitable partner, we are arranged for a date here on the Hongniang's Tea Gathering Day.
Jack:	Now that you can try to find a marriage partner through TV or newspaper, why do you come to a teahouse for this reason?
Mr. Qian:	It's a convenient place for a chat, and the price is reasonable.
Miss Zhang:	To do it through TV or newspaper is not only expensive, but also makes yourself look like a fool. It's very embarrassing and I do not have the courage.
Mr. Qian:	It's not crowded here, and very quiet too. You can set a date to meet here, sit together, listen to Beijing opera and chat over a cup of tea. How comfortable and informal! It is a rest and a serious matter at the same time, killing two birds with one stone.
Jenny:	Miss, have you taken a fancy to each other?
Miss Zhang:	You'd better ask him.
Mr. Qian:	Yes, yes, we have.
Jenny:	Is it that easy? Then I should also come and register.
Jack:	What? Do you want to get a Chinese young man too?
Jenny:	Why? Can't I?

Jack:	It isn't that you can't. I'm afraid you may not have the courage to do so.
Jenny:	Manager, how did you hit upon the idea of holding a Hongniang's Tea Gathering?
Manager:	Oh, the Chinese like to while away their time at teahouses. They may stay as long as half a day. They chat over a cup of tea about domestic trivia, interesting news of the city, important events in the world and what not. We have many people coming here, and naturally the teahouse becomes a place for the exchange and spreading of information.
Jack:	It seems that Lao She Teahouse doesn't have a Hongniang's Tea Gathering.
Manager:	You're right. Now Beijing has many teahouses or tea-drinking places, and each of them has its own characteristics. Lao She Teahouse can be called a cultural teahouse.
Jenny:	And yours can be called a Hongniang teahouse then?
Manager:	Yes.
Yamaguchi:	Then, are there other types of teahouses?
Manager:	Yes. For instance there is a kind of "public relations teahouse", where the customers can exchange information about the market condition and changes in supply and demand. They can also carry out business negotiations. Some of these teahouses have had computers installed. People can get information from the Internet whenever they want.
Jenny:	Do people go there to exchange information and hold business talks?
Manager:	Yes, of course. The volume of business is quite large too, and the teahouse has a thriving business.
Jack:	It seems to me that the most important thing in running a shop is to develop its own characteristics.

Lesson 41   The Taste Is Great (I)

(In class)

Professor Wang: Everybody, do you know the importance of trademarks and commercials?

Jack: I know. A trademark represents the quality and reputation of a commodity.

Yamaguchi: A trademark is also the property and life of an enterprise.

Jenny: It is also a means for the commodity to compete in the market.

Professor Wang: All of you are right. Can you give one or two examples?

Yamaguchi: Panasonic electric appliances, Mercedes-Benz cars and Coca-Cola are all world-famous. Their trademarks represent quality, good reputation and strong competitiveness.

Jack: I hear that the Coca-Cola trademark is worth 70 billion US dollars, accounting for three quarters of the company's assets.

Jenny: When people buy a commodity, they often look at the trademark first. The better the reputation of the trademark, the easier it will win over customers. When I buy, I aim for famous brands only.

Professor Wang: This is a universal consumer psychology.

Jack: That is the reason why entrepreneurs, amidst fierce market competition, go all out to advertise so as to increase the fame of their commodities and trademarks. Is that right?

Professor Wang: That's right. Now, the Chinese market is brisk, and you can see ads everywhere. Can you mention some trademarks and ads that have made the deepest impression on you?

Yamaguchi: Jack, do you know what is the most widespread ad in China currently?

Jack: Yes, I do. "Mm, the taste is great!"

Jenny: You look so pleased with yourself that I would like to have a cup of Nescafé now.

Yamaguchi: This applies not just to Nescafé. Now both men and women,

	old and young, no matter what they eat, if you ask them how it is and if they feel satisfied, they will say: "Mm, the taste is great!"
Jenny:	It is a really good message.
Yamaguchi:	There are many more good messages. The largest household appliance manufacturer in China—Haier—has a loud message that goes...
Jack:	"Haier, made in China!"
Yamaguchi:	The message for Midea air conditioning goes like this...
Jack:	"It turns out that life can be more pleasant (homophone of 'Midea' in Chinese)!"
Yamaguchi:	And for Coca-Cola?
Jack:	"Forever Coca-Cola, forever the taste!"
Yamaguchi:	For Macro water heaters?
Jack:	"Macro makes myriad households happy."
Yamaguehi:	Lenovo computers?
Jack:	"Lenovo makes the world a better place."
Yamaguchi:	Jack really knows a lot.
Jack:	To learn Chinese, you can't help remembering these extremely clever words.

Lesson 42   The Taste Is Great (II)

(After class)

Jenny:	Yamaguchi, come and have a look at the characters written on the shopfront.
Yamaguchi:	"Guixiangcun", this is a food shop selling Chinese and Western pastries and sweets.
Jenny:	What do these two lines of characters say?
Yamaguchi:	"The color, fragrance and taste of famous pastries gather here."
Jack:	Er, I'm a bit hungry. Yamaguchi, how about giving us a treat by buying 250 grams of light refreshments? Seeing

	this message, I know that the taste must be excellent.
Yamaguchi:	250 grams? I won't even buy an ounce. We have just come out and you want to eat whatever you see? Let's go.
Jenny:	Yamaguchi, look. This is a restaurant.
Yamaguchi:	"With a smile, we welcome guests from all places, and you will have satisfaction of being in the capital."
Jack:	Let's go in and see whether we will be satisfied.
Yamaguchi:	Again? Let's go. There is the Xindong'an Market at Wangfujing. Not only can you buy things there, you can also find different styles of snacks. Let's go there to satisfy your craving for delicious food.
Jack:	Fine!
Jenny:	Wow, what a big, bustling shopping mall!
Yamaguchi:	Look here. "Buy one, get one free." And here, "spend 200 *yuan* and get 80 *yuan* returned" and "Clearance sale". There, "For a lucky start in business, we offer a 30% discount. Come and make your choice!" And there, "A prize-winning sale. A lucky draw on the spot. We wish you good luck!"
Jack:	"A prize-winning sale." That's good. Let's go and try our luck.
Jenny:	Jack, smell it. What a nice smell! Shouldn't you go get a bite to eat first?
Jack:	No hurry, no hurry. First let's go and try our luck. Maybe we can win a laptop computer.
Jenny:	You're daydreaming!
Jenny:	Gosh! After walking for a full day, I'm dog-tired. I just want to sit down and watch TV.
Yamaguchi:	Me too. Let me turn the TV on.
Jenny:	Commercials again! You watch and watch, but it's always the same old stuff. I'm tired of it.
Yamaguchi:	But there are many good commercials too, and I like

	watching them. Listen, "Stomach (homophone of 'hello' in Chinese), how are you?" "Take the white pill during the day, you won't feel sleepy; take the black one at night, you will have a sound sleep."
Jenny:	How come all the ads you like are for medicines?
Yamaguchi:	Sidashu cures stomach troubles, and White & Black is for the cold. I can't live without them.
Jenny:	Well, I remember some too. "I only use Lux." And, "L'Oréal of Paris, you deserve to have it."
Yamaguchi:	Why are you interested in these ads?
Jenny:	These ads feature movie stars who are adored by the Chinese people. These beauties use excellent cosmetics. What a feast for the eyes!
Yamaguchi:	Now I understand. No wonder more and more movie and singing stars are making ads. It is because of audiences like you.
Jenny:	Hey, I've always adored stars. And I think taking advantage of the charm of stars to promote sales is a smart practice. What do you think?

Lesson 43 Never Say "No" (I)

(In class)

Yamaguchi:	Professor, why do some shop assistants quarrel with customers? Didn't they undertake to "serve with a smile" and "look after customers with good manners"?
Jenny:	I once heard a customer mention "using money to buy a rage". What does that mean?
Jack:	That means the person spent money to buy things angrily.
Professor Wang:	Yes. At present the service in quite a number of shops is of poor quality and the customers are not satisfied. As a matter of fact, the Chinese businessmen have a tradition of first-rate service.

English Translation of the Texts

Jack:	I know that the Chinese merchants often say: "Amiability begets riches."
Professor Wang:	That's right. And "When business comes to the door, welcome it with a smile", "Even when the transaction is not concluded, friendship remains", "When friendly feelings are kept, they pave the way for the next meeting". Even if one doesn't buy this time, he will come again next time. In this way, you leave the door open for business.
Yamaguchi:	As you say, it is better to serve with a smile and look after customers with good manners. The more customers come back to buy, the more prosperous the business will become.
Professor Wang:	How do you think one can do a good job in "serving with a smile" then?
Jenny:	For a shop to do well in serving with a smile, the most important thing is never to say "no" to the customers. Jack, do you think so?
Jack:	Yes, that's right, because the customers' requirements are always reasonable.
Jenny:	OK then. Now I'm the customer and you are the shop assistant. You can't reject my requests and can't say "no" to me. And you are not supposed to use such words as "not have", "there isn't", or "don't".
Jack:	That's easy. If you don't believe me, we can give it a try.
Professor Wang:	Jack and Jenny, you can give us a demonstration.
Jack:	Sure.
Jack:	Hello, Miss. These are all the latest styles in this year. Come in and take a look.
Jenny:	This pair of shoes looks good.
Jack:	This is a famous brand, very popular now. You've got a sharp eye.
Jenny:	May I try them on?
Jack:	Sure. Here is one shoe. Please…, please step on this

	cardboard box lest it gets dirty.
Jenny:	Why don't you say "don't get the shoes dirty"?
Jack:	I am sure our customers will take good care of the new shoes.
Jenny:	Good. Let's go on. This pair is a bit small and it pinches. Please change...
Yamaguchi:	Hello, Jack!
Jack:	Oh, Yamaguchi, it's you.
Yamaguchi:	Are the Shanghai leather shoes that were on sale last time available today?
Jack:	They came in yesterday, but were sold out as soon as they were put on the counter.
Jenny:	Sir, you haven't changed the shoes for me yet.
Jack:	You...
Jenny:	Didn't you see...?
Jack:	Oh, I'm sorry. I've got something urgent to attend to. Please wait for a moment.
Jenny:	Good for you. The word "no" was on your lips and you swallowed it.
Jack:	Yamaguchi, this batch of shoes are even better than those you saw last time.
Yamaguchi:	Why didn't you keep one pair for me?
Jack:	As close as we are, how could I not? I've already wrapped a pair up for you. Here you are.
Jenny:	Sir, please change this pair of shoes for me...
Yamaguchi:	Jack, you are a true friend. I'd like to treat you to a movie tonight.
Jack:	Well, what movie, and where?
Yamaguchi:	It's an American movie, at the Capital Cinema.
Jenny:	Hey, sir! I've been waiting for a long time. Can't you save the chatter until later?
Jack:	Who is chatting? She is here to buy shoes too.
Jenny:	Weren't you talking about going to a movie?

Jack:	Who's talking about going to a movie? Did you make a recording?
Jenny:	Why are you being so utterly unreasonable?
Jack:	Are you being reasonable?
Jenny:	How can you talk like this? How can you treat your job, and your customer like this?
Jack:	What did I do wrong? You tell me how I should work! And how I should treat my customers!
Jenny:	Where is your manager? I want to make a complaint against you.
Jack:	Make a complaint? Please, go ahead. Miss, here is the suggestion book. As if I care!
Jenny:	You! Your service attitude is very bad. I would suggest that your manager have you fired.
Jack:	I'm wanting to start up my own business to make big money anyway. Just have me fired. I have been thinking of not doing this job for a long time.
Jenny:	Ha, ha. You finally used the word "not".
Jack:	Oh, did I really use the word "not"?!

Lesson 44 Never Say "No" (II)

(After class)

Jenny:	Yamaguchi, please come and have a look. What bad luck I have!
Yamaguchi:	What's the matter?
Jenny:	This is the trench coat I bought yesterday. Look, there is a run at the back. What should I do?
Yamaguchi:	A little, but not very obvious. It doesn't matter.
Jenny:	But wearing it is very disappointing.
Yamaguchi:	Then go and return it.
Jenny:	Return it? Can I do that?
Yamaguchi:	Probably.

Jenny: But I have heard that many shops announce "No returns on goods sold".

Yamaguchi: That was in the past. Now the market competition is becoming more and more intense and the businessmen are becoming wiser.

Jenny: There are new stipulations and new practices now?

Yamaguchi: Right. When a customer asks to return goods, they always have a reason. What the businessmen do now shows that they have customers' interests at heart.

Jenny: Exactly. Who would make a fuss over nothing and return satisfactory goods, thus getting oneself down?

Yamaguchi: So a shop which truly takes the customers into consideration would agree to return merchandise and respect the customers' right of selection.

Jenny: Well, the reasoning does go like that, but I don't know if they follow it.

Yamaguchi: We'll go and have a try.

Jenny: Great!

Jenny: Miss, this is the trench coat I bought here yesterday. It's faulty. Can I exchange it?

Shop assistant: Oh, I'm really sorry that you had to come again because of this. Let me have a look.

Yamaguchi: You see, what good service attitude she has!

Jenny: Don't praise her yet. She hasn't agreed to exchange it.

Shop assistant: Oh, it is of inferior quality. I'll go and exchange it for you. Please wait a moment.

Yamaguchi: How's that? I didn't put it wrong, did I? The Chinese market is brilliant. You can have new discovery every day.

Jenny: Why hasn't she come back after such a long time?

Yamaguchi: Maybe she was going to the storeroom to get it for you.

Shop assistant: Miss, I'm really sorry, but trench coats of this style have already been sold out.

Jenny:	Is there anything you can do? I like this trench coat very much. Can't you get in contact with the factory?
Shop assistant:	I got in contact with the factory just now. They only produce a small batch for each style, and now they have turned to other styles. This style is out of production.
Jenny:	If it can't be exchanged for another one, then I will have to return it.
Shop assistant:	What about we give you a discount?
Jenny:	But I don't feel good about paying several hundred *yuan* for an inferior product.
Yamaguchi:	Can't we return it? We can pay the service charge.
Shop assistant:	Of course you can return it. You don't need to pay any money. It's just that this young lady likes it so much. Though there is a flaw, it's not obvious. It's a pity to return it.
Yamaguchi:	I think it's better to return it. Yon can buy a new one next time you see something that fits. What do you say, Jenny?
Jenny:	Yes, Miss, please return it for me anyway.
Shop assistant:	OK. Please wait a minute.

Lesson 45 After Making a Promise (I)

(In class)

Jenny:	Mr. Wang, I often see on the walls of malls these words: "The shopping mall makes a solemn promise...". What does it mean?
Yamaguchi:	I sometimes hear customers say to the salesperson: "You should fulfill your promise."
Professor Wang:	Yes, many shopping malls now make promises to the customers. You can check the dictionary to see what "promise" means.
Jack:	Oh, I see. The shopping malls' "promise" is to ensure what kind of goods and services they provide for the customers.
Professor Wang:	You are right. Can you give an example?

Jack:	Exchange or refund is available when buying things online. Is that a promise?
Yamaguchi:	"Free installation of air conditioners" is also a promise, right?
Jenny:	And "replaceable within one year from the date of sale if anything goes wrong in regular use".
Professor Wang:	Yes, it seems that you know a lot.
Jenny:	Sir, can all these promises be fulfilled?
Professor Wang:	Most of them can.
Jack:	Yes. Take the exchange and refund service I mentioned for example. The online shops promise that goods can be exchanged or returned freely within seven days.
Jenny:	What if they fail to do so?
Jack:	Then they have to pay a fine.
Jenny:	Who pays?
Jack:	The online shop, of course!
Jenny:	That's great! Then I will not hesitate to buy things online anymore. I can buy whatever I want since I can return what I don't like freely.
Jack:	But you have to look at them carefully before purchase, for some goods, such as food, cannot be returned.
Yamaguchi:	Yes, although the businessmen make a promise, the customers should still think it over before buying to avoid trouble.
Jenny:	What if a physical store breaks a promise?
Yamaguchi:	You can make a complaint.
Jenny:	To whom?
Professor Wang:	To the local consumer associations and relevant departments. Now, the supervision is strengthened in all ways and the market order is regulated. Once a promise is made, the businessmen have to fulfill it.
Jenny:	It's good to have a promise!
Jack:	Of course. The customers can reason with the businessmen

	according to their promises. If they still find out all sorts of excuses and refuse to fulfill their promises, they may face a complaint or fine.

Professor Wang: Now in the buyer's market, the promise is forced out due to fierce competition. To attract more customers, the businessmen have to be honest and keep their word while improving management and service to win the trust of customers.

Jack: The businessmen can also improve themselves if the customers supervise them to fulfill their promises.

Yamaguchi: A promise also helps protect the customers' rights. We must know the promises before buying or doing things in the future.

Lesson 46 After Making a Promise (II)

(After class)

Jack: Will you really go traveling rather than go back home during the holiday?

Yamaguchi: Of course. It is the best chance to learn about China and learn Chinese.

Jenny: Jack, come with us!

Jack: Why? You want a labor force?

Jenny: Cash-for-work, OK?

Jack: Good! I'll carry your luggage and you bear all the costs of my travel.

Jenny: You wish! Is your labor worth so much?

Jack: I can also provide other services for you, such as making travel plans, booking tickets, arranging accommodation, buying tickets in tourist attractions, acting as the tour guide, and so on.

Yamaguchi: And seriously, will you go or not?

Jack: Of course I will. But where do you want to go?

Jenny:	Shanghai. Shanghai is a world-renowned international metropolis and shopping paradise with developed commerce.
Yamaguchi:	I also want to go to Suzhou and Hangzhou. Jenny said that they had beautiful scenery!
Jack:	But I want to go to Xishuangbanna in Yunnan, where the ethnic minorities' customs are quite appealing.
Yamaguchi:	Let's go to them all.
Jenny:	OK, that's a deal!
Yamaguchi:	Then how to save money and trouble in trip arrangements?
Jack:	Let's go self-guided. You can just enjoy yourselves. I'll take care of everything else.
Jenny:	You said it. Don't break your promise then.
Jack:	I won't!

(Two days later)

Jack:	Yamaguchi, Jenny, I have made the travel plan. If you agree, we can start immediately!
Jenny:	You do keep your word!
Jack:	Of course I do! First we go to Shanghai. It takes four to five hours from Beijing to Shanghai by high-speed rail.
Jenny:	Then we can leave in the morning and arrive in the afternoon.
Jack:	Right. I also booked a four-star hotel online which is not far from the Bund. We can have a rest after arriving in the afternoon, and then enjoy the beautiful night scene of the Bund!
Jenny:	This arrangement is great!
Jack:	Then we go to Suzhou and Hangzhou by train.
Yamaguchi:	Suzhou Gardens and Hangzhou's West Lake are among China's most famous scenic spots. I must take a lot of pictures!
Jack:	No problem. I'll be your photographer then!
Jenny:	How do we get to Xishuangbanna from Hangzhou? Also by

	train?
Jack:	Hangzhou is too far from Xishuangbanna, so we will take the plane.
Yamaguchi:	What's fascinating about Xishuangbanna?
Jack:	The scenery there is very beautiful. You can enjoy the tropical atmosphere different from Suzhou and Hangzhou, and participate in some interactive activities to experience them personally.
Jenny:	Interesting!
Yamaguchi:	I heard that there were elephant performances there. Can we interact with elephants, too?
Jack:	Of course we can!
Yamaguchi:	That is fascinating!
Jenny:	Jack, it seems that you really have prepared a lot. You are truly trustworthy!
Jack:	Of course I am! You need to keep your promise, right?

Lesson 47 A Career in Public Relations (I)

(In class)

Professor Wang:	Everybody, do you know what public relations work is about?
Jack:	Yes, I do. It's about establishing relationships.
Yamaguchi:	What did you say, Jack?
Jack:	At home one depends on one's parents, and away from home one relies on friends. To get things done, one has to have relations. When people meet, they talk about friendly relations. Anything can be done if one has good relations and wide contacts. That's the same no matter which country you are in.
Yamaguchi:	I don't think that's necessarily right.
Jack:	Not necessarily right? For instance, you work in a company that has imported electronic products which are extremely

	popular and difficult to obtain. Then I send you two bottles of expensive wine and treat you to a sumptuous dinner, so as to establish a relationship. Then I ask you to provide me with a batch of these goods. How could you turn down the request?
Yamaguchi:	It would be really difficult to reject it.
Jack:	Then I would trouble you, requesting you to help me.
Jenny:	And things get done like this?
Jack:	Of course. What's more, you lose your tongue after eating a dinner offered by others, and your hands get weak after taking gifts. How can you not comply with their requests?
Professor Wang:	Jack, what you mentioned just now belongs to unhealthy social phenomena, and is not the real PR work.
Yamaguchi:	Professor, what is the real PR work then?
Professor Wang:	Since you all have rich experiences, I'll let you discuss it among yourselves.
Jenny:	I once read a book about public relations. It says that PR work includes receiving clients, meeting and seeing them off, arranging accommodation, accompanying guests on tours and entertainments, and sending them champagne and fresh flowers, etc.
Yamaguchi:	These look like minor matters, but it is no easy job to handle these minor matters politely and appropriately so as to facilitate the success of the enterprise.
Jack:	That's right. Take banquets for example. The warmth, consideration and humor on the part of the host can always bring a light and joyful atmosphere to a serious negotiation, and enhance the emotional exchange of the two parties so that business talks can go well.
Yamaguchi:	Nevertheless, as Japanese businessmen look at it, friendship is friendship and business is business. For quality goods, it's the buyer who entreats the seller. For inferior goods,

English Translation of the Texts

	it's the seller who beseeches the buyer. At a banquet, if you are being too solicitous, it would be regarded as purposely currying favor. The other party would think you have acted in such a way because you want his help. And he has to think twice whether or not he should enter into this transaction.
Jenny:	Then the business just falls through?
Yamaguchi:	Most likely.
Jack:	Therefore, the most important thing in public relations work is to understand and respect each other.
Jenny:	Maybe that's also the most difficult part in handling public relations. Different countries have different cultures and different customs. How can one understand all of them?
Jack:	So we have to learn more. For example, gifts cannot be sent in pairs in some countries, and in some other countries odd numbers are regarded as inauspicious.
Jenny:	I've also heard that people in some countries do not like the white color, and some do not like black. In different countries, the preferences are different.
Jack:	From this we can see how important it is to understand and respect each other. If you incur the other party's displeasure or even hurt their feelings because of some trifles, how can the transaction be concluded?
Yamaguchi:	It follows that the real PR work contributes to the establishment of true friendship and good relationship between cooperative partners by way of polite and appropriate reception as well as friendly contacts.

Lesson 48 A Career in Public Relations (II)

(After class)

Yamaguchi:	Happy birthday to you!
Jack:	Happy birthday to you!

243

Jenny:	Thank you, thank you.
Yamaguchi:	Now Jenny, today's birthday girl, will you please blow out the candles and cut the cake?
Jack:	Listen! There seems to be someone knocking at the door.
Jenny:	Please come in.
Attendant:	Miss, someone has sent you this bunch of flowers.
Yamaguchi:	Wow, what a big bunch! Very beautiful indeed! Is it from your boyfriend?
Jenny:	He is in France. How could he send me flowers?
Yamaguchi:	Perhaps he ordered it from an online florist's.
Jack:	No more guessing now. You can just read the greeting card so that you'll know.
Yamaguchi:	That's right. Please read it to us.
Jenny:	"Happy Birthday, Miss Jenny! Wish you always as beautiful and charming as fresh flowers! PS: There will be an opening ceremony for a culinary festival at 7 o'clock tomorrow evening at our restaurant. You and your friends are all invited. Best regards, from Liu Jingjing."
Yamaguchi:	Oh, what beautiful flowers and what sweet and warm words!
Jack:	Who is Liu Jingjing?
Yamaguchi:	You've forgotten her? She is the PR manager of Yingbin Restaurant.
Jenny:	Yes, it's her! But I never mentioned my birthday to her. How did she find out? I'm really moved.
Jack:	That's the skill of a PR manager.
Yamaguchi:	Are you going to the opening ceremony of tomorrow's culinary festival?
Jenny:	Of course I am. I must express my thanks to her in person. Why not come with me? She has also invited you guys.
Liu Jingjing:	Jenny, Yamaguchi, welcome, welcome!

English Translation of the Texts

Jenny:	Hello, Miss Liu. Thank you for the flowers and birthday card you sent me yesterday. I will never forget your great kindness.
Yamaguchi:	We were all deeply moved. Thank you for your kind invitation.
Liu Jingjing:	Don't mention it. Please come in. Hi, Jack. I'm so glad that you come.
Jack:	Oh, Miss Liu, you still remember me?
Liu Jingjing:	How could I forget you? An outstanding student from the United States. We have met twice. You're very optimistic and full of humor.
Jack:	I'm very glad you put it that way. Thank you for the compliment.
Liu Jingjing:	Please make yourselves at home. See you later. I have to go and attend to other guests.
Jack:	Jenny, when did we meet Miss Liu?
Yamaguchi:	At least half a year ago.
Jenny:	At that time we had just arrived in Beijing and were unfamiliar with the people and the places here. She took the initiative to help us.
Jack:	She said she met us twice before.
Jenny:	Twice it was, once in the karaoke room of their restaurant, and the other time near Huiqiao Hotel.
Jack:	Look, as soon as she saw us, she could call out our names and talk about our characters. What a good memory she has!
Yamaguchi:	If you listen attentively, you'll find that Miss Liu can tell the name, position, and workplace of every guest. She can also mention some happy past events.
Jack:	That's not easy. How do you feel?
Jenny:	It's really heart-warming, just like being home.
Yamaguchi:	Me too. As soon as she greets me, I know my position in

	the eyes of our hostess. How cordial and gratifying it is!
Jack:	That's true. As soon as she meets you, she can accurately recall your name and then engage you in small talk. This creates an atmosphere that makes the guests feel at home. Who won't be moved? Who won't have an especially favorable impression of this place?
Jenny:	Jingjing is really an outstanding PR manager.
Liu Jingjing:	Ladies and gentlemen, welcome to this grand gathering tonight. Now I declare the culinary festival open. I hope you all will have a very pleasant evening.

Lesson 49   Choose the Right "God" (I)

(In class)

Professor Wang:	There is a foreign saying that goes like this: "The customer is God." It is very popular in China too. Do you think that it makes sense?
Yamaguchi:	The customer is "God". If he doesn't love you, the store will have to close down and the enterprise will go bankrupt.
Jack:	So the Hilton Hotel in the United States is famous for its service with a smile.
Yamaguchi:	Yes, a friendly attitude will make customers feel at home, thus attracting more customers.
Jenny:	The customer is "God", and a difficult one too.
Yamaguchi:	Jenny is right. There are all kinds of customers, men and women, old and young, rich and poor.
Jenny:	And they are of different nationalities, with different cultures, different levels of education, and different preferences.
Yamaguchi:	In a word, different customers have different requirements, and it is very difficult for stores and enterprises to satisfy them all.
Jack:	This probably equates to the Chinese saying "It is difficult

	to cater to all tastes." Turnips and cabbages—people have different preferences. Such being the case, we can't attempt to cater to the tastes of all "gods". We can only choose some of the customers as our "gods".
Professor Wang:	Therefore, each enterprise or store must choose its own "gods", and it must choose the right ones too. If you have chosen the right ones, then you have made the right choice as to the orientation of your business. Only by doing so, can the enterprise flourish and prosper.
Jenny:	Jack, do you have any brilliant ideas concerning the selection of "God"?
Jack:	Naturally one has to do a market investigation.
Yamaguchi:	Apart from a market investigation, more attention should be paid to the study of the data.
Jack:	Right. We have to do the market investigation and analyze it. I heard that KFC carried out a large-scale market investigation before it started its business in Beijing.
Yamaguchi:	How did they do it?
Jack:	First, they noticed that Beijing at that time was faced with three big problems—housing, dining out, and transportation. So they concluded that KFC would create enormous market demands in Beijing.
Yamaguchi:	Mm, understanding this is very important. With no market, we cannot speak of anything else.
Jack:	After that, they went to eat in almost every restaurant in Beijing, large or small, so as to become familiar with the varieties of food offered by these restaurants, the tastes of Beijingers, their levels of education and income, etc.
Yamaguchi:	What conclusion did they come to this time?
Jenny:	Don't ask for the conclusion yet. Let's look at what they did next.
Jack:	On the basis of what they had learned, they immediately

	developed samples of KFC that conformed to the Chinese conditions, provided them for people from all social strata to have a taste free of charge, and asked for their opinions.
Yamaguchi:	What questions did they ask?
Jack:	How does it taste? What price can ordinary Chinese afford? What's the best selection of materials and the best match of colors? What are the requirements regarding business hours and the dining environment...
Yamaguchi:	They did make intensive inquiries and analyses. Well, we don't have to talk about their conclusion anymore. I think I now understand how to select the "God".

Lesson 50 Choose the Right "God" (II)

(After class)

Jenny:	Yamaguchi, I've found you are quite interested in KFC's market investigation. Why is that?
Jack:	Do you want to develop a catering business in Beijing in the future?
Yamaguchi:	You've guessed right. I do have such a plan. How about we go to have a look around the city today, and try to understand the catering market in Beijing?
Jenny:	OK, let's go.
Yamaguchi:	We've walked a long time. Have you noticed what food is popular?
Jenny:	I've found that people in Beijing love noodles. As you see, there are many noodle and bun restaurants on the street.
Yamaguchi:	Yes. Look, here is a noodle restaurant. Let's go to talk with the customers.
Yamaguchi:	Hello, sir. Do you often come here to eat?
Customer:	Yes.

Yamaguchi:	There are several cheap noodle restaurants on this street. Why do you choose this one?
Customer:	I think the dining environment here is better.
Yamaguchi:	Do you attach great importance to the dining environment?
Customer:	Of course.
Jenny:	Then, you also often go to KFC and McDonald's?
Customer:	Yes, but I like noodles better.
Yamaguchi:	Why?
Customer:	Because I don't like cold drinks. I'm much more accustomed to eating hot noodles in warm soup.
Jenny:	Thank you.
Yamaguchi:	Jack, what impression do you have after hearing that customer's words?
Jack:	Today, restaurants, big and small, are spread all over Beijing. And the fast food business is developing particularly fast.
Yamaguchi:	Then what do you think of the prospect of developing a catering business in China?
Jack:	I don't think the prospect is bright.
Yamaguchi:	My view is just the opposite.
Jack:	Oh, really?
Yamaguchi:	Yes. Even though quite a lot of foreign fast foods have entered the Chinese market, they are not entirely to the taste of the Chinese people. China has a long-standing culinary culture, and everyone is a gourmet. The Chinese people will not give up their culinary traditions.
Jack:	You're right, and I didn't think of that. For foreigners to start a catering business in China, they have to take that into full consideration.
Yamaguchi:	So I think there is still a bright prospect for the development of catering business in China. But a new trail must be blazed in the introduction of popular fast foods that suit Chinese conditions.

Jenny:	That's a very good idea. Now be quick and tell us what the new trail is.
Yamaguchi:	The quality and speed of foreign fast foods, the traditions and tastes of Chinese food, and the prices which ordinary customers can afford.
Jenny:	Excellent idea! Yamaguchi, splendid!
Jack:	It's easier said than done. That may have to be accomplished by the Chinese people themselves.
Yamaguchi:	We might also try. Otherwise, how can we gain a firm foothold in the Chinese market?
Jenny:	Nevertheless, Chinese fast foods are also emerging. Yonho soybean milk and Laojia meat pie, for example, are both Chinese-style fast foods.
Yamaguchi:	That's nothing to be afraid of. I like competition. There will be no development without competition.

Lesson 51   Skillful Salesmanship (I)

(In class)

Professor Wang:	For a commodity to occupy the market, what else must it depend on, apart from the superiority in quality and price?
Jenny:	On advertising.
Yamaguchi:	On after-sales service.
Jack:	On superb salesmanship. The opportunity to make money is everywhere. It all depends on whether you can seize it, utilizing all means to push and promote sales.
Yamaguchi:	Jack has a point. The Japanese cars, watches and household electric appliances sell well all over the world only after arduous promotion.
Jack:	The more abundant the commodities, and the fiercer the competition, the more the promotion will be the key to success.
Professor Wang:	Then how can one do a good job in promoting sales?

Jenny:	I think the most important thing is to be good at studying the psychology of customers, and then in the light of such psychology, to employ salesmanship skillfully.
Jack:	No wonder many shops in Beijing have hired female shopping guides. Has anybody seen any male shopping guides?
Yamaguchi:	What do you mean?
Jack:	Don't you understand? Women are more understanding and they can more easily have a grip on their "gods".
Jenny:	Oh, you now admit that men are not reasonable. Ha, ha...
Yamaguchi:	We are talking about serious matters, and you are joking again.
Jack:	To tell the truth, I admire saleswomen. For many commodities, saleswomen can bring better results.
Jenny:	That's just natural. Take cosmetics for example. Saleswomen can demonstrate in person, showing an ideal effect of the makeup. They can also put on makeup for their female customers free of charge. Isn't this more effective than a salesman holding cosmetics in his hand and explaining how to use them?
Jack:	You're right. However, sometimes salesmen have their own advantages.
Jenny:	Do they?
Jack:	For example, wouldn't men's clothes, pants, supplies, etc. be sold better if promoted by salesmen?
Yamaguchi:	This is true.
Jack:	There used to be a type of jeans whose ad featured a female model. After the ad was broadcast, the jeans did not sell well.
Jenny:	What happened then?
Jack:	The jeans company found through surveys that most people who bought the jeans were men and then made another ad: a dark-eyed, rough-skinned, wild-looking man in jeans with

	his sleeves rolled up. This is the picture. What do you think of it?
Yamaguchi:	He is really handsome!
Jack:	That's it. After the ad was broadcast, the sales of the jeans increased by 60%, and the company became a big one.
Yamaguchi:	In fact, both of you are right. Different products need different marketing methods.
Jack:	I know. Everyone has his own trick. It depends on the salesperson's own ability.

Lesson 52 Skillful Salesmanship (II)

(After class)

Manager:	Xiao Luo, this is Jack, a foreign student who comes here for an internship. Please take care of him.
Xiao Luo:	Welcome! Feel free to ask me if you have any questions.
Jack:	Thank you. Just receive customers as you always do. I will stand aside to learn first and ask you if I have any questions.
Xiao Luo:	Hello, Miss, can I help you?
Young woman:	I want to buy a cell phone of the lastest type.
Xiao Luo:	As you see, this is the latest phone that has just appeared on the market. It is small and stylish with multiple functions.
Young woman:	Is there any phone with a larger screen? It doesn't matter if the price is higher.
Xiao Luo:	The phones over here have larger screens and you can have a look. What functions do you like?
Young woman:	I like to travel, so it would be better if it can take good photos.
Xiao Luo:	Then this one is particularly suitable for you. The front and rear cameras both have high pixel density and will help you take great pictures of people and landscapes. It can also beautify photos.

Young woman:	How about listening to music and watching videos?
Xiao Luo:	It has stereo speakers and a high-resolution screen with great image quality. You can enjoy yourself with it anytime and anywhere.
Young woman:	How about its standby time?
Xiao Luo:	It can last two days if you only make calls and take photos.
Young woman:	Can I have a try?
Xiao Luo:	Yes, of course.
Young woman:	Very good. It is sensitive and runs smoothly. I will take this one. Please give me a receipt.
Xiao Luo:	OK.
Old man:	Hello, young man.
Xiao Luo:	Hello, sir. Can I help you?
Old man:	I want to buy a computer.
Xiao Luo:	What do you want to use it for?
Old man:	I just want to go online to buy things and chat with my children.
Xiao Luo:	Then why don't you buy a smartphone with Internet access? You can make calls and connect to the Internet with the phone. It is very convenient.
Old man:	The characters on the phone are too small. I am old and find it hard to look at them. A computer is more useful.
Xiao Luo:	You are right. Then you can take a look at this computer. It has a large screen and nice color.
Old man:	Does it have a bigger font size?
Xiao Luo:	Yes, of course. The font size is middle now and I can change it into large. How about now?
Old man:	Great. I can see it clearly. I need to learn to use it after purchase. Or else it would become an ornament of no value like a sample in the store.
Xiao Luo:	That's OK. You will get familiar with it after a few days. Computers nowadays are very easy to operate.

Old man:	How about its quality? I cannot stand it if it goes wrong every now and then.
Xiao Luo:	Computers of this brand have great quality and are guaranteed for three years. Don't worry!
Old man:	Is it expensive?
Xiao Luo:	No, only a bit more than three thousand *yuan*.
Old man:	OK, I will take one.
Jack:	Xiao Luo, you took the initiative to introduce a high-end mobile phone to the young lady but an inexpensive computer to the old man. Why?
Xiao Luo:	As different customers have different living environments and needs, the goods introduced to them are not the same. The young lady liked phones with multifunctions and a big screen, and the latest phone should be recommended to her. The old man did not expect too much, so I introduced an inexpensive computer of good quality to him.
Jack:	In other words, sales of goods depend on the targets.
Xiao Luo:	Of course. The customers will only be satisfied when you recommend products in accordance with their needs. Only with customer satisfaction can the business get better and better.
Jack:	It seems that marketing skills also vary from person to person.

Lesson 53   Express Delivery and Takeout (I)

(In class)

Professor Wang:	Have you used express delivery?
Yamaguchi:	Of course. The books, clothes and computer I bought online are all delivered to me by express.
Professor Wang:	Did you have dealings with the delivery guys?
Jenny:	Sir, do you mean the couriers?

Professor Wang:	Yes, we generally call those who deliver parcels "delivery guys" cordially. Do you think they are busy?
Jack:	Very busy. They have to race against time to send one parcel, and then rush to the next one. They also need to work in the wind and rain all the year round and I've never seen them rest.
Professor Wang:	Jack is right. For express delivery, the most important thing is "fast". The intact goods should be delivered to the customers quickly, safely, and soundly. Do you know when the first parcel of "Double 11th Shopping Carnival" this year was delivered?
Yamaguchi:	I don't.
Jenny:	I do. I saw it on the Internet. It was a cell phone bought by a young lady at 00:00 and delivered to her after 20 minutes. At the time, she was eating in a restaurant with her friends!
Yamaguchi:	Express delivery in China is really fast. If you make an order in the morning, often you can receive your goods in the afternoon. If the goods are sent from other places, it would take three days at the soonest.
Jack:	I've also seen that many Chinese students only take a small bag when going home on holidays. The big luggage is delivered to their home address. When they arrive home, the parcel arrives too. It is obvious that express delivery brings great convenience to our lives!
Jenny:	I've heard that now many countries and regions in the world have Chinese express delivery business. As express delivery is getting more and more convenient, my friends also start to buy things on Chinese websites.
Yamaguchi:	Sir, how many parcels does a Chinese courier need to send each day?
Professor Wang:	Normally more than one hundred a day. However, during holidays, especially the "Double 11th", they become much

	busier. The "Double 11th" is followed by the "Double 12th", Christmas, New Year's Day and the Spring Festival, when they are the busiest in a year and need to send an average of over 300 parcels a day.
Yamaguchi:	No wonder I have never seen a female courier. The labor intensity is too much for a woman.
Jenny:	Sir, the couriers go out early and come back late and cannot even take a break at mealtimes. Are they not tired?
Professor Wang:	Someone once asked the question. They replied that despite the hard work, the job was meaningful. While delivering the goods fast, they also pass their true feelings.
Jack:	Quite right. The couriers bring us a comfortable and convenient life. I will thank them sincerely next time I receive a parcel.

Lesson 54   Express Delivery and Takeout (II)

(After class)

Yamaguchi:	Jenny, Jack, will you go to the canteen for lunch?
Jenny:	No, I want to eat hamburgers. Jack, do you want to eat hamburgers?
Jack:	I've eaten hamburgers for several days and feel a bit tired of them.
Yamaguchi:	Then what will we eat?
Jack:	A Sichuan specialty restaurant was newly opened near the campus. I've heard that the taste is very authentic and that takeout service is available. I want to have a try.
Jenny:	Tell us about the specialties of the restaurant.
Jack:	Fish filets in hot chili oil, hot and sour rice noodles, hot-spicy pot…
Yamaguchi:	I have not even heard of these dishes. We still do not know what they are if you introduce them like this.
Jack:	It doesn't matter. Let's look at the introduction to their

dishes online, and you will know what these dishes look like.

Yamaguchi:	These dishes look very spicy.
Jack:	Yes, Sichuan cuisine is famous for being spicy and hot.
Jenny:	Great. I like spicy food very much.
Jack:	Well, you are lucky today.
Jenny:	Is this the fish filets in hot chili oil you just introduced? It looks really hot!
Jack:	Why? You dare not eat it?
Jenny:	Who said that? I will have one!
Jack:	Yamaguchi, what do you want to eat?
Yamaguchi:	I want to eat noodles.
Jack:	How about this, the "dandan noodles"?
Yamaguchi:	It looks good and not too spicy. I'll have this.
Jack:	I will order Mapo tofu. OK, the order is placed. You see, here shows that the order has been taken, and there will be a delivery guy to deliver our food later.
Yamaguchi:	Ordering takeout is really convenient. We can receive the food at home without going out. How long does the delivery usually take?
Jack:	About half an hour, but not always. It is the rush hour of delivery now, and the number of guests in the restaurants is the largest.
Jenny:	Yes, due to the fast-paced life now, a lot of white-collar workers have only a short time to rest at noon and mostly order takeouts online. Ordering time is basically around 12:00 at noon, so the delivery time is uncertain.
Jack:	The delivery guys also want to deliver every order on time. But it is easier said than done. They will inevitably be late on rainy and windy days.
Jenny:	I saw in the news yesterday that a delivery guy needed to climb 12 floors to send the food due to elevator maintenance

	in a building.
Yamaguchi:	The delivery guys' work is not easy. We should be more tolerant and understand each other.
Jack:	After our food is delivered, let's leave the delivery guy a positive comment.

生词总表

Vocabulary List

生词	拼音	课号

A

爱好	àihào	49
爱好者	àihàozhě	29
爱惜	àixī	43
安静	ānjìng	40
安排	ānpái	46
安装	ānzhuāng	40
岸	àn	30
按劳付酬	àn láo fù chóu	46

B

巴黎	Bālí	33
白	bái	34
白菜	báicài	49
白加黑	Báijiāhēi	42
摆	bǎi	31
摆设	bǎishè	52
拜托	bàituō	47
办	bàn	40
棒	bàng	30
包	bāo	37
包	bāo	46
包子	bāozi	32
保修	bǎoxiū	52
保障	bǎozhàng	45
保证	bǎozhèng	45
抱歉	bàoqiàn	43
背	bèi	44
被	bèi	48
呗	bei	40
奔驰	Bēnchí	41
本来	běnlái	42
本事	běnshi	34
逼	bī	45
比	bǐ	37
比较	bǐjiào	29
彼此	bǐcǐ	40
必须	bìxū	50
壁画	bìhuà	30
变化	biànhuà	33
便捷	biànjié	53
遍	biàn	49
遍布	biànbù	50
表演	biǎoyǎn	34
宾至如归	bīnzhì-rúguī	48
饼	bǐng	39
播出	bōchū	51
不错	búcuò	29
不论	búlùn	41
不光	bùguāng	49
不仅	bùjǐn	35
不然	bùrán	50
不如	bùrú	38

步	bù	49	承诺	chéngnuò	45
部分	bùfen	49	（承）认	(chéng)rèn	44
部门	bùmén	45	承受	chéngshòu	39
簿	bù	43	诚实	chéngshí	45
			吃不消	chībuxiāo	53
			吃惊	chījīng	34

C

			驰名	chímíng	33
猜	cāi	48	充分	chōngfèn	50
材料	cáiliào	49	充满	chōngmǎn	37
财产	cáichǎn	41	冲	chōng	38
踩	cǎi	43	冲动	chōngdòng	38
菜	cài	31	冲浪	chōnglàng	30
菜品	càipǐn	54	冲	chòng	41
参加	cānjiā	41	抽	chōu	42
参谋	cānmóu	34	抽丝	chōusī	44
餐饮业	cānyǐnyè	50	出发	chūfā	46
操作	cāozuò	52	出色	chūsè	48
层次	céngcì	49	出现	chūxiàn	45
茶馆	cháguǎn	39	出行	chūxíng	36
产生	chǎnshēng	48	初	chū	37
尝	cháng	32	除了	chúle	51
场所	chǎngsuǒ	40	传播	chuánbō	40
超	chāo	54	传统	chuántǒng	37
超过	chāoguò	37	吹	chuī	47
潮流	cháoliú	33	春节	Chūnjié	37
炒菜	chǎocài	31	次品	cìpǐn	44
炒鱿鱼	chǎo yóuyú	43	伺候	cìhou	49
车牌	chēpái	36	从来	cónglái	48
称心如意	chènxīn rúyì	44	粗糙	cūcāo	51
称为	chēng wéi	53	促进	cùjìn	45
撑	chēng	32	促销	cùxiāo	37
成败	chéngbài	51	脆	cuì	32
成交额	chéngjiāo'é	37			

| 村 | cūn | 38 |
| 错过 | cuòguò | 34 |

D

搭配	dāpèi	49
达	dá	41
达到	dádào	29
打扮	dǎban	34
打发	dǎfa	37
打交道	dǎ jiāodao	53
打入	dǎ rù	50
打算	dǎsuàn	29
大巴	dàbā	1
大概	dàgài	31
大观园	Dàguān Yuán	36
大象	dàxiàng	46
大众化	dàzhònghuà	50
待	dāi	43
代表	dàibiǎo	41
待机	dàijī	52
单	dān	53
单车	dānchē	35
单身	dānshēn	37
单位	dānwèi	48
担	dàn	54
耽误	dānwu	32
当场	dāngchǎng	42
当家菜	dāngjiācài	39
当面	dāngmiàn	48
当时	dāngshí	49
挡	dǎng	33
当作	dàngzuò	49
档	dàng	33
导购	dǎogòu	51
导游	dǎoyóu	46
倒闭	dǎobì	49
倒霉	dǎoméi	44
到处	dàochù	31
倒	dào	33
得意	déyì	34
登	dēng	36
登记	dēngjì	40
地道	dìdao	54
地区	dìqū	37
地铁	dìtiě	1
地位	dìwèi	48
点菜	diǎn cài	31
点击	diǎnjī	36
点心	diǎnxin	42
电脑	diànnǎo	40
电商	diànshāng	37
电梯	diàntī	54
电子	diànzǐ	36
调查	diàochá	49
订购	dìnggòu	48
定位	dìngwèi	35
丢人	diūrén	35
丢人现眼	diūrén xiànyǎn	40
东京	Dōngjīng	33
动	dòng	31
都市	dūshì	40
豆腐	dòufu	54
豆浆	dòujiāng	32
独一无二	dúyī-wúèr	41

度假	dùjià	30		非常	fēicháng	34
端午节	Duānwǔ Jié	37		费	fèi	35
短	duǎn	34		费劲	fèijìn	52
断定	duàndìng	49		费心	fèixīn	47
锻炼	duànliàn	29		费用	fèiyong	46
堆	duī	38		分	fēn	41
对待	duìdài	38		分辨率	fēnbiànlǜ	52
对方	duìfāng	47		粉	fěn	54
对象	duìxiàng	40		份儿	fènr	32
兑现	duìxiàn	45		丰富	fēngfù	35
敦煌	Dūnhuáng	30		风格	fēnggé	34
顿	dùn	31		风景	fēngjǐng	30
多样	duōyàng	52		风情	fēngqíng	46
多元化	duōyuánhuà	39		风俗	fēngsú	47
				风味	fēngwèi	32
E				疯狂	fēngkuáng	38
额	é	40		逢年过节	féngnián-guòjié	53
饿	è	31		否则	fǒuzé	38
二维码	èrwéimǎ	35		服	fú	42
				服务	fúwù	46
F				俯瞰	fǔkàn	36
发（表）	fā(biǎo)	39		父母	fùmǔ	47
发布会	fābùhuì	33		富（裕）	fù(yù)	49
发达	fādá	37				
发票	fāpiào	52		**G**		
发现	fāxiàn	33		高铁	gāotiě	29
发展	fāzhǎn	35		改天	gǎitiān	32
罚	fá	45		干吗	gànmá	32
烦	fán	42		赶	gǎn	32
反感	fǎngǎn	47		赶紧	gǎnjǐn	53
反正	fǎnzhèng	45		赶上	gǎnshàng	54
方向	fāngxiàng	49		敢	gǎn	54

感恩节	Gǎn'ēn Jié	37	古代	gǔdài	30
感（觉）	gǎn (jué)	34	古老	gǔlǎo	39
感到	gǎndào	34	股	gǔ	31
感动	gǎndòng	48	故障	gùzhàng	45
感情	gǎnqíng	47	顾	gù	32
感受	gǎnshòu	48	雇用	gùyòng	51
感想	gǎnxiǎng	50	雇员	gùyuán	39
感谢	gǎnxiè	53	关键	guānjiàn	51
高才生	gāocáishēng	48	关门	guānmén	49
高峰	gāofēng	54	关于	guānyú	47
高见	gāojiàn	49	观光	guānguāng	47
高论	gāolùn	39	观景台	guānjǐngtái	36
高速	gāosù	30	观众	guānzhòng	42
高速公路	gāosù gōnglù	29	广大	guǎngdà	39
糕点	gāodiǎn	42	归	guī	47
搞	gǎo	43	规定	guīdìng	44
各	gè	29	规范	guīfàn	45
根本	gēnběn	38	规模	guīmó	49
根据	gēnjù	45	桂香村	Guìxiāngcūn	42
更	gèng	41	锅	guō	54
更加	gèngjiā	35	国际	guójì	46
公道	gōngdào	40	国家	guójiā	29
公共交通	gōnggòng jiāotōng	1	国贸大厦	Guómào Dàshà	34
			国子监	Guózǐjiàn	36
公关	gōngguān	40	过分	guòfèn	47

H

功能	gōngnéng	52
供求	gōngqiú	40
共享	gòngxiǎng	35	海	hǎi	30
贡献	gòngxiàn	36	海尔集团	Hǎi'ěr Jítuán	41
购买	gòumǎi	51	海南	Hǎinán	30
够	gòu	38	含	hán	39
姑娘	gūniang	30	汉堡包	hànbǎobāo	31

行	háng	42
行情	hángqíng	40
杭州	Hángzhōu	30
毫不	háo bù	34
毫无	háo wú	38
好处	hǎochù	30
好感	hǎogǎn	48
好评	hǎopíng	54
好运	hǎoyùn	42
号	hào	52
好奇心	hàoqíxīn	31
合理	hélǐ	39
合作	hézuò	47
和气	héqì	43
河	hé	30
贺卡	hèkǎ	48
恨不得	hènbude	31
红火	hónghuo	31
红娘	Hóngniáng	40
后悔	hòuhuǐ	38
互动	hùdòng	46
互联网+	hùliánwǎng jiā	35
花	huā	33
化妆	huàzhuāng	51
化妆品	huàzhuāngpǐn	51
画质	huàzhì	52
环保	huánbǎo	36
环节	huánjié	46
环境	huánjìng	50
回答	huídá	31
回头客	huítóukè	43
惠侨饭店	Huìqiáo Fàndiàn	48

昏	hūn	38
馄饨	húntun	32
活跃	huóyuè	41
伙伴	huǒbàn	29
或者	huòzhě	35
货品	huòpǐn	35
货物	huòwù	53

J

几乎	jīhū	49
机会	jīhuì	34
机遇	jīyù	51
基本上	jīběn shang	54
激烈	jīliè	45
吉	jí	42
极	jí	30
集中	jízhōng	54
挤	jǐ	1
记性	jìxing	48
继续	jìxù	32
加强	jiāqiáng	45
夹脚	jiā jiǎo	43
家长里短	jiācháng-lǐduǎn	40
家电	jiādiàn	41
家家户户	jiājiāhùhù	37
价位	jiàwèi	52
价值	jiàzhí	39
假期	jiàqī	29
艰苦	jiānkǔ	51
监管	jiānguǎn	45
煎饼果子	jiānbingguǒzi	32
减少	jiánshǎo	36

简直	jiǎnzhí	31	精确	jīngquè	35
见面	jiànmiàn	40	景点	jǐngdiǎn	46
见识	jiànshi	31	竞争	jìngzhēng	45
建立	jiànlì	47	敬	jìng	48
建议	jiànyì	36	究竟	jiūjìng	31
江南	jiāngnán	30	举	jǔ	41
江苏	Jiāngsū	30	举行	jǔxíng	48
将来	jiānglái	50	拒绝	jùjué	43
讲解	jiǎngjiě	46	据说	jùshuō	39
讲理	jiǎnglǐ	43	卷	juǎn	51
奖	jiǎng	42	绝妙	juémiào	41
交流	jiāoliú	31	君	jūn	42
交情	jiāoqing	47			
交谈	jiāotán	40	**K**		
教育	jiàoyù	49	开发	kāifā	50
接待	jiēdài	47	开幕式	kāimùshì	48
接受	jiēshòu	37	开业	kāiyè	42
接着	jiēzhe	43	开展	kāizhǎn	40
街道	jiēdào	30	看法	kànfǎ	50
节	jié	48	看重	kànzhòng	50
节制	jiézhì	38	扛	káng	46
节奏	jiézòu	54	考虑	kǎolǜ	38
结果	jiéguǒ	38	烤	kǎo	39
结论	jiélùn	49	靠	kào	39
解馋	jiěchán	42	科幻	kēhuàn	1
解决	jiějué	35	瞌睡	kēshuì	42
进行	jìnxíng	49	可见	kějiàn	29
进展	jìnzhǎn	47	可怕	kěpà	34
经过	jīngguò	51	可惜	kěxī	33
经历	jīnglì	47	客户	kèhù	53
经营	jīngyíng	45	肯	kěn	37
精彩	jīngcǎi	34	肯德基	Kěndéjī	31

肯定	kěndìng	35	累	lèi	29
空调	kōngtiáo	41	累	lèi	42
空气	kōngqì	36	冷静	lěngjìng	38
口福	kǒufú	54	冷饮	lěngyǐn	50
库房	kùfáng	44	李维斯公司	Lǐwéisī Gōngsī	33
夸	kuā	44	理解	lǐjiě	45
快递	kuàidì	53	理想	lǐxiǎng	51
快递员	kuàidìyuán	53	理性	lǐxìng	38
快捷	kuàijié	29	理由	lǐyóu	45
快乐	kuàilè	48	力度	lìdù	38
快速	kuàisù	53	力士	Lìshì	42
筷子	kuàizi	31	历史	lìshǐ	30
宽容	kuānróng	54	立体声	lìtǐshēng	52
款	kuǎn	45	利用	lìyòng	37
款式	kuǎnshì	33	例子	lìzi	41
狂欢	kuánghuān	37	连	lián	54
亏	kuī	34	联系	liánxì	44
困难	kùnnan	47	联想	Liánxiǎng	41
			良好	liánghǎo	47

L

			量	liàng	39
拉关系	lā guānxi	47	聊（天儿）	liáo(tiānr)	40
拉面	lāmiàn	50	林荫道	línyīndào	36
蜡烛	làzhú	48	灵活	línghuó	32
辣	là	54	灵敏	língmǐn	52
来宾	láibīn	48	领导	lǐngdǎo	33
来往	láiwǎng	30	另（外）	lìng(wài)	51
兰州	Lánzhōu	30	刘京京	Liú Jīngjīng	48
劳动力	láodònglì	46	流	liú	30
老家肉饼	Lǎojiā Ròubǐng	50	流畅	liúchàng	52
老舍	Lǎo Shě	39	流传	liúchuán	41
乐	lè	41	流行	liúxíng	33
乐观	lèguān	48	龙舟	lóngzhōu	37

旅途	lǚtú	29
旅行	lǚxíng	29
伦敦	Lúndūn	33
萝卜	luóbo	49

M

麻	má	54
马上	mǎshàng	36
麦当劳	Màidāngláo	31
满	mǎn	38
满	mǎn	42
满意	mǎnyì	36
满足	mǎnzú	31
忙活	mánghuo	37
毛衣	máoyī	33
美的	Měidì	41
美好	měihǎo	30
美丽	měilì	48
美滋滋	měizīzī	39
门票	ménpiào	46
迷路	mílù	36
迷人	mírén	48
米饭	mǐfàn	31
秒	miǎo	39
妙	miào	50
民族	mínzú	34
名牌	míngpái	33
名堂	míngtang	32
明智	míngzhì	44
模特儿	mótèr	34
魔术	móshù	39
某	mǒu	47

目光	mùguāng	51

N

内	nèi	45
男士	nánshì	51
男子汉	nánzǐhàn	34
难道	nándào	31
难怪	nánguài	42
难免	nánmiǎn	54
难题	nántí	49
难为情	nánwéiqíng	40
能（够）	néng(gòu)	50
腻	nì	54
年纪	niánjì	52
念	niàn	48
牛肉	niúròu	39
牛仔裤	niúzǎikù	33
农历	nónglì	37
弄	nòng	43
女士	nǚshì	48
女性	nǚxìng	53

O

欧莱雅	Ōuláiyǎ	42
欧洲	Ōuzhōu	29

P

拍照	pāizhào	52
攀谈	pāntán	48
泡	pào	40
陪同	péitóng	47
佩服	pèifú	51

批	pī	43	瞧	qiáo	31
批量	pīliàng	44	巧妙	qiǎomiào	51
皮肤	pífū	51	切	qiē	48
皮鞋	píxié	33	亲切	qīnqiè	48
片	piàn	42	亲身	qīnshēn	46
票	piào	34	亲自	qīnzì	51
品	pǐn	39	青年	qīngnián	40
品尝	pǐncháng	49	轻松	qīngsōng	39
品种	pǐnzhǒng	33	清仓	qīngcāng	42
平均	píngjūn	53	清洁	qīngjié	39
平时	píngshí	38	清晰	qīngxī	52
平台	píngtái	37	清新	qīngxīn	36
平稳	píngwěn	30	情况	qíngkuàng	29
屏幕	píngmù	52	情谊	qíngyì	43
婆	pó	54	请教	qǐngjiào	52
普遍	pǔbiàn	41	穷	qióng	44
普通	pǔtōng	39	趣闻	qùwén	40
铺	pù	50	全部	quánbù	46
			权（利）	quán(lì)	44
Q			却	què	29
			雀巢	Quècháo	31
其实	qíshí	33	确实	quèshí	39
其余	qíyú	46	裙	qún	34
旗袍	qípáo	33	群众	qúnzhòng	50
气氛	qìfēn	37			
洽谈	qiàtán	40	**R**		
千万	qiānwàn	38			
前景	qiánjǐng	50	惹	rě	43
强度	qiángdù	53	热带	rèdài	46
墙	qiáng	45	热乎乎	rèhūhū	48
抢	qiǎng	38	热情	rèqíng	39
敲门	qiāo mén	48	热水器	rèshuǐqì	41
桥	qiáo	30	人情	rénqíng	43

人物	rénwù	52
忍	rěn	31
认为	rènwéi	43
如何	rúhé	33
软	ruǎn	32

S

赛	sài	37
三天两头儿	sāntiān-liǎngtóur	52
扫描	sǎomiáo	35
色	sè	31
色彩	sècǎi	49
沙滩	shātān	30
善解人意	shàn jiě rényì	51
善于	shànyú	51
伤害	shānghài	47
商标	shāngbiāo	33
商务	shāngwù	38
赏心悦目	shǎngxīn-yuèmù	42
上班族	shàngbānzú	35
上帝	Shàngdì	49
烧饼	shāobing	32
少数民族	shǎoshù mínzú	46
少	shào	41
舍不得	shěbude	33
社会	shèhuì	35
摄像头	shèxiàngtóu	52
摄影师	shèyǐngshī	46
身心	shēnxīn	36
深	shēn	33
深沉	shēnchén	51
深刻	shēnkè	34
深入	shēnrù	49
甚至	shènzhì	47
生	shēng	48
生产商	shēngchǎnshāng	41
生活	shēnghuó	41
生命	shēngmìng	41
生意经	shēngyijīng	34
省	shěng	36
圣诞节	Shèngdàn Jié	37
盛会	shènghuì	48
盛情	shèngqíng	48
什么的	shénmede	45
石窟	shíkū	30
时代	shídài	34
时段	shíduàn	54
时髦	shímáo	33
时尚	shíshàng	52
时速	shísù	29
时装	shízhuāng	33
实惠	shíhuì	50
实习	shíxí	52
实在	shízai	30
食材	shícái	37
食品	shípǐn	32
使用	shǐyòng	35
示范	shìfàn	51
世界	shìjiè	41
市场	shìchǎng	33
事业	shìyè	47
视频	shìpín	52

适应	shìyìng	35		虽然	suīrán	50
收入	shōurù	49		随便	suíbiàn	40
收摊儿	shōutānr	32		随地	suídì	52
手段	shǒuduàn	41		随时	suíshí	51
手续费	shǒuxùfèi	44		所	suǒ	49
守信	shǒuxìn	45		所有	suǒyǒu	49
首都	shǒudū	43				
首先	shǒuxiān	49		**T**		
寿星	shòuxing	48				
受	shòu	43		态度	tàidù	39
舒畅	shūchàng	36		谈情说爱	tánqíng-shuōài	40
舒适	shūshì	30		谈吐	tántǔ	47
熟悉	shúxi	31		糖	táng	32
属于	shǔyú	47		糖果	tángguǒ	42
薯条	shǔtiáo	39		趟	tàng	44
术	shù	51		桃红柳绿	táo hóng liǔ lǜ	30
帅	shuài	51		讨好	tǎohǎo	47
双	shuāng	37		套餐	tàocān	39
水平	shuǐpíng	33		套近乎	tào jìnhu	47
水乡	shuǐxiāng	30		特色	tèsè	54
睡懒觉	shuì lǎnjiào	32		特殊	tèshū	48
顺手	shùnshǒu	38		提高	tígāo	29
说明	shuōmíng	44		提供	tígōng	46
司机	sījī	36		体验	tǐyàn	46
丝绸	sīchóu	34		天津	Tiānjīn	32
私家车	sījiāchē	29		天堂	tiāntáng	30
斯达舒	Sīdáshū	42		挑选	tiāoxuǎn	37
四川	Sìchuān	54		调	tiáo	52
四通八达	sìtōng-bādá	29		铁路	tiělù	29
苏州	Sūzhōu	30		停产	tíng chǎn	44
速度	sùdù	29		挺	tǐng	34
酸	suān	54		通过	tōngguò	47
				通情达理	tōngqíng-dálǐ	51

同意	tóngyì	36		温馨	wēnxīn	48
痛快	tòngkuài	36		文化	wénhuà	30
头脑	tóunǎo	38		闻	wén	31
投放	tóufàng	52		闻名	wénmíng	54
投诉	tóusù	45		乌篷船	wūpéngchuán	30
土豆	tǔdòu	39		乌镇	Wū Zhèn	30
团聚	tuánjù	37		污染	wūrǎn	36
团圆	tuányuán	37		物美价廉	wù měi jià lián	37
推出	tuīchū	38				
推销	tuīxiāo	42		**X**		
退	tuì	44				
				西餐	xīcān	31
W				西湖	Xīhú	46
				西双版纳	Xīshuāngbǎnnà	46
袜子	wàzi	33		西服	xīfú	33
外卖	wàimài	35		吸引	xīyǐn	37
外滩	Wàitān	46		希尔顿饭店	Xī'ěrdùn Fàndiàn	49
完	wán	34		习惯	xíguàn	31
完好无损	wánhǎo wúsǔn	53		戏法	xìfǎ	51
碗	wǎn	32		系统	xìtǒng	35
万家乐	Wànjiālè	41		吓	xià	34
王国	wángguó	29		吓唬	xiàhu	43
网店	wǎngdiàn	45		先进	xiānjìn	35
网购	wǎnggòu	35		鲜花	xiānhuā	48
网络	wǎngluò	36		鲜亮	xiānliang	34
网站	wǎngzhàn	53		闲聊	xiánliáo	40
往事	wǎngshì	48		嫌	xián	38
微笑	wēixiào	39		显示	xiǎnshì	54
维修	wéixiū	54		显眼	xiǎnyǎn	44
伟大	wěidà	30		现象	xiànxiàng	47
味	wèi	31		相当	xiāngdāng	50
味道	wèidao	31		相反	xiāngfǎn	50
胃	wèi	42		相中	xiāngzhòng	40

香	xiāng	31	兴旺	xīngwàng	49
香槟	xiāngbīn	47	兴许	xīngxǔ	48
详细	xiángxì	34	星巴克	Xīngbākè	1
享受	xiǎngshòu	30	行李	xíngli	46
响	xiǎng	33	形	xíng	31
像	xiàng	35	形状	xíngzhuàng	31
像素	xiàngsù	52	兴趣	xìngqù	42
消费	xiāofèi	33	性	xìng	41
消费者	xiāofèizhě	38	性格	xìnggé	48
消极	xiāojí	36	休闲	xiūxián	36
销路	xiāolù	34	袖子	xiùzi	51
销售	xiāoshòu	42	需求	xūqiú	35
小吃	xiǎochī	31	需要	xūyào	38
小调	xiǎodiào	30	许多	xǔduō	29
小伙子	xiǎohuǒzi	40	宣布	xuānbù	48
小巧	xiǎoqiǎo	52	选择	xuǎnzé	29
效果	xiàoguǒ	51	迅速	xùnsù	50
效益	xiàoyì	32	逊色	xùnsè	34
校园	xiàoyuán	35			
歇	xiē	53		**Y**	
协会	xiéhuì	45	咽	yàn	43
鞋	xié	43	严格	yángé	39
心理	xīnlǐ	37	严肃	yánsù	47
心仪	xīnyí	38	沿	yán	36
欣赏	xīnshǎng	39	沿途	yántú	30
新东安市场	Xīndōng'ān Shìchǎng	42	沿线	yánxiàn	36
			研究	yánjiū	49
信任	xìnrèn	45	颜色	yánsè	31
信息	xìnxī	36	眼光	yǎnguāng	43
信誉	xìnyù	41	宴请	yànqǐng	47
兴隆	xīnglóng	40	阳光	yángguāng	30
兴起	xīngqǐ	50	样品	yàngpǐn	49

样子	yàngzi	43	迎宾饭店	Yíngbīn Fàndiàn	48
要求	yāoqiú	39	迎合	yínghé	49
邀请	yāoqǐng	34	赢得	yíngdé	39
咬	yǎo	31	拥有	yōngyǒu	42
要不	yàobu	38	雍和宫	Yōnghé Gōng	36
要么	yàome	29	永和豆浆	Yǒnghé Dòujiāng	50
也许	yěxǔ	33			
野性	yěxìng	51	永远	yǒngyuǎn	39
业务	yèwù	40	勇气	yǒngqì	40
夜景	yèjǐng	46	用品	yòngpǐn	51
夜宵	yèxiāo	53	优点	yōudiǎn	51
衣服	yīfu	34	优惠	yōuhuì	42
医药	yīyào	42	优势	yōushì	51
一旦	yídàn	45	幽默	yōumò	47
（一）概	(yí)gài	44	悠久	yōujiǔ	50
一溜儿	yíliùr	32	尤其	yóuqí	53
一样	yíyàng	35	由	yóu	51
遗憾	yíhàn	44	犹豫	yóuyù	45
以	yǐ	49	油条	yóutiáo	32
以免	yǐmiǎn	43	游泳	yóuyǒng	30
艺术品	yìshùpǐn	31	友善	yǒushàn	39
一经	yìjīng	44	有关	yǒuguān	45
一连	yìlián	54	诱惑	yòuhuò	33
一年到头	yìnián-dàotóu	53	于	yú	42
意见	yìjiàn	43	鱼	yú	54
意义	yìyì	53	娱乐	yúlè	37
因人而异	yīnrén'éryì	52	愉快	yúkuài	39
音乐	yīnyuè	30	与	yǔ	50
音效	yīnxiào	52	与其	yǔqí	38
殷勤	yīnqín	47	预约	yùyuē	36
引起	yǐnqǐ	47	元旦	Yuándàn	53
印象	yìnxiàng	33	元素	yuánsù	37

园林	yuánlín	46
原来	yuánlái	41
原因	yuányīn	44
约	yuē	40
月饼	yuèbǐng	37
越	yuè	41
云集	yúnjí	42
云南	Yúnnán	46
运动	yùndòng	29
运动鞋	yùndòngxié	38

Z

脏	zāng	43
糟心	zāoxīn	44
早出晚归	zǎochū-wǎnguī	53
早市	zǎoshì	32
造	zào	41
啧啧	zézé	31
增进	zēngjìn	47
赠	zèng	48
炸糕	zhágāo	32
展示	zhǎnshì	34
占	zhàn	41
占领	zhànlǐng	51
站稳	zhànwěn	50
招待	zhāodài	48
招牌菜	zhāopáicài	39
着迷	zháomí	34
照常	zhàocháng	52
照片	zhàopiàn	51
折腾	zhēteng	44
折(扣)	zhé(kòu)	42

浙江	Zhèjiāng	30
针对	zhēnduì	51
真诚	zhēnchéng	47
真情	zhēnqíng	53
真正	zhēnzhèng	47
争分夺秒	zhēngfēn-duómiǎo	53
征婚	zhēnghūn	40
征求	zhēngqiú	49
正常	zhèngcháng	45
正经	zhèngjing	46
正式	zhèngshì	48
郑重	zhèngzhòng	45
之	zhī	41
支付	zhīfù	35
知名度	zhīmíngdù	41
值得	zhídé	42
职务	zhíwù	48
只管	zhǐguǎn	52
只要	zhǐyào	36
纸盒	zhǐ hé	43
指	zhǐ	53
至少	zhìshǎo	34
制造	zhìzào	37
治	zhì	42
秩序	zhìxù	45
智能	zhìnéng	52
中餐	zhōngcān	31
中秋节	Zhōngqiū Jié	37
中央电视塔	Zhōngyāng Diànshì Tǎ	36
终生	zhōngshēng	48

终于	zhōngyú	43	准确	zhǔnquè	33
种	zhǒng	44	桌子	zhuōzi	31
众口难调	zhòngkǒu--nántiáo	49	着想	zhuóxiǎng	44
			字眼	zìyǎn	43
周到	zhōudào	39	自在	zìzai	40
周围	zhōuwéi	35	自助	zìzhù	46
周庄	Zhōuzhuāng	30	宗旨	zōngzhǐ	39
诸	zhū	48	总之	zǒngzhī	36
主动	zhǔdòng	48	粽子	zòngzi	37
煮	zhǔ	54	走俏	zǒuqiào	47
住宿	zhùsù	46	嘴快	zuǐ kuài	40
注意	zhùyì	48	最终	zuìzhōng	37
祝	zhù	42	尊重	zūnzhòng	47
抓	zhuā	51	作用	zuòyòng	47
撞	zhuàng	42	做法	zuòfǎ	44
准（许）	zhǔn(xǔ)	43	做梦	zuòmèng	42